The contributors to this book have opened up a controversial and fascinating subject, so far hardly explored: the father-daughter relationship seen from the daughter's point of view. *Fathers* is a collage of memoirs and polemic, stories, photographs and poems, bringing together testimony and insights from childhood, family life, religion, literature, psychology, anthropology, and much else. The contributors' ages range from thirteen to sixty-four. Many of them are novelists and poets, others are journalists, historians, anthropologists and literary critics. Several of them teach, and one is a schoolgirl. Most of the contributions are highly personal, and each begins with an autobiographical note.

Ursula Owen was born in 1937. Her parents lived in Berlin until 1938 when, as German Jews, they had to emigrate to Britain. She went to school in London and took a degree in Physiology at Oxford University. Before going into publishing she was a social worker and researcher, and also spent several years in the Middle East and America. A founder member and joint managing director of Virago, she has a daughter and lives in London.

If you would like to know more about Virago books, write to us
at 41 William IV Street, London WC2N 4DB for a full catalogue.

Please send a stamped addressed envelope

VIRAGO
Advisory Group

Book Tokens

**Give them
the pleasure of choosing**
Book Tokens can be bought
and exchanged at most
bookshops

FATHERS

Reflections by Daughters

EDITED BY
URSULA OWEN

Virago

Published by Virago Press Limited 1983
41 William IV Street, London WC2N 4DB

British Library Cataloguing in Publication Data
Fathers reflections by daughters.
    1. Fathers and daughters
    I. Owen, Ursula
    306.8′742   HQ755.85

    ISBN 0-86068-394-X

Photoset by Rowland Phototypesetting Limited
Bury St Edmunds, Suffolk

Printed in Great Britain by litho at
St Edmundsbury Press, Bury St Edmunds.

CONTENTS

CONTENTS

ACKNOWLEDGEMENTS

Thanks to Hugh Brody, Jane Cousins, Livy Harris, Julia Vellacott and Bill Webb for reading parts of the manuscript, and for many conversations.

'Cap O' Rushes' is taken from *English Fairy Tales*, collected and rewritten by Joseph Jacobs (David Nutt, London 1895); the contribution by Doris Lessing first appeared as 'My Father' in *A Small Personal Voice* (Vintage, 1975); the contribution by Julia O'Faolain first appeared in a slightly different version in the *London Magazine* (Issue June 1980); Michèle Roberts' poem 'memories of trees' is taken from *Licking the Bed Clean* (Teeth Imprints, 1978); Stevie Smith's poem 'Papa Love Baby' is taken from *Collected Poems* (Allen Lane 1979), and is reproduced by permission of James MacGibbon; Elaine Feinstein's poem 'Dad' is taken from her collection *Some Unease and Angels* (Hutchinson, 1981); the contribution by Adrienne Rich first appeared in a slightly different version in *Nice Jewish Girls* (Persephone Press, 1982); 'A Conversation with my Father' by Grace Paley first appeared in *Enormous Changes at the Last Minute* (Virago, 1978).

Extracts from books are taken from the following sources: Virginia Woolf, *Three Guineas* (Penguin 1977); Simone de Beauvoir, *The Second Sex* (Penguin 1974); May Sinclair, *The Three Sisters* (Virago 1982) and *Life and Death of Harriett Frean* (Virago 1980); Ann Douglas, *The Feminisation of American Culture* (Knopf 1979); Rebecca West, *The Fountain Overflows* (Macmillan 1957); Emily Holmes Coleman, *The Shutter of Snow* (Virago 1981); *The Journals of Anais Nin, Vol III* (Quartet 1974); Margaret Walker, 'On Being Black, Female and Free', from *A Writer and her Work*, ed. Janet Sternburg (Norton 1980); Arthur Wing Pinero, *The Second Mrs Tanqueray* (French); Mary Gordon, 'The Parable of the Cave or: In Praise of Watercolors', from *A Writer and her Work*, ed. Janet Sternburg (Norton 1980); Antonia White, *The Lost Traveller* (Virago 1979); E. E. Maccoby and C. N. Jacklin, *The Psychology of Sex Differences* (Stanford University Press

1975); Nancy Chodorow, *The Reproduction of Mothering* (University of California Press 1979); Mary Gordon, *Final Payments* (Corgi 1978); John and Elizabeth Newsom, *Four Years Old in an Urban Community* (Penguin 1970); N. and J. MacKenzie, eds, *The Diary of Beatrice Webb, Vol I (Virago 1982); George Eliot, The Mill on the Floss* (Penguin 1979); Sigmund Freud, *On Sexuality* (Penguin 1953); Sigmund Freud, *Case Histories I* (Penguin 1953); Janine Chasseguet Smirgel, *Female Sexuality* (Virago 1981); Dinah Brook, *Games of Love and War* (Cape 1976); Naomi Mitchison, *Small Talk: Memories of an Edwardian Childhood* (Bodley Head 1973); Antonia White, *The Hound and the Falcon* (Virago 1980); Marjorie Leonard, 'Fathers and Daughters (*International Journal of Psychoanalysis*); Elizabeth Von Arnim, *Vera* (Virago 1983) and the *Pastor's Wife* (Macmillan, 1914); H. G. Wells, *Ann Veronica* (Virago 1980); Christina Stead, *For Love Alone* (Virago 1978); Olive Schreiner, *The Story of an African Farm* (Penguin 1982); Adrienne Rich, *Of Woman Born* (Virago 1977); Paule Marshall, *Brown Girl, Brownstones* (Virago 1982).

All photographs reproduced by kind permission of the authors. The photograph of Adrienne Rich's parents was kindly supplied by Rita Dibbert. The photograph of Sigmund Freud and Sophie Freud-Halberstadt reproduced by kind permission of Sigmund Freud Copyrights Ltd, England.

❤

*For Bill Webb, whose idea it was,
and who knows something about the subject.*

INTRODUCTION

In 1951, when I was fourteen years old, I came across a photograph of my father in British army uniform. For a child of my time, this should not have been strange, but for me it was. My father was an immigrant, a German Jew; he had never been in the British army. But as a German-speaking industrialist, he'd been sent by the British government as soon as the war ended to look at the state of German industry, and they'd dressed him up in colonel's uniform to make him look the part.

But for me the photograph always had another, special significance. Because it was odd, I looked at it closely. I was a teenager battling with an autocratic if benevolent father who very much expected his will to be done. And here was this same man, in uniform, looking uncharacteristically ill at ease, anxious, even sheepish. The expression on his face was one I didn't recognise. After a while I realised what it was: my father looked vulnerable.

The photographer had caught him off guard. Now I'd seen it once, I began to see that expression on his face more often. The way I looked at my father altered, and the way I felt about him changed too: I still loved him very much, he still seemed an immensely powerful person, and I was still at times afraid of him. But now I realised that he wasn't always in control and, what's more, that I knew things he didn't – because I was a woman. As the eldest daughter I'd already been initiated into the world of women, where feelings are more freely expressed. By the time I left home a few years later, I recognised that much of this vulnerability lay in the fact that, like many men, he seemed ill at ease with his own emotions.

In a sense that photograph is the kernel of this book: when the idea was suggested to me, I remembered that image.

The father as patriarch, apparently invulnerable, in control, is one of our most powerful mythologies. We may know them intimately, feel at ease with them, but fathers do represent something beyond this intimacy: social power; and the bond inevitably raises fundamental questions for daughters. It is striking that, though women have written a great deal recently about their mothers, and there is beginning to be a veritable industry in theories of fathering and fatherhood, there is much less information from the receiving end of this embattled and intense relationship. What *do* daughters feel about their fathers?

Writing about a parent is never easy: our parents lie at the heart of our innermost feelings, and are part of our most important inner debates. For daughters writing about fathers, this difficulty seems to be acute. For one thing, apart from fiction, there's no tradition within which to write such an account, which may leave a certain freedom but – like so many freedoms – also induces a sort of vertigo.

In our century, there are two idioms in which the father–daughter bond has been expressed. The first is Freud's and that of the psychoanalysts who came after him. However little Freudian ideas are accepted or even understood, the Oedipus complex, with its central focus on the sexual feelings a daughter has for her father, is now part of our stock in trade. The second idiom is to be found in writings about patriarchy, the institutionalised power of the fathers. The consequences of living in a patriarchal society have begun to be explored in the last fifteen years or so. Adrienne Rich puts it well: 'For the first time in history we are in a position to look at the country of fathers and see it for what it is and has been. What we see is the one system which recorded civilisation has never actively challenged and which is so universal as to appear a law of nature. Patriarchy is the power of the fathers, a familial, social and political system in which men . . . determine what part women shall or shall not play and in which the female is everywhere subsumed under the male.'

For most women, the starting point of being thus subsumed is their relationship to their fathers. The purpose of this book could be summarised as an opportunity for women to try and find their own idiom for this most complicated of relationships, to explore their own experience of paternal authority. The contributors are almost all writers, though this is not a 'literary' book. Nor is it intended to supply answers. The women here felt they had something to say, and I decided to record their voices rather than attempt the highly problematic task of finding a representative cross-section of women. *Fathers*, in fact, began with many conversations and the subject provoked a remarkably strong response. Some women even decided to write something whether it would be included in the book or not, out of a sheer sense of discovered need. There were those who simply refused, finding it too painful, or fearing it would stir up old family dramas best left alone, or would hurt the people involved. And for many women who agreed to contribute, there turned out to be anxieties which took them by surprise.

Loyalty is always a problem when writing about families, and this created particular difficulties for every writer whose father was alive. It was a sign of the emotional complexity of the work that while several contributors talked of an overwhelming desire to fragment, compress or disregard information that lay in painful areas, at the same time most wanted urgently to get to grips with the subject – to 'break the taboos', as Michele Roberts puts it. Several women spoke of how difficult it was to put the most ordinary events into writing – they turned out to be not so ordinary after all. In some essays the absences and silences are almost as eloquent as what is said. The loyalties induced in daughters turn out to be formidably strong, and are sometimes based on fear as well as love.

The tensions came out in conversations with the authors: 'It's been the most difficult thing I've ever written'; 'It's the kind of intimacy which seems to bring out contradictory and murderous thoughts in me'; 'While I'm writing about him I feel as if I'm pushing something uphill'. Several said that the moment their pen touched the paper they felt they were betraying their history; one said that her mother, brothers and sisters seemed to appear as shadows over her shoulder, restraining her. It's no accident, then, that people often approached the subject in a sideways fashion, and there is much that can be read between the lines: a taboo subject indeed. And the struggle, always, for an idiom.

So little has been said, so much has been seen and not heard in this area, that we don't really know the questions to which answers are needed. So the brief for this book was left wide – fathers: reflections by daughters. The results are wide-ranging, too, and the form of the contributions is very varied. There are memoirs, stories, poems, polemics. And there are many kinds of father here – shadowy, attentive, absent, overpowering, charming, loyal, gentle, violent, or a mixture of many of these and other characteristics. Some women describe the closest and most loving relationships, others bitter-sweet or unresolved ties, others again angry and painful encounters, including the darkest of them all, incest. That it is a problematic bond, full of ambivalences and longings, comes out in many of these essays. It also, incidentally, comes out in conversations with fathers, who quite often have equally intense feelings about this relationship. But that is another book. Some daughters remain incorrigibly anxious about their fathers: others express particular joy at being cherished as a child or forming close ties with a father later in life, or grief because a father has died before these were made. Anne Boston describes

11

the strangeness of growing up fatherless; Dinah Brooke writes about coming to terms with an unstable father from whom she longed for support; Michèle Roberts was as a young girl unashamedly in love with hers. Sara Maitland deals with her father's godlike qualities by creating a mythic father; Cora Kaplan looks again at one of the most famous parent-child encounters, between Edward Barrett and Elizabeth Barrett Browning, and the idea of the 'wicked' father. Rose Rider gives a powerful account of incest; Angela Carter talks of a father who never used fear as a means of control, and Julia O'Faolain quietly interviews her father on the craft she shares with him.

Perhaps there are as many father-daughter relationships as there are daughters, but there are recurring themes here. Several accounts convey a daughter's huge need to please, the desire to win approval, which may never be given. Whether this drives a woman to try harder and harder, a common enough cliché, is difficult to gauge. It may be no more the case than for the favoured daughter, the one in whom all in invested, who must reflect everything the father holds most dear *and* all that's best in womanhood. In exchanged for being this chosen one, for protection and entry into his world, the favoured daughter often has to offer an extraordinary loyalty to her father. Daughters in the 1980s may have gained independence in a way their mothers and grandmothers would never have dreamed of, but the sense of having failed a father by going against his will or being critical seems hardly to have diminished. We remain very much in the kingdom of the fathers. And there's something else at work here too, very familiar to many women. It is the fear that, by being critical, women reveal their competence and independence: we're afraid of desexing ourselves, of no longer seeming to be 'real' women to our fathers, and so losing their seemingly essential protection.

The strange thing is that fathers – the essential protectors – are often absent, especially during a child's early years. Fathers are special, moving in another world which obliges them constantly to leave home – a pattern vividly described by Olivia Harris. Even though many mothers work outside the home, and especially now, in the recession, are often the main breadwinners in the family, fathers are still the symbolic link to the outside world, to the market place, to 'out there'. The mother's world is the everyday, the home, the meeting of daily needs, and the girl's own future.

The presence of the mother looms large in many of these essays. For some she is a powerfully felt absence: or she is a model of a strong woman for the daughter; sometimes she is a person who naturally enters the scene when the father is discussed. There will be many reasons for this, and a consideration of one parent, whether in writing or in one's thoughts, often drives attention towards the other. But one reason stands out: responsibility for the care of children is left largely to mothers, and it is she who mediates between the daughter and the father – and then may be ignored for her pains. Again and again there is a late recognition of a mother's stoicism, particularly where the daughter and father have been very close. Daughters who idolised their fathers when they were children talk of undervaluing their mothers, being blind to their qualities. Perhaps this is a natural product of the difficulties and intensities of family life. But it is also confirmation that mothers and fathers symbolise quite different aspects of experience in children's early lives – far beyond those which biology lays down.

There are some notable absences. Some of these accounts give a sense of the reality of Oedipal attraction, but there is surprisingly little about the moment when a woman transfers her affection to a lover or husband – the time supposed to be especially fraught for the father-daughter relationship. And there's little speculation here on whether, or how, the choice of a lover is affected by that father-daughter relationship. Perhaps these daughters are negotiating with their fathers on their own territory, as independent people, rather than as lovers and wives. Or perhaps, as with many near-clichés about women, this one is being dismantled by women themselves. The authors of this book know that their mother often influences their future loving as much as their father.

In our culture, mothering is a job and fathering is a hobby. It may turn out to be a lifelong passion, but it is still a hobby, and fathers who want to alter this find no real model available to them. A father can choose his duties: there is no normal or essential behaviour which defines him as a father or predetermines the nature of his fathering. He can be attentive and cherishing or neglectful and violent, but he still remains simply a father. There is no such flexibility with mothering. The job is laid down, defined, set in cement. If mothers break the rules they are called to order, their status as mothers is questioned: for fathers, there are no such clear rules to break.

Except perhaps one. Some women have felt that fathers can make or break a daughter's confidence in her own power. The favoured daughter is often recognisable for her confidence, her refusal to accept powerlessness. Women know more now about how fathers can affect their sense of themselves, and it is possible that daughters are beginning to make some ground rules for fathering.

Two last points: this book has turned out to be a sort of collage, and I have linked the contributions with quotations from fiction, psychoanalysis, sociology and poetry which reflect other ways of talking about fathers and daughters. I have also included photographs of the contributors with their fathers. This produced a minor but interesting revelation: almost everyone had difficulty in finding one. Why? 'Because Dad always takes the photograph.' What does that vignette tell us about family life? There's a great deal still to be read between the lines. This is only a beginning.

Ursula Owen, London, 1983

CAP O' RUSHES

from English Fairy Tales

Collected and rewritten by Joseph Jacobs

Well, there was once a very rich gentleman, and he'd three daughters, and he thought he'd see how fond they were of him. So he says to the first, 'How much do you love me, my dear?'

'Why,' says she, 'as I love my life.'

'That's good,' says he.

So he says to the second, 'How much do *you* love me, my dear?'

'Why,' says she, 'better nor all the world.'

'That's good,' says he.

So he says to the third, 'How much do *you* love me, my dear?'

'Why, I love you as fresh meat loves salt,' says she.

Well, but he was angry. 'You don't love me at all,' says he, 'and in my house you stay no more.' So he drove her out there and then, and shut the door in her face.

Well, she went away on and on till she came to a fen, and there she gathered a lot of rushes and made them into a kind of a sort of a cloak with a hood, to cover her from head to foot, and to hide her fine clothes. And then she went on and on till she came to a great house.

'Do you want a maid?' says she.

'No, we don't,' said they.

'I haven't nowhere to go,' says she, 'and I ask no wages, and do any sort of work,' says she.

'Well,' said they, 'if you like to wash the pots and scrape the saucepans you may stay,' said they.

So she stayed there and washed the pots and scraped the saucepans and did all the dirty work. And because she gave no name they called her 'Cap o' Rushes'.

Well, one day there was to be a great dance a little way off, and the servants were allowed to go and look on at the grand people. Cap o' Rushes said she was too tired to go, so she stayed at home.

15

But when they were gone she offed with her cap o' rushes, and cleaned herself, and went to the dance. And no one there was so finely dressed as she.

Well, who should be there but her master's son, and what should he do but fall in love with her the minute he set eyes on her. He wouldn't dance with any one else.

But before the dance was done Cap o' Rushes slipt off, and away she went home. And when the other maids came back she was pretending to be asleep with her cap o' rushes on.

Well, next morning they said to her, 'You did miss a sight, Cap o' Rushes!'

'What was that?' says she.

'Why, the beautifullest lady you ever see, dressed right gay and ga'. The young master, he never took his eyes off her.'

'Well, I should have liked to have seen her,' says Cap o' Rushes.

'Well, there's to be another dance this evening, and perhaps she'll be there.'

But, come the evening, Cap o' Rushes said she was too tired to go with them. Howsoever, when they were gone she offed with her cap o' rushes and cleaned herself, and away she went to the dance.

The master's son had been reckoning on seeing her, and he danced with no one else, and never took his eyes off her. But, before the dance was over, she slipt off, and home she went, and when the maids came back she pretended to be asleep with her cap o' rushes on.

Next day they said to her again, 'Well, Cap o' Rushes, you should ha' been there to see the lady. There she was again, gay and ga', and the young master he never took his eyes off her.'

'Well, there,' says she, 'I should ha' liked to ha' seen her.'

'Well,' says they, 'there's a dance again this evening, and you must go with us, for she's sure to be there.'

Well, come this evening, Cap o' Rushes said she was too tired to go, and do what they would she stayed at home. But when they were gone she offed with her cap o' rushes and cleaned herself, and away she went to the dance.

The master's son was rarely glad when he saw her. He danced with none but her and never took his eyes off her. When she wouldn't tell him her name, nor where she came from, he gave her a ring and told her if he didn't see her again he should die.

Well, before the dance was over, off she slipt, and home she went, and when the maids came home she was pretending to be asleep with her cap o' rushes on.

16

Well, next day they says to her, 'There, Cap o' Rushes, you didn't come last night, and now you won't see the lady, for there's no more dances.'

'Well, I should have rarely liked to have seen her,' says she.

The master's son he tried every way to find out where the lady was gone, but go where he might, and ask whom he might, he never heard anything about her. And he got worse and worse for the love of her till he had to keep to his bed.

'Make some gruel for the young master,' they said to the cook. 'He's dying for the love of the lady.' The cook she set about making it when Cap o' Rushes came in.

'What are you a-doing of?' says she.

'I'm going to make some gruel for the young master,' says the cook, 'for he's dying for love of the lady.'

'Let me make it,' says Cap o' Rushes.

Well, the cook wouldn't at first, but at last she said yes, and Cap o' Rushes made the gruel. And when she had made it she slipped the ring into it on the sly before the cook took it upstairs.

The young man he drank it and then he saw the ring at the bottom.

'Send for the cook,' says he.

So up she comes.

'Who made this gruel here?' says he.

'I did,' says the cook, for she was frightened.

And he looked at her.

'No, you didn't,' says he. 'Say who did it, and you shan't be harmed.'

'Well, then, 'twas Cap o' Rushes,' says she.

'Send Cap o' Rushes here,' says he.

So Cap o' Rushes came.

'Did you make my gruel?' says he.

'Yes, I did,' says she.

'Where did you get this ring?' says he.

'From him that give it me,' says she.

'Who are you, then?' says the young man.

'I'll show you,' says she. And she offed with her cap o' rushes, and there she was in her beautiful clothes.

Well, the master's son he got well very soon, and they were to be married in a little time. It was to be a very grand wedding, and everyone was asked far and near. And Cap o' Rushes' father was asked. But she never told anybody who she was.

But before the wedding she went to the cook, and says she: 'I want you to dress every dish without a mite o' salt.'

'That'll be rare nasty,' says the cook.

'That doesn't signify,' says she.

'Very well,' says the cook.

Well, the wedding day came, and they were married. And after they were married all the company sat down to the dinner. When they began to eat the meat, it was so tasteless they couldn't eat it. But Cap o' Rushes' father tried first one dish and then another, and then he burst out crying.

'What is the matter?' said the master's son to him.

'Oh!' says he, 'I had a daughter. And I asked her how much she loved me. And she said, "As much as fresh meat loves salt." And I turned her from my door, for I thought she didn't love me. And now I see she loved me best of all. And she may be dead for aught I know.'

'No, father, here she is!' says Cap o' Rushes. And she goes up to him and puts her arms round him.

And so they were all happy ever after.

Lear: . . . *What can you say, to draw*
A third, more opulent than your Sisters? Speak.
Cordelia: *Nothing, my Lord.*
Lear: *Nothing?*
Cordelia: *Nothing.*
Lear: *Nothing will come of nothing, speak again.*
Cordelia: *Unhappy that I am, I cannot heave*
My heart into my mouth: I love your Majesty
According to my bond, nor more nor less.

King Lear, Act I, Scene 1

Shall we press the old word 'freedom' once more into service? . . . Let 'freedom
from unreal loyalties' then stand as the fourth great teacher of the daughters of
educated men.

Virginia Woolf, *Three Guineas*

ANGELA CARTER

Sugar Daddy

I was born in 1940. 'Carter' is the name of my first husband, not that of my father. His family trekked from the feudal darkness of the West Highlands to the Protestant ethic of the east coast of Scotland some time in the eighteenth century but, through several generations, contrived to retain certain specifically regional characteristics of loquacity, squalor and mythomania which have served me well in my career as writer of fiction and freelance journalism.

Two of my seven novels (*The Magic Toyshop*, 1967, and *The Passion of New Eve*, 1977) have recently been published as Virago Modern Classics. I have also published two collections of short stories, the most recent of which is *The Bloody Chamber* (King Penguin, 1981), and a nonfiction monograph, *The Sadeian Woman*, Virago, 1979. In 1982, Virago published a collection of my journalism, *Nothing Sacred*, most of which originally appeared in the magazine, *New Society*, to which I am a regular contributor. My work has been translated into the major European languages.

I live in South London and use the same public library in which my mother studied for a grammar school scholarship in 1917.

I would say my father did not prepare me well for patriarchy; himself confronted, on his marriage with my mother, with a mother-in-law who was the living embodiment of peasant matriarchy, he had no choice but to capitulate, and did so. Further, I was the child of his mid-forties, when he was just the age to be knocked sideways by the arrival of a baby daughter. He was putty in my hands throughout my childhood and still claims to be so although now I am middle-aged myself whilst he, not though you'd notice, is somewhat older than the present century.

I was born in 1940, the week that Dunkirk fell. I think neither of my parents were immune to the symbolism of this, of bringing a little girl-child into the world at a time when the Nazi invasion of England seemed imminent, into the midst of death and approaching dark. Perhaps I seemed particularly vulnerable and precious and that helps to explain the overprotectiveness they felt about me, later on. Be that as it may, no child, however inauspicious the circumstances, could have been made more welcome. I did not get a birthday card from him a couple of years ago; when I querulously rang him up about it, he said: 'I'd never forget the day you came ashore.' (The card came in the second post.) His turn of phrase went straight to my heart, an organ which has inherited much of his Highland sentimentality.

He is a Highland man, the perhaps atypical product of an under-developed, colonialised country in the last years of Queen Victoria, of oatcakes, tatties and the Church of Scotland, of four years' active service in the First World War, of the hurly burly of Fleet Street in the twenties. His siblings, who never left the native village, were weird beyond belief. To that native village he competently removed himself ten years ago.

He has done, I realise, what every Sicilian in New York, what every Cypriot in Camden Town wants to do, to complete the immigrant's journey, to accomplish the perfect symmetry, from A to B and back again. Just his luck, when he returned, that all was as it had been before and he could, in a manner of speaking, take up his life where it left off when he moved south seventy years ago. He went south; and made a career; and married an Englishwoman; and lived in London; and fathered children, in an enormous parenthesis of which he retains only sunny memories. He has 'gone home', as immigrants do; he established, in his seventh decade, that 'home' has an existential significance for him which is not part of the story of his children's independent lives. My father lives now in his granite house filled with the souvenirs of a long and, I think, happy life. (Some of them bizarre; that framed certificate from an American tramp, naming my father a 'Knight of the Road', for example.)

He has a curious, quite unEnglish, ability to live life in, as it were, the *third person*, to see his life objectively, as a not unfortunate one, and to live up to that notion. Those granite townships on the edge of the steel-grey North Sea forge a flinty sense of self. Don't think, from all this, he isn't a volatile man. He laughs easily, cries easily, and to his example I attribute my conviction that tears, in a man, are a sign of inner strength.

He is still capable of surprising me. He recently prepared an electric bed for my boyfriend, which is the sort of thing a doting father in a Scots ballad might have done had the technology been available at the time. We knew he'd put us in separate rooms – my father is a Victorian, by birth – but not that he'd plug the metal base of Mark's bed into the electric light fitment.

21

Mark noticed how the bed throbbed when he put his hand on it and disconnected every plug in sight. We ate breakfast, next morning, as if nothing untoward had happened, and I should say, in the context of my father's house, it had not. He is an enthusiastic handyman, with a special fascination for electricity, whose work my mother once described as combining the theory of Heath Robinson with the practice of Mr Pooter.

All the same, the Freudian overtones are inescapable. However unconsciously, as if *that* were an excuse, he'd prepared a potentially lethal bed for his daughter's lover. But let me not dot the i's and cross the t's. His final act of low, emotional cunning (another Highland characteristic) is to have lived so long that everything is forgiven, even his habit of referring to the present incumbent by my first husband's name, enough to give anybody a temporary feeling.

He is a man of immense, nay, imposing physical presence, yet I tend to remember him in undignified circumstances.

One of my first memories is how I bust his nose. I was, perhaps, three years old. Maybe four. It was on a set of swings in a public park. He'd climbed up Pooterishly to adjust the chains from which the swings hung. I thought he was taking too long and set the swing on which I sat in motion. He wasn't badly hurt but there was a lot of blood. I was not punished for my part in this accident. They were a bit put out because I wanted to stay and play when they went home to wash off the blood.

They. That is, my father and my mother. Impossible for me to summon one up out of the past without the other.

Shortly after this, he nearly drowned me, or so my mother claimed. He took me for a walk one autumn afternoon and stopped by the pond in Wandsworth Common and I played a game of throwing leaves into the water until I forgot to let go of one. He was in after me in a flash in spite of the peril to his gents' natty suiting (ever the dandy, my old man) and wheeled me dripping in my pushchair home to the terrible but short-lived recriminations of my mother. Short-lived because both guilt and remorse are emotions alien to my father. Therefore the just apportioning of blame is not one of his specialities, and though my mother tried it on from time to time, he always thought he could buy us off with treats and so he could and that is why my brother and I don't sulk, much. Whereas she –

She has been dead for more than a decade, now, and I've had ample time to appreciate my father's individual flavour, which is a fine and gamey one, but, as parents, they were far more than the sum of their individual parts. I'm not sure they understood their instinctive solidarity against us, because my mother often tried to make us take sides. Us. As their child, the product of their parenting, I cannot dissociate myself from my brother, although we did not share a childhood for he is twelve years older than I and sent off, with his gas mask, his packed lunch and his name tag, as an evacuee, a little hostage to fortune, at about the time they must have realised another one was on the way.

I can only think of my parents as a peculiarly complex unit in which neither bulks larger than the other, although they were very different kinds of people and I often used to wonder how they got on, since they seemed to have so little in common, until I realised that was *why* they got on, that not having much in common means you've always got something interesting to talk about. And their children, far from being the raison d'être of their marriage, of their ongoing argument, of that endless, quietly murmuring conversation I used to hear, at night, softly, dreamily, the other side of the bedroom wall, were, in some sense, a sideshow. Source of pleasure, source of grief; not the glue that held them together. And neither of us more important than the other, either.

Not that I suspected this when I was growing up. My transition from little girl to ravaged anorexic took them by surprise and I thought they wanted my blood. I didn't know what they wanted of me, nor did I know what I wanted for myself. In those years of ludicrously overprotected adolescence. I often had the feeling of being 'pawns in their game' . . . in *their* game, note . . . and perhaps I indeed served an instrumental function, at that time, rather than being loved, as it were, for myself.

All this is so much water under the bridge. Yet those were the only years I can remember when my mother would try to invoke my father's wrath against me, threaten me with his fury for coming home late and so on. Though, as far as the 'and so on' was concerned, chance would have been a fine thing. My adolescent rebellion was considerably hampered by the fact that I could find nobody to rebel with. I now recall this period with intense embarrassment, because my parents' concern to protect me from predatory boys was only equalled by the enthusiasm with which the boys I did indeed occasionally meet protected themselves against me.

It was a difficult time, terminated, inevitably, by early marriage as soon as I finally bumped into somebody who would go to Godard movies with me and on CND marches and even have sexual intercourse with me, although he insisted we should be engaged first. Neither of my parents were exactly overjoyed when I got married, although they grudgingly did all the necessary. My father was particularly pissed off because he'd marked me out for a career on Fleet Street. It took me twenty years more of living, and an involvement with the women's movement, to appreciate he was unusual in wanting this for his baby girl. Although he was a journalist himself, I don't think he was projecting his own ambitions on me, either, even if to be a child is to be, to some degree, the projective fantasy of its parents. No. I suspect that, if he ever had any projective fantasies about me, I sufficiently fulfilled them by being born. All he'd wanted for me was a steady, enjoyable job that, perhaps, guaranteed me sufficient income to ensure I wouldn't too hastily marry some nitwit (a favourite word of his) who would displace him altogether from my affections. So, since from a child I'd been good with words, he apprenticed me to a suburban weekly newspaper when I was eighteen, intending me to make my traditional way up from there. From all this, given my natural perversity, it must be obvious why I was so hell-bent on getting married – not, and both my parents were utterly adamant about this, that getting married meant I'd give up my job.

In fact, it *did* mean that because soon my new husband moved away from London. 'I suppose you'll have to go with him,' said my mother doubtfully. Anxious to end my status as their child, there was no other option and so I changed direction although, as it turns out, I *am* a journalist, at least some of the time.

As far as projective fantasies go, sometimes it seems the old man is only concerned that I don't end up in the workhouse. Apart from that, anything goes. My brother and I remain, I think, his most constant source of pleasure – always, perhaps, a more positive joy to our father than to our mother, who, a more introspective person, got less pure entertainment value from us, like all mothers, though partly for reasons within her own not untroubled soul. As for my father, few souls are less troubled. He can be simply pleased with us, pleased that we exist, and, from the vantage point of his wonderously serene and hale old age, he contemplates our lives almost as if they were books he can dip into whenever he wants. His back pages, perhaps.

As for the books I write myself, my 'dirty books', he said the other day: 'I was a wee bitty shocked, at first, but I soon got used to it.' He introduces me in the third person: 'This young woman . . .' In his culture, it is, of course, a matter of principle to express pride in one's children. It occurs to me that this, too, is not a particularly English sentiment.

Himself, he is a rich source of anecdote. He has partitioned off a little room in the attic of his house, constructed the walls out of cardboard boxes, and there he lies, on a camp bed, listening to the World Service on a portable radio with his cap on. When he lived in London, he used to wear a trilby to bed but, a formal man, he exchanged it for a cap as soon as he moved. There are two perfectly good bedrooms in his house, with electric blankets and everything, as I well know, but these bedrooms always used to belong to his siblings, now deceased. He moves downstairs into one of these when the temperature in the attic drops too low for even his iron constitution, but he always shifts back up again, to his own place, when the ice melts. He has a ferocious enthusiasm for his own private space. My mother attributed this to a youth spent in the trenches, where no privacy was to be had. His war was the War to end Wars. He was too old for conscription in the one after that.

When he leaves this house for any length of time, he fixes up a whole lot of burglar traps, basins of water balanced on the tops of doors, tripwires, bags of flour suspended by strings, so that we worry in case he forgets where he's left what and ends up hoist with his own petard.

He has a special relationship with cats. He talks to them in a soft, chirruping language they find irresistible. When we all lived in London and he worked on the night news desk of a press agency, he would come home on the last tube and walk, chirruping, down the street accompanied by an ever-increasing procession of cats, to whom he would say good night at the front door. On those rare occasions, in my late teens, when I'd managed to persuade a man to walk me home, the arrival of my father and his cats always caused consternation, not least because my father was immensely tall and strong.

He is the stuff of which sit-coms are made.

His everyday discourse, which is conducted in the stately prose of a thirties *Times* leader, is enlivened with a number of stock phrases of a slightly eccentric, period quality. For example:
On a wild night: 'Pity the troops on a night like this.'
On a cold day: 'Cold, bleak, gloomy and glum,
                 Cold as the hairs on a polar bear's –'
The last word of the couplet is supposed to be drowned by cries of outrage. My mother always turned up trumps on this one, interposing: 'Father!' on an ascending scale.
At random: 'Thank God for the navy, who guard our shores.'
On entering a room: 'Enter the fairy, singing and dancing.' Sometimes, in a particularly cheerful mood, he'll add to this formula: 'Enter the fairy, singing and dancing and waving her wooden leg.'

Infinitely endearing, infinitely irritating, irascible, comic, tough, sentimental, ribald old man, with his face of a borderline eagle and his bearing of a Scots guard, who, in my imagination as when I was a child, drips chocolates from his pockets as he strides down the road bowed down with gifts, a cat dancing in front of him crying: 'Here comes the Marquis of Carrabas!' The very words, 'my father', always make me smile.

But why, when he was so devilish handsome – oh, that photograph in

battledress! – did he never marry until his middle thirties? Until he saw my mother, playing tennis with a girlfriend on Clapham Common, and that was it. The die was cast. He gave her his card, proof of his honourable intentions. She took him home to meet her mother. Then he must have felt as though he were going over the top, again.

In 1967 or 1968, forty years on, my mother wrote me: 'He really loves me (I think).' At that time, she was a semi-invalid and he tended her, with more dash than efficiency, and yet remorselessly, cooking, washing up, washing her smalls, hoovering, as if that was just what he'd retired from work to do, up to his elbows in soapsuds after a lifetime of telephones and anxiety. He'd bring her dinner on a tray with always a slightly soiled traycloth. She thought the dirty cloth spoiled the entire gesture. And yet, and yet . . . was she, after all those years, still keeping him on the hook? For herself, she always applauded his ability to spirit taxis up as from the air at crowded railways stations and also the dexterous way he'd kick his own backside, a feat he continued to perform until he was well into his eighties.

Now, very little of all this has to do with the stern, fearful face of the Father in patriarchy, although the Calvinist north is virtually synonymous with that ideology. Indeed, a short-tempered man, his rages were phenomenal; but they were over-in the lightning flash they resembled, and then we all had ice cream. And there was no fear. So that, now, for me, when fear steps in the door, then love and respect fly out the window.

I do not think my father has ever asked awkward questions about life, or the world, or anything much, except when he was a boy reporter and asking awkward questions was part of the job. He would regard himself as a law-and-order man, a law-abiding man, a man with a due sense of respect of authority. So far, so in tune with his background and his sense of decorum. And yet somewhere behind all this lurks a strangely free, anarchic spirit. Doorknobs fall from doors the minute he puts his hand on them. Things fall apart. There is a sense that anything might happen. He is in a law-and-order man helplessly tuned in to misrule.

And somewhere in all this must lie an ambivalent attitude to the authority, to which he claims to defer. Now, my father is not, I repeat, an introspective man. Nor one prone to intellectual analysis; he's always got by on his wits so never felt the need of the latter. But he has his version of the famous story, about one of the Christmas truces during the First World War, which was *his* war, although, when he talks about it, I do not recognise Vera Brittain's war, or Siegfried Sassoon's war, or anything but a nightmarish adventure, for, as I say, he feels no fear. The soldiers, bored with fighting, remembering happier times, put up white flags, moved slowly forward, showed photographs, exchanged gifts – a packet of cigarettes for a little brown loaf . . . and then, he says, 'some fool of a First Lieutenant fired a shot'.

When he tells this story, he doesn't know what it *means*, he doesn't know what the story shows he really felt about the bloody officers, nor why I'm proud of him for feeling that; nor why I'm proud of him for giving the German private his cigarettes and remembering so warmly the little loaf of bread; and proud of him for his still undiminished anger at the 'nitwit' of a boy whom they were all forced to obey just when the ranks were in a mood to pack it in and go home.

Of course, the old man thinks that, if the rank and file *had* packed it in and gone home in 1915, the Tsar would still rule Russia and the Kaiser Germany, and the sun would never have set on the British Empire. He is a man of grand simplicities. He still grieves over my mother's leftish views; indeed, he grieves over mine, though not enough to spoil his dinner. He seems, rather, to regard them as, in some way, genetically linked. I have inherited his nose, after all, so why not my mother's voting patterns?

She never forgave him for believing Chamberlain. She'd often bring it up, at moments of stress, as proof of his gullibility. 'And, what's more, you came home from the office and said: "There ain't gonna be a war."'

See how she has crept into the narrative, again. He wrote to me last year: 'your mammy was not only very beautiful but also very clever'. (Always in dialect, always 'mammy'.) Not that she did anything with it. Another husband might have encouraged her to work, or study, although, in the nineteen thirties, that would have been exceptional enough in this first generation middle-class family to have projected us into another dimension of existence altogether. As it was, he, born a Victorian and a sentimentalist, was content to adore, and that, in itself, is sufficiently exceptional, dammit, although it was not good for her moral fibre. She, similarly trapped by historic circumstance, did not even know, I think, that her own vague discontent, manifested by sick headaches and complicated later on by genuine ill health, might have had something to do with being a 'wife', a role for which she was in some respects ill-suited, as my father's tribute ought to indicate, since beauty and cleverness are usually more valued in mistresses than they are in wives. For her sixtieth birthday, he gave her a huge bottle of Chanel No. 5.

For what it's worth, I've never been in the least attracted to older men – nor they to me, for that matter. Why *is* that? Possibly something in my manner hints I will expect, nay, demand, behaviour I deem appropriate to a father figure, that is, that he kicks his own backside from time to time, and brings me tea in bed, and weeps at the inevitability of loss; and these are usually young men's talents.

Don't think, from all this, it's been all roses. We've had our ups and downs, the old man and I, for he was born a Victorian. Though it occurs to me his unstated but self-evident idea I should earn my own living, have a career, in fact, may have originated in his experience of the first wave of feminism, that hit in his teens and twenties, with some of whose products he worked, by one of whose products we were doctored. (Our family doctor, Helen Gray, was eighty when she retired twenty years ago, and must have been one of the first women doctors.)

Nevertheless, his Victorianness, for want of a better words, means he feels duty bound to come the heavy father, from time to time, always with a histrionic overemphasis: 'You just watch out for yourself, that's all.' 'Watching out for yourself' has some obscure kind of sexual meaning, which he hesitates to spell out. If advice he gave me when I was a girl (I could paraphrase this advice as 'Kneecap them'), if this advice would be more or less what I'd arm my own daughters with now, if I had any, it ill accorded with the mood of the sixties. Nor was it much help in those days when almost the entire male sex seemed in a conspiracy to deprive me of the opportunity to get within sufficient distance. The old man dowered me with too much self-esteem.

But how can a girl have *too much* self-esteem?

Nevertheless, not all roses. He is, you see, a foreigner; what is more, a Highland man, who struck further into the heartland of England than Charles Edward Stewart's army ever did, and then buggered off, leaving his children behind to carve niches in the alien soil. Oh, he'd hotly deny this version of his life; it is my own romantic interpretation of his life, obviously. He's all for the Act of Union. He sees no difference at all between the English and the Scots, except, once my mother was gone, he saw no reason to remain amongst the English. And his always unacknowledged foreignness, the extraversion of his manners, the stateliness of his demeanour, his fearlessness, guiltlessness, his inability to feel embarrassment, the formality of his discourse, above all, his utter ignorance of and complete estrangement from the English system of social class, make him a being I puzzle over and wonder at.

It is that last thing – for, in England, he seemed genuinely classless – that may have helped me always feel a stranger, here, myself. He is a perfectly good petty bourgeois stock; my grandfather owned a shoe shop although, in those days, that meant being able to make the things as well as sell them, and repair them, too, so my grandfather was either a shopkeeper or a cobbler, depending on how you looked at it. The distinction between entrepreneur and skilled artisan may have appeared less fine, in those days, in that town beside the North Sea which still looks as if it could provide a good turn-out for a witch burning.

There are all manner of stories about my paternal grandfather, whom I never met; he was the village atheist, who left a fiver in his will to every minister in the place, just in case. I never met my Gaelic-speaking grandmother, either. (She died, as it happens, of toothache, shortly before I was born.) From all the stories I know they both possessed in full measure that peculiar Highland ability, much perplexing to early tourists, which means that the meanest, grubbing crofter can, if necessary, draw himself up to his full height and welcome a visitor into his stinking hovel as if its miserable tenant were a prince inviting a foreign potentate into a palace. This is the courtly grace of the authentic savage. The women do it with an especially sly elegance. Lowering a steaming bowl onto a filthy tablecloth, my father's sister used to say: 'Now, take some delicious kale soup.' And it was the water in which the cabbage had been boiled.

It's possible to suspect they're having you on, and so they may be; yet this formality always puts the visitor, no matter what his or her status, in the role of supplicant. Your humiliation is what spares you. When a

Highlander grovels, then, oh, then, is the time to keep your hand on your wallet. One learns to fear an apology most.

These are the strategies of underdevelopment and they are worlds away from those which my mother's family learned to use to contend with the savage urban class struggle in Battersea, in the nineteen hundreds. Some of my mother's family learned to cynically manipulate the English class system and helped me and my brother out. All of them knew, how can I put it, that a good table with clean linen meant self-respect and to love Shakespeare was a kind of class revenge. (Perhaps that is why those soiled traycloths upset my mother so; she had no quarrel with his taste in literature.) For my father, the grand gesture was the thing. He entered Harrods like the Jacobite army invading Manchester. He would arrive at my school to 'sort things out' like the wrath of God.

This effortless sense of natural dignity, of his own unquestioned worth, is of his essence; there are noble savages in his heredity and I look at him, sometimes, to quote Mayakovsky, 'like an Eskimo looking at a train'.

For I know so little about him, although I know so much. Much of his life was conducted in my absence, on terms of which I am necessarily ignorant, for he was older than I am now when I was born, although his life has shaped my life. This is the curious abyss that divides the closest kin, that the tender curiosity appropriate to lovers is inappropriate, here, where the bond is involuntary, so that the most important things stay undiscovered. If I am short-tempered, volatile as he is, there is enough of my mother's troubled soul in me to render his very transparency, his psychic good health, endlessly mysterious. He is my father and I love him as Cordelia did, 'according to my natural bond'. What the nature of that 'natural bond' might be, I do not know, and, besides, I have a theoretical objection to the notion of a 'natural bond'.

But, at the end of *King Lear*, one has a very fair notion of the strength of that bond, whatever it might be, whether it is the construct of culture rather than nature, even if we might all be better off without it. And I do think my father gives me far more joy than Cordelia ever got from Lear.

The life of the father has a mysterious prestige: the hours he spends at home, the room where he works, the objects he has around him, his pursuits, his hobbies, have a scared character. He supports the family, and he is the responsible head of the family. As a rule his work takes him outside, and so it is through him that the family communicates with the rest of the world: he incarnates that immense, difficult and marvellous world of adventure; he personifies transcendence, he is God.

Simone de Beauvoir, *The Second Sex*

She hated it. She hated the whole house. It was so built that there wasn't a corner in it where you could get away from Papa. His study had one door opening into the passage and one into the dining-room. The window where he sat raked the garden on the far side. The window of his bedroom raked the front; its door commanded the stairhead. He was aware of everything you did, of everything you didn't do. He could hear you in the dining-room; he could hear you overhead; he could hear you going up and downstairs. He could positively hear you breathe. She drew in her breath lest he should hear it now.

May Sinclair, *The Three Sisters*

Children were like their father's family or their mother's, and Cordelia had taken her inheritance from Papa. That gave her some advantages, it did indeed. Mary had black hair and I had brown, and so had many other little girls. But though Papa was so dark there was red hair in his family, and Cordelia's head was covered with short red-gold curls, which shone in the light and made people turn round in the street. There was something more to that than mere heredity, too, which made it harder to bear. It was at Papa's insistence that Mamma kept Cordelia's hair short at a time when that was a long-forgotten fashion, not to be renewed for years. At his home in Ireland there had been a portrait of his Aunt Lucy, with her hair dressed in the fashion known as à la Bacchante, and as Cordelia was very like her he got Mamma to get her curls cut in as nearly the same style as puzzled hairdressers in South Africa and Edinburgh could manage.

Mary and I were not pleased about this. It made us feel that Cordelia was not only closer to Papa than we were, owing to an unfair decision of Nature, but that she was also an object on which he had worked to bring her up to the standards of his taste. He had not done that to us.

Rebecca West, *The Fountain Overflows*

SARA MAITLAND

Two for the Price of One

I was born in 1950, the second of six children. After being excessively well educated in expensive girls' schools in London and Wiltshire, I went to Oxford in 1968. There, *inter alia*, I read English and discovered the women's movement, socialism and friendship. In 1972 I married someone who is now an Anglican priest and with whom I share a marriage, two children and a passionate commitment to extreme Anglo-Catholicism. Possibly because of my proven inability to do anything else very efficiently I started describing myself as a writer in about 1975 and since then have written a novel, *Daughter of Jerusalem* (Blond and Briggs, 1978); a book about feminism and Christianity, *A Map of the New Country* (Routledge and Kegan Paul, 1983); a number of short stories – some of which I wrote in collaboration with Zoe Fairbairns, Valerie Miner, Michele Roberts and Michelene Wandor and were published in *Tales I Tell My Mother* (Journeyman, 1978), and some more which are being published in my own collection *Telling Tales* (Journeyman, 1983). Also some articles, journalism, reviews and sermons. Recently I have been working with Jo Garcia on editing a collection of writings on spirituality from within the women's movement, *Walking on the Water* (Virago, 1983). Now I want to write another novel, which is proving difficult. I don't like being in my thirties much, and am looking forward to being fifty, and better still seventy-five.

I have two fathers.

I have a material, biological father. His name was Adam Maitland; he was born in 1913; his earliest memory was of waiting on a station platform for his father (a serving officer) to come home on leave; he had an odd unlovely childhood; he went to Cambridge, served in the war; in 1948 he married my mother, it was a very strong and happy marriage; he had six children; at the age of fifty he retired from his job as managing director of a large London printing press and went home to south west Scotland to manage his inherited acres instead; in March 1982, in his own home, after 'a long illness bravely borne', as they say, he died of cancer.

I have another father. This one is alive and well and rampaging inside me. He never goes away, although sometimes he is silent; he is never ill, never weakened, never leaves me alone. He lurks about under other names – God, Husband, Companion, and all those relationships are made possible (which is nice) and impossibly difficult and conflicting because of the Father who is in and under and through them all. In my late teens I fled away from my father's house; it has taken me a long time to realise that I carried with me the Father from whom I could not escape by escaping childhood, from whom I have not yet escaped, and from whom I have had, and still have, to wrest my loves, my voice, my feminism and my freedom. It is this Father that I have hated loving and loved hating. It is this Father that I want to kill, and dare not

In the eighteen months between the diagnosis of my father's cancer and his death it became vital for me to separate the two fathers, because – of course – I did not want to kill my father. I really did not want to; because in the last ten years or so of his life I had come to respect this person who happened to be my father – an unusual, distinguished and in many ways admirable man. I liked him. And also because his death, his absence, was going to mean that I could no longer use the childish device of blaming him for everything that was difficult in my life. The years of evasion and projection were coming to an end, the dark Father in my head was coming into consciousness, was putting on the pressure. I do not know how to use that Father. I want him out. I don't want to kill my father but my guilt rose up and indicted me: at one point I actually believed that his cancer had developed *because* I had started seeing a therapist – in a new attempt to subdue and vanquish the wild Father inside my own self.

I wanted to separate the fathers not just to allay my own guilt, but because I honestly learned that they were not the same person. When he became ill, my brothers and sisters and I talked of him in a new way, recalling him through memories and anecdotes and stories, shoring up his presence. I noticed something odd: what I had thought of as literal chronological memories were either so absent from their heads that they could not believe that the episodes I remembered had ever happened (and vice versa); or the incidents remained, but flavoured with such different emotions and meanings as to render them almost unrecognisable. I had to see that we, who all shared the same historical father, all had different fathers inside our heads. Between the six of us we had seven fathers.

Quite soon before he died I realised that I had a special bequest from him. He gave us many gifts, and among them he gave me a real knowledge and deep love for mythology. I started with his classical pantheon and with the tales from the Old Testament, and these have been tools of my thinking and working ever since. In Jane Lazarre's book *On Loving Men* I read that in classical mythology, that bloody and treacherous web of connections and hatreds, there is no story in which the daughter kills the father. I was taken aback. I searched high and low. I sifted through the equally blood-strewn corpus of the Bible. I extended my research into other mythologies. I thought to myself, 'Oh ho, here is male dominance at work, this is the one tale They cannot afford to know.' Then I started looking at historical murders, the ones that make it to the sleazy annals of crime literature. Women, I discovered, after travelling in some pretty gruesome places, do not murder their fathers. Or do so very seldom, and under very bizarre circumstances. It is an extremely rare crime. Women murder men – their lovers, their employers, their children, their rapists, their ancient uncles, and the victims of stray meetings on the street. Clytemnestra drowned Menelaus in the bath; Jael made a bloody mess of Sisera; Myra Hindley mutilated children. Nothing can be universally claimed about women's gentleness, their lack of violence, their tender loving hearts; but they don't kill their fathers. If we don't kill our fathers then I could not have killed mine. Why did he, who taught me so many things, never teach me that my anger would not kill him? Or me? Or our love?

I think of this little fact as a gift because it set me free of some fears and helped me begin to separate the fathers. But it is not easy, and learning to separate them means also learning how they are joined. They grow from one root and it cannot be severed. To canonise my biological father at the expense of my mythic father, to absolve my physical father by projecting onto the interior father every dark thing that *father* means in a sexist society, will bring me no nearer to the truth – about myself, or him, or fathers, or daughters.

I am my father's daughter. I cannot love myself unless I love him.

I am a woman. I cannot be free while I am a daughter possessed by the Father inside my head.

He was just a man, I tell myself. He was a man whom I loved, as it happens. He was my father; he was the most influential person in my life. He was a man who introduced me into a male-dominated world.

One of my problems with my father is that he really did correspond to the archetype of the Father. Many women grow out of their father when they discover that he is not really like what fathers are supposed, imaginatively, mythologically to be: he is weak, or a failure, or dishonest, or uninterested, or goes away. My father was not a perfect person, but he was very Father-like.

He was one of the Old Gods – Zeus, Yahweh, Odin. The mediaeval Christian God-the-father was distant and unapproachable, above and beyond emotions. The oriental god is pure impersonal spirit-in-the-cosmos. The modern God suffers humbly with his poor (and may even be imaged as female). But the Old Gods were in there with their people: emotional, excitable, passionate, the administrators of a deeply partial justice, jealous of their prerogatives, zealously prejudiced in favour of their own, vengeful and dangerous when crossed, and delightedly generous when pleased by services rendered. They were powerful, and willing to use that power.

That might be a thumbnail sketch of my father.

Of course his power was partly social. On grounds of class and wealth he had a simple confidence about who he was, where he came from, and his ability to give his children what he wanted. It was physical – he was strong and very good-looking; he could not tolerate physical weakness, his own or other people's. It was personal too; he had 'presence', a sort of shining inflexibility which, while it could and did infuriate people, also commanded a respect.

He was not a distant father. He cared. His energy was directed at us in flood waves. He held a responsible and demanding job; he was an intelligent man and friends with influential and powerful people; he was actively interested in politics (Conservative), philanthropy and, with limitations, culture. But we came first. He came home from the office every day and ate high tea with his family. He bathed his babies, climbed trees, kicked footballs, hugged, kissed and played with his children. Above all he *taught* us, but close to, not from far away. It started at dawn; whichever of us was at that stage of education went to get dressed in his dressing room. While he shaved he taught us our times tables, his face visible only in the mirror registering pleasure or irritation at our answers. When we knew our times tables impeccably, and the boys went off to prep school he turned his attention to me and to wider fields of knowledge. With him, at seven-thirty in the morning, I learned by heart irregular Latin verbs, the dates of the Kings of England and Scotland and – along with quantities of other Victorian verse – the whole of 'How Horatius Kept the Bridge in the Brave Days of Old' from MacCauley's *Lays*

of Ancient Rome. When I was in interminable labour with my first child I found myself muttering, 'And how can man die better/than by facing, fearful odds/For the ashes of his fathers/and the temples of his Gods.' There are seventy verses, I found I still knew them all and was comforted. He was a master pedagogue, full of zeal, enthusiasm and the expectation and demand that we would perform well. We did.

He really came into his own when we went to live in Scotland. There the split between business and family, work and play, inside and outside disappeared. We were organised, energised, empowered by him, with scarcely a moment's break. I can easily understand how the ancient Hebrews did not believe in an individual soul, but only in the spirit of the community – Yahweh and my father seem to have had a lot in common and the driving force was 'the tribe in activity'. Now we were communally involved in high-energy activities as much of the time as possible:

gardening, planting trees, playing tennis, playing bridge, climbing hills, rowing boats, dancing reels, entertaining visitors, shooting, fishing, fighting, laughing, teasing. (He encouraged us, and joined us almost to the point of brutality in the permitted ranges of teasing – so long as it was witty it was fine. Simple rude abuse was not allowed but to be funny at someone else's expense was 'good for them'. How long you could stand it without bursting into tears and rushing from the dining room was a measure of merit.) He was the direct force. Because the boys went away to school, and because too of a natural affinity of mind, there was at least a time when I was the central recipient of his energetic love.

He was partial. There was nothing cold about either his justice or his loyalty, nor about what he expected in return. He had an extraordinary sense of family, not particularly snobbish, but he lived in the home of his ancestors and saw himself – and all other members of his brood – in a curiously tribal way; simply one link in a chain which should not be broken. He handed on to us what he had received from them: education, pride, class privileges and class responsibility, a wealth of belonging as much as of belongings. He delighted to see that continue; he certainly deprived himself and my mother of many material luxuries (and some basic comforts) in order to hand on intact a promise of a future for the family estate. His grandchildren gave him a special joy. In the last few days of his life when speech had become impossible and when a great weariness seemed his main emotion, he still wanted to have the babies – mine and my sister's smallest children were then only months old – on the bed with him, or playing on the floor around him.

Yahweh made a deal with the children of Israel: his devotion and loyalty in exchange for their keeping his law. It was like that for us. We were disciplined hard. He was on the side of grown-up civilisation against childhood anarchy, but he was on our side against the world. He did not teach too much respect for other authorities: we were praised for being critical of governments and powers – especially bureaucracies; impertinence towards them was not an unforgivable sin. He wanted us independent, especially physically, to travel, to look after ourselves, to be brave, courageous, not afraid of the universe and its conventions. He never (to our embarrassment) hid his scorn of the petty disciplines of girls' school life. But the bright independence, the questioning intelligence he taught us was not to be used against him. And like the Old Gods, infringements were punished with a ferocious and wild wrath. Thunderbolts were hurled, there was roaring in the heavens. Punishments of the most unsuitable nature were dealt out, blows and humiliations were part of his repertoire, and they were not confined necessarily to domestic privacy.

We were punished for tantrums by his tantrums. We were punished for any loss of control by his abandoning of control. It was confusing, to put it mildly.

It was made still more confusing by his godlike assumption that everything he did was somehow *right*, not on a personal level, but by some objective law of the universe. This is how it was, and is and evermore shall be. Moving only a step or two away from him, it became obvious that not everyone in the whole world believed what he believed, acted as he acted, and that those who did not were not damned to an eternity of chaos, stupidity, unhappiness and immorality. But when one moved into his orbit it was impossible to remember this.

Because of the overwhelming sense that he knew best I couldn't just disagree with him and let it go, I needed his endorsement. When I first opposed the Vietnam war I wrote him screeds and screeds about why; I put an enormous amount of energy in trying to get him to admit at least that I wasn't stupid to feel this war was wrong – a hopeless task and one I never gave up on. Right up to the end of his life I wanted his approval. The size of the family gave an added weight to this sense of his rightness; even if two or three of us were at odds with him at the same time it was inevitably on different grounds, and the unspoken pressures to keep the family united were immense.

That is why I have found this article nearly impossible to write. Nothing I have done has sat so heavy on my fingers – I have to drag the words away from my family. They do not want me to write this. I know this, even though I haven't told any of them that I'm going to do so. To try and *look* at my family means that I'm withdrawing from it; I'm taking something away, I'm challenging not just my father but the whole code by which we live, as a family. I do not want to betray them. I feel that I am betraying them, committing an act of disloyalty, and family loyalty was at the centre of my childhood, because my father was loyal to us, to his own code and to his idea of family.

In return for this loyalty and hard work and involvement he wanted ours. It was impossible to measure up. I never felt that anything I did was quite good enough. His standards weren't just high, they were mountainous, above me. When I got into Oxford, I felt strongly that it wasn't Cambridge. 'We' always went to Cambridge. I had failed to get into Cambridge and failure wasn't good enough. While I was berated and teased for being a bookworm and withdrawn from the family and physically clumsy, other family members were harassed for not doing well enough in school or not reading enough. Later my family found the great majority of my friends 'uncouth' (and that was after I had hand-picked the more presentable ones for them to meet!) but my sisters' friends, who were definitely 'couth', indeed substantially 'county', were regarded as frivolous and stupid. Of course everyone was received with hospitality and charm. It was I, not they, who had failed. My father wanted brains and accomplishments, and beauty and charm and good manners and independence and imagination and originality and conventionalism and clear thinking and obedience and health and virtue and success and self-discipline, self-control, orderliness. Perfection, simply.

I bought his model. I believed if I tried harder I could manage it: such was the charm that he had for me as a child and in my early teens. I wanted to be Pallas Athene to his Zeus. In some ways he encouraged this identification. When I was fifteen he took me, just me alone, that was part of the magic, to Italy. For a fortnight we toured the classical and Renaissance high spots of Rome and Florence. This was our shared heritage and he gave it to me with warmth and wit. It was probably the two weeks of most unalloyed, simple happiness of my whole life. For any child from a large family, extended time alone with a parent is a real treat; but this was something more. I wanted to be that rational woman, the powerful father-identified companion, the daughter who was worthy of love. The weeks in Italy were as near as I ever got.

In the end I could not pull it off. As I approached a delayed adolescence with an older brother who had many of the necessary skills and a younger sister who had a very successful relationship with my mother already established, there was little room for manoeuvre. Moreover there were a number of things I could not give proper consideration to. My father loved my mother very much; with a richness and fullness and companionship that was in some ways complete. You cannot be a father-identified daughter and treat your mother with respect and devotion; it just isn't possible, not if your mother is creatively housewifely, with six children, a warm kitchen, considerable intelligence and an adored and adoring husband. I know some daughters who feel their fathers turned to them to substitute for the deficiencies in their wives; that is simply not the case with my father. He loved the child, not the woman. Because I did not treat my mother well he was furious with me too often. My mother did not protect me from his fury, so I treated her still less well and he was even more furious.

My father taught me to be independent and cocky, and free-thinking, but he could not stand it if I disagreed with him. I do not know how that can be resolved. What I did learn was that he would not love me unless I loved him completely, and he would not love me if I loved him completely. After much yelling and screaming on both sides, I ran away, and kept running but never left. I did and felt things just because they were things he would not want me to do and feel. It did me little good.

Now I want to tell stories about him all the time. I am told sometimes that I sentimentalise him, but I don't think this is true. I want to tell these stories not just to remember him, but to individualise him, to separate him from the faceless Father inside my head – the man who is without weakness, without history.

The Father inside my head runs a protection racket – the God Father. He is not as principled as my other father and he is very much more powerful. For a very high price, he does provide protection. The price is behaviour: if I am good – the way my father wanted me to be – then the Father will say, 'This is my beloved daughter, in whom I am well pleased,' and will both present me with the world and protect me from it. The potential rewards for a fully paid-up daughter are greater than those for a son. The Fathers adore a well-brought-up daughter. Sons come cheaper and without the sweetness of victory. Sons may grow up and become fathers, but daughters never will, though they can if necessary be bestowed on a younger man as a gift and a reward. The Father in my head holds me in a double blackmail: if you are good I will cherish you *and* if you are bad I will punish you. But I will never ignore you or leave you alone or let you go your own way. I pay and pay and pay. In exchange for the rewards, the punishments and the constant attention I am strong and never ill, and I am industrious and look after my husband and children, and I am professional and competent and tough. I never get too angry, too sad or too mad. I exercise control and charm and good manners and I do not run off to the woods at night when the moon is full to grunt and wallow with the sows or howl with the wolf cubs. I ignore, or spank, the little girl who wants to scream or sulk or play in the mud or eat too many ice creams. I have to persuade myself that I am superwoman, and, knowing that I'm not, continue to act as though I were: I have to be everything my mother is, plus everything the boys are, plus something extra. Pallas Athene was goddess of peace and war, fully armed and always calm, never foolish, never in love, never a child, never naughty, never in the wrong.

This internal Father monitors my relationships with others and with myself. My feelings about my women friends is deeply ambivalent. I find them exciting at every level, but part of that excitement is the danger of it; when the Father notices he will be very angry. Women's approval, companionship, makes me feel happy, but it does not ever make me feel virtuous, safe, or good. Men's approval, which does make me feel virtuous, does not make me feel happy, safe or good. And in this conflict between being happy and being virtuous I am never at peace. Virtue, far from being its own reward, becomes tortuously its own punishment. I punish myself for happiness too, both by destroying it – not doing the things that would make me happy (from simple little things like never indulging myself with cream buns through to never making space to do the writing I most want to do) – and by punishing myself, with guilt, for things I have enjoyed. I fret about this masochism in myself but I do not know how to change it.

My father planted the seeds of this Father in my head, but it was watered and manured and nourished and trained by society and by circumstance. There is so much that was, and ought to be, positive in what my real father gave me, but I feel shadowed by the negatives; his power and his standards and his image were affirmed everywhere, even by other women. And in the end the daughters cannot pay enough; everywhere, finally, the fathers decide for the sons and not for the daughters. In the end you cannot win this one, girls. My father, who brought us up to believe in equality, in human rights for women, in equal education and equal value, in the end divided his estate between his sons – he dealt generously with his daughters, and it seems mean to complain (a quick apologetic aside). But his heirs – his real, social heirs – are his boys. The love that my father had for me and expressed so fully and so generously has soured in me. It was so exactly, uncannily, precisely that paternal love which a deeply anti-woman society uses to control its uppity women. I suppose it's not his fault. But should he have known?

And where are the mothers? In a sane society the power of the Mother inside would protect the daughters from the unleashed power of the Fathers, would balance the Fathers with their own power, and we could receive our fathers' love without being broken by it. There is nothing flimsy about my mother; she is tough and loving and knows and uses her real power and she loves her children. But she's a woman in history – she used her strength and energy for my father and for us. I think this was genuinely fulfilling for her and that she was happy. But the Mother in my head says, 'Serve the father and the children; protect the father from what might scare him in the mother; don't ask for too much for yourself, and be contented.' So she cannot counterbalance the power of the father, but only further it. Where will we find the powerful mother?

One last story about my father. Last year I met some old friends of my parents. I had not seen them for a long time, though we had known them well as children. We chatted away, and inevitably talked about my parents and suddenly they were saying, 'It used to make us laugh how frightened your father was of his mother?' I was amazed. My grandmother *was* a frightening woman, a bizarrely terrible old lady and we had all been scared of her, including my mother. But my *father*? My father frightened of his mother, my father so frightened that his friends, who incidentally had not known him as a child, but only after he was grown up, knew about it.

In a way it increased my affection for him. But there is something else. I have compared him to the Old Gods. There is an ancient secret: the Old Gods were always terrified of the Older Mother, the Goddess who had been before them and was waiting, dispossessed but dangerous. I have always liked the metaphor of feminism as a new incarnation of the Older Goddess, the Oldest Gods. Her power will cast out the mighty from their seats. The power of feminism will cast out the Father in my head who rules and controls me. Feminism will set me free. But I also want feminism to leave alone my splendid father, the man of honour who taught me so much about so much – even how to die with dignity. I don't know if it's possible to make terms with, to lay conditions on, this abstraction of the Great Goddess. This frightens me; I want to protect my father and my love for him. I do not want to kill him, to see him dead. I want to set the man free from having to be a father.

Is this real? Or is it one more price that the power of the Fathers is demanding that I pay?

The child expected protectiveness, loyalty, comfort, attention, help, teaching, guidance, companionship. His failure to be reassuring, present even, accessible, approving, companionable, dictated the judgement. If I had known him as a playmate with whom roughhousing and games might be treacherous, dangerous even, and a matter of pitting one's energy and skills, or sharing adventures, he would have been my companion in dangerous experiences. Instead he became the awesome figure of the no-praise man, creating in me such a need of approval.
The Journals of Anaïs Nin

Ever since I was a little girl I have wanted to write and I have been writing. My father told my mother it was only a puberty urge and would not last but he encouraged my early attempts at rhyming verses just the same, and he gave me the notebook or daybook in which to keep my poems together. When I was eighteen and had ended my junior year in college, my father laughingly agreed it was probably more than a puberty urge. I had filled the 365 pages with poems.
Margaret Walker, in A Writer on Her Work,
ed. Janet Sternburg

Fathers appear to want their daughters to fit their image of a sexually attractive female person, within the limits of what is appropriate for a child, and they play the masculine role vis-à-vis their daughters as well as their wives. This may or may not generate rivalry between mother and daughter, but there can be little doubt that it is a potent force in the girl's development of whatever behaviour is defined as 'feminine' by her father.
Maccoby and Jacklin, The Psychology of Sex Difference

The young girl (and the woman she becomes) is willing to deny her father's limitations (and those of her lover or husband) as long as she feels loved. She is more able to do this because his distance means that she does not really know him. The relationship, then, because of the father's distance and importance to her, occurs largely as fantasy and idealization, and lacks the grounded reality which a boy's relation to his mother has.
Nancy Chodorow, The Reproduction of Mothering

ANNE BOSTON

Growing Up Fatherless

Much of my background is described in the chapter about my father, but a few more facts: I am thirty-eight, a freelance journalist, and live in North London. After taking a degree in International Relations at Sussex University I worked for a news agency, book publishers and *Nova* and *Cosmopolitan* magazines before going freelance. Besides writing for magazines and newspapers, I am *Cosmopolitan's* fiction editor. I'm always hoping to find a Great New Talent among the hundreds of unsolicited short stories – just as I always intend to write a book of short stories myself. For the past three years I have been involved in the campaign for nuclear disarmament; looking ahead seems positively quixotic under the circumstances, yet one still makes plans for the future.

On my fifth birthday an announcement was made at morning prayers by one of the two small, portly sisters who ran the school where my brother and I were pupils. It was Anne's birthday, said Miss Galley, and today everybody must be nice to me because 'Anne doesn't have a Daddy'.

In retrospect, it's odd that I should have been singled out with that magnificently tactless non sequitur, since fatherless families could hardly have been unusual in the post-war years. Whatever Miss Galley's motives, that was the first time I can remember registering that my family was 'different' from others. While I felt a brief flush of self-importance at the unexpected attention, it came as a surprise to hear that we deserved sympathy – I adored my mother and brother, and was delighted with our move to a new house and school. No father existed in my experience. Why, at five, should you grieve over a person you never knew? What his absence would mean to my brother and me, in the shaping of our lives and selves as we grew up, would be quite another matter.

Dad, Daddy, Father – the words, the concept are foreign territory. I've never called anybody by any of those names, except for gabbled pleas to Our Heavenly Father in school prayers. Even referring to 'my father' seems stilted: our mother always spoke of him as David, and so, by way of imitation, did I.

David, then, was killed on the first of May 1945, a last-minute casualty of the war. He left his armoured car to inspect a shell crater in the road ahead; in the crater was a live landmine which blew up when he approached. My mother received the news in a telegram with bells printed on it, the Post Office's contribution to Victory Day celebrations. I was born two weeks later, a posthumous baby – right on time to the day, according to my mother's calculations.

By a quirk of fate I was not only without a father, but without either grandfather after the age of six. My childhood was, I hasten to say, a wonderfully contented one – if there's anything to be learned from the experience it's the absurdly obvious (but often forgotten) point that not all happy families are nuclear families. As a result, I've always tended to discount the effects of being without a father – quite wrongly, I think now. There were effects, and they continued to influence my entire life, if anything increasingly so.

On what level does an infant absorb its parent's grief in the first, unremembered years? If the rest of my childhood was to become as charmed as it now seems in retrospect, that must have been *despite* David's death – for, make no mistake, it was a disaster for my mother. He'd been the most loved, most important person in her life, and there would be no replacement for him. But I (and my brother Simon) had been dealt two major advantages. First, we'd lost a father we'd never known, which was a great deal less painful than the loss would have been after familiarity had bound us close! For us, death had scythed off David's life as cleanly as if (apart from the fact of our existence) he had never been. And second, we were brought up by a mother who refused to cast herself as a victim – of fate, tragedy, misfortune, what you will. In time she would come to enjoy and even prefer the independence and self-reliance which had been forced upon her; but even when I was very small, she somehow created an illusion of emotional strength and safety round us.

Although his parental role so far as I was concerned was strictly biological, the fact that I was able to draw on a ready-made mythology about my father was an essential part of my security. Virtually everything I heard about him (apart from his letters, which I read much later) came filtered through the memories of his mother, and mine – they talked about him, not in a reverential 'your sainted father' sort of way, nor as a conventional figure of parental authority which of course he'd never been, but as they'd known him.

Granny, an incurable romantic, was a great storyteller and regaled Simon and me with dozens of 'tales' about David as a small boy; the only child, he'd been a delicate, thoughtful, bookish boy, dreadfully cosseted by his mother. She always told these tales in exactly the same words, so often repeated that the punch lines became chorused refrains. My mother, who had a built-in resistance to Granny's romancifying, didn't actually talk about David much but vivid fragments of her past with him would emerge from time to time – how they'd met in the Quaker Friends' Ambulance Unit early in the war (David had been a pacifist at that time), their digs in blacked-out Soho, celebratory meals in Greek Street and cooking rook pie for friends, the long waits to see him on leave after he'd joined up.

Their favourite photographs of David reflect the difference in their attitudes towards him. Granny had soft-focus neo-Victorian portraits, carefully posed and taken by Grandpa (an accomplished amateur photographer), of herself reading to the infant David who nestled, entranced, by her side. My mother has dog-eared snapshots, cherished for the way they catch a particular moment: David leaning up against a corn stook, smoking a pipe and looking contemplatively at the camera, both of them laughing together over a shared picnic. So there he is, devoted son and wartime lover: inappropriate yet oddly sustaining images for a child to remember her father by.

I'm grateful for those comforting impressions. They helped to fend off the potent threat left by my absent father, which lurked on the edges of conscious thought. Occasionally strange images would surface like oil slicks in dreams. How old was I, for instance, when I dreamed my father returned from the war? I could see him in the distance as he walked down the road where we lived, past one side of the field and the gate where Nobby the horse stood, to the corner where our row of cottages started, and I knew as he drew closer that I would have to kill him with my knife which I held ready in my hand. . . . And surely the unspeakable childhood terror of ghosts which haunted my nights and made some of the most innocuous fairy stories insupportable must have been buried deep in my knowledge of his death, and fear of his return. 'You cannot turn your back upon a dream,/For phantoms have their reasons when they come.'*

I'm told I am very like David, and I can see this from the photographs:

*From 'The Ghost (after Sextus Propertius)' by Robert Lowell.

the straight nose and square jaw, the heavy-lidded eyes and (unfortunately) the short sight, are all reproduced in me. My mother has sometimes been startled to see his gestures repeated by both my brother and
myself, though we never saw their originals, and she recognises distinct
likenesses in temperament. By all accounts I'm unmistakably my father's
daughter. Of course I have a romanticised view of him. He didn't come
back from the war, a stranger, to reclaim my mother from me. He didn't
become disappointed, disillusioned, middle-aged; I never saw him brow-
beaten by his mother or arguing with mine (who has wondered, on
occasion, how he would have withstood the rival pull of their demanding
personalities if he had lived). Idealised or not, I've every reason to believe
we would have got on very well together. But it's no reflection on David to
say that I could hardly have enjoyed a more contented first ten years than
I did without him.

The reverse side of David's absence from our lives was our mother's presence. Inevitably, without David the imprint of her character on ours would be doubly strong; in fact she *replaced* him and became both parents to us, so that – at any rate up to adolescence – far from feeling deprived I had a great sense of completeness in my family.

It's impossible for me to describe my upbringing without David without including my mother: she was Family Personified, and absolutely central in the world of my childhood affections. Comparing my attitude towards her with the way friends regard their parents, I realise that it's been more than a matter of our being unusually fond of one another: she stood for more, and fulfilled a far more complex role. Besides being the person who fed and cared for and comforted me, she was the provider and mentor; the head of the family; to be emulated as well as loved. Too good to be true, isn't it? Only characters in Victorian novels have mothers that marvellous. But mine was no defenceless child widow, but an attractive, resourceful young woman with a strong streak of Yorkshire practicality, who was determined to carve out the best opportunities and – even more important – the most enjoyable life she could for the three of us.

Why does misfortune apparently strengthen some people's reserves of endurance, yet shatter others? Just as the repercussions of David's death were to ripple invisibly but endlessly through my life, although I never consciously missed him, my mother must have been profoundly affected by her past. It was extraordinary enough, in an unsensational way – she'd been brought up without father *or* mother, having been orphaned at the age of five.

Her family came from comfortably off Yorkshire stock, in the local Sheffield business of silver and cutlery manufacturing. My mother's parents were childhood friends and half of a double match, two sisters marrying two brothers. I'd very much like to have known them. Photographed in Egypt, where grandfather Cooper was posted as an army vet and where my mother was born, neither of them looks in the least prepared for tragedy: on the contrary, they've every appearance of being an extrovert and jolly couple – a good Yorkshire antidote to the lavish vein of Victorian melancholy which ran through my father's family. But my grandfather died of heart failure in Egypt when my mother was five; and his wife survived only six months before succumbing to pneumonia. My mother and her older sister were brought up by their uncle and aunt, the other half of their parents' double match, who treated them with kindness and affection, if not with love.

My mother was very bright academically, but wasn't sent to university (something she greatly regretted later, with the result that she was determined that I and my brother would have every opportunity to go). She stayed on at her old school, Ackworth, to work as the school secretary, then joined the Quaker Friends' Ambulance Unit in London when the war broke out – and met David under a table during an air raid.

Cut to David's death, and you can see why everything depended on our ma. With my arrival she had two babies under eighteen months old to cope with, no home, no money to speak of, and no immediate family to call on for help. (Even my birthplace seems to have been haphazard: my mother was staying with friends in West Kirby, Cheshire, somewhere she's never been before or since.) I've always thought of my childhood as profoundly secure; but that's ignoring those first two years, which stay obstinately locked outside all our memories. My mother doesn't talk about that time. Certainly, our physical circumstances were anything but stable.

We seem to have spent the first years after David's death in a kind of limbo. The obvious place for us to settle was with David's parents in the Midlands, but the undertow of friction between Granny and my mother was too strong for this to be a permanent solution; so we shunted between friends and relations-in-law, with occasional trips back to the aunt and uncle who'd brought up my mother. Not until I was nearly three did we set up house alone together, when my mother rented an isolated cottage on the Welsh border near Shrewsbury.

My first and strongest impression of Home is of the Welsh cottage. That landscape is my childhood pastoral, the border mountains are my Blue Remembered Hills. It was a Cold Comfort cottage – no electricity or running water, rats scrabbling in the attic, nearest shops a bus ride away. But the abrasive physical discomfort was therapeutic for my mother. It made her start to fight back. During that time she must have made the awful wrench out of grief, when even to think of the future seems treachery and betrayal, and have reached some kind of acceptance of her position. Whatever had been dealt out in the past, from then on *she* was the one who would make things happen. At the end of the year we moved to the Thames Valley, near close friends of hers with three boys roughly the same age as Simon and me.

Maidenhead, with its faded riverside splendours, was a comfortable enough place to grow up in, though I can't say we put down roots there: after we moved to London in my late teens I never went back. With some difficulty my mother had arranged a mortgage (it had to be signed by a male guarantor) on, 7 Chauntry Road, a small, cramped terraced house with a leaking glass-roofed lean-to kitchen slapped on the back. The front bedroom looked across the road straight on to a massive railway bank carrying the main-line Great Western Railway, and whenever an express thundered down the near side all speech was blotted out – to this day I find the sound of trains intensely evocative.

'When we say a woman is of a certain class, we really mean that her husband or father is,' said the author Zoe Fairbairns recently. It's an interesting generalisation; but what happens to families which have neither? We were extraordinarily short of men anywhere in the family – even David's father, Grandpa Caulkin, quietly died while I was still small. Like clergymen's families, our living was often at odds with the people we mixed with. I suppose our circumstances put us into the category of 'distressed gentlefolk', except that my mother rejected the pathos of the part. In fact, we probably enjoyed far greater freedom from social restrictions than if our status had been conventionally defined, which had advantages for all of us. My mother's way of life wasn't dramatic or self-conscious enough to be bohemian but was distinctly individual – 'arty', as school friends put it later. We flourished, somehow, on the edges of respectability, mildly disapproved of by my mother's sister and cousin.

My mother was determined at any rate that our education would be respectable. Now that my brother and I were learning the two R's – both Miss Galleys were defeated by arithmetic – at our small private school, she had a full-time secretarial job at the nearby Taplow hospital. She gradually enlarged the work to include teaching French to the long-stay child patients, administration and so on; but it wasn't well paid, and she had the added cost of a childminder for us till she finished work. She says now that to the extent that she worried at all about money it was that lack of it would deprive us of 'opportunities', especially as we got older, but we were unaware of these dragging anxieties and I don't remember a single occasion when it prevented either of us children from doing anything we wanted.

'Soft management' would be the business terminology for the way my mother ran our lives. Her system was unorthodox but practical. Whenever the various spheres in her life – family, friends, work – threatened to conflict, her policy was not to separate but to combine them, with the overriding proviso that Family Came First. So on holidays when I was at a loose end I'd spend whole days with her at the hospital, crayoning pictures in the medical library or inspecting the rabbits and white rats in the animal house attached to the pathology lab. This habit of including family and friends in her work has been lifelong – she still looks after her grandson George in the office as she once did me. The policy worked well; my brother and I saw no threat in her work, and were more prepared to help her out at home. (None of us liked housework – my mother especially can be sensationally untidy – but it was accepted that we each had to do a minimum. The idea that a woman's place is in the home, or that my mother ought to be a full-time housewife and mum, never entered my head.)

My mother has a genuine talent for friendship, and seems to have got on equally well with men and women. Her relentless policy of including us children in everything she did carried through to her social life, and I grew very fond of some of her friends. They were a delightfully mixed bunch – no wonder I was to find boarding school so dull after home. Our house was still a retreat from the outside world, but it was also a place to meet people; whether or not my mother consciously used her friends to dilute the potential claustrophobia of the family, that was the effect. I became familiar with adult company, and enjoyed it.

To make ends meet, and I imagine partly because she enjoyed the company, my mother took in a series of lodgers – this must have been mostly after Simon had gone to boarding school, because there was barely enough room for the three of us as it was. Even so the lodgers had a pretty uncomfortable time of it since they were installed either in my miniscule bedroom or, if I refused to budge, in my brother's room which happened to be the passage to the bathroom – we both remember startling one or other lodger stark naked as we barged through. But in spite of the discomfort and gross lack of privacy some of them stayed for months, and were added to the general company.

Men who had more than friendly intentions had to be determined, because my mother made few concessions. Wherever she went my brother and I went too, and we guarded her like Scylla and Charybdis against anyone we disliked. A smooth operator called Tim once took us all to Whipsnade Zoo for a weekend treat; we travelled in unheard-of luxury, in his grey Jaguar with a walnut dashboard and dove-coloured plush upholstery. On the way home the excitement went to my stomach and I was spectacularly sick all over the back – that was the last my mother saw of him, which for my part more than compensated for the ruined afternoon.

She never remarried, but aside from friends we weren't brought up in a household without men. I'm not, I'm afraid, someone who can claim total childhood recall; scenes start, stop and shift into one another with the discontinuity of dreams. So I don't remember how my mother met Ray; but there he was, by the time I was six or so, and I remember the time he spent with us with great affection.

Ray was a Yorkshireman, younger than my mother, good-looking with a long face and a great quiff of thick springy brown hair. He enjoyed clowning, and one of my sharpest pictures is of him sitting at the upright piano singing 'The Foggy Foggy Dew' and 'I Attempt from Love's Sickness to Fly-hy-hy-hy-hy-hy-hy-hy I-hin Va-hain' in mock-tragic falsetto. He taught at the local art college, and was wonderful at making things. On Valentine's day he painted a circle of blue forget-me-nots on a card for my mother; for Christmas he made my brother and myself papier-mâché puppets – a skeleton on strings for Simon, a ghoulish witch hand puppet for me. He came on holidays with us – to the Norfolk Broads, and on another houseboat holiday the summer I Fell In Seven Times. In short, he became part of our lives, and right on cue I fell in love with him.

This story did not have the traditional happy ending, though I did my best to make it so, thereby (I still believe) causing the very opposite of what I wanted to happen. 'Ray, why don't you marry Mummy?' I piped, out cycling with him and Simon one Sunday afternoon. Where had the idea come from? I don't think I ever considered him as my father, so much as wanted to make sure he was *ours*. At any rate that evening, when I was in bed, I could hear their voices indistinctly downstairs. Before long he left, slamming the front door. My mother came upstairs to my bedroom and sat on the bed; it was one of the very few times I had seen her cry. He had asked her to marry him, and she had refused.

There were a number of lessons to be learned from this episode – for instance, 'Don't interfere' – and exhumed in the future. The one which stuck, I'm afraid, was that affairs of the heart are never permanent – I've always had notoriously low expectations in this direction, though happily I haven't always been proved right.

Strangely enough I don't remember pining for Ray after he'd moved out of our lives and back to Yorkshire, much as I'd adored him. In time, my mother would become involved in other relationships. These never meant quite so much to me as Ray had, but I'm not aware of resenting her attachment to anyone until my adolescence, when a hopeless, all-pervasive sense of inadequacy made me jealous of everybody, friends and all. Before that nothing could jolt my sense of coming first, with my brother, in her affections.

The triangle is an inherently stable structure in physical terms, since each side touches and is held together by the other two. The emotional dynamics of our family were equally powerful: mother, son, daughter, we were joined by equal and opposite ties and there was no breaking out of them. The umbilical cord between children and mother might never have been cut – our lives still overlap constantly through physical proximity and shared friends, welded together by the exasperating, intransigent bonds of familiarity. But the links between my brother and me were also forged to last.

There were just eighteen months between us, my brother's early homicidal intentions towards me soon disappeared, and by the time we were old enough to play by ourselves we became almost as close as twins. We had our separate friends at school but at home we fought, squabbled and entertained ourselves for hours. Being the younger and smaller I always lost or came last in everything, with a perpetual whine of, 'It isn't *fair!*' At the same time there was a strong element of hero worship in my attitude towards Simon which must have been gratifying to him, and he was protective towards me with his older friends.

His departure for boarding school when he was ten was utterly traumatic for the three of us, and he and I both went down with psychosomatic illnesses – I had my first and most dramatic migraine ever. After my own start at boarding school, and with the confusing onset of adolescence, we were doubly distanced from each other. Even so, then as now we could be hypersensitive to each other's moods and often thought alike, which we took for granted but other people found striking – we couldn't be put on opposite sides in party games like charades, for instance, because one of us would guess the other's word the moment they made the first gesture. Even now we see each other almost absurdly often and our respective partners have each previously been the close friend of the other sibling.

At boarding school I had at least three fatherless friends from all-female families, with sisters but no brothers; tremendous tensions often erupted into furious rows between them, and at home during these scenes their mothers made it desperately clear how much they missed a masculine influence. Looking back, I see now that my brother's presence strengthened the structure of our family and diffused whatever jealousy and rivalry might have come between my mother and me. He wasn't inclined to take on the part of 'little father', and wasn't overburdened with extra responsibilities by my mother, who treated us both scrupulously as equals. Nonetheless, as the youngest I surely transferred to him some of the affection and admiration that would have been David's, and today I probably rely on him more than he would like. Claustrophobic though we sometimes find our attachment, it's not one to escape easily. After all, it's been lifelong.

My brother was sent to boarding school at ten, and as my mother was working full time it seemed more sensible to send me too. We both went to schools which made grants available for fatherless children: Simon to the Bluecoat School, Christ's Hospital, and I to a smaller mixed school in Surrey, where I learned to be miserable.

With adolescence you pass through a kind of sound barrier which separates your adult self from childhood. At the same time I was deeply unhappy at boarding school. The two together were a devastating death blow to childhood. I experienced all the usual emotions there – boredom, homesickness, alienation. They didn't fade with time. I was treated like a child as never before at home, with the added torture of having nowhere, ever, to escape to on my own. All this was compounded by being academically, but not emotionally, precocious and the youngest by two years in my class – a sprout among cabbages, I was. I can see now that all my fledgling nonconformist bias, so much of it absorbed at home, was at odds with consensus views there, but all I knew then was that I was a misfit. I'd never learned to theorise or defend my beliefs with arguments at home. Aside from the probability that I wouldn't have been sent to boarding school at all had David lived, a father might have helped me to think things out objectively and assert my individuality, rather than try to hide the aspects of myself that didn't conform.

Much later, I would begin to enjoy my status as the only boarder girl in the sixth form – most of my friends left at fifteen; but during this time of early adolescence other effects of being brought up without a father began to emerge. I don't mean that one was made to feel deprived by other children who had the regulation set of parents; at both my own and my brother's school there was an above-average proportion of children in a situation like ours, and our best friends were often from one-parent families. In any case, other children's fathers had left me deeply unimpressed. They went, in my experience, with large houses and cars: oversized, unconvincing creatures who made brief, booming appearances as you were about to leave your friends' houses. They tended to tease you in a heavy-handed manner which made you feel desperately uncomfortable. No, all this made me very relieved I didn't have one.

I see it differently now. Watching friends with their children, I find myself fascinated by the teasing familiarity between fathers and daughters. All that complicated shadow-boxing and shaping of sexual identity which goes on during those early encounters within the family – no wonder I react as an outsider, amused, shocked, envious. Looking back, I really *was* more than ordinarily awkward as a teenager – there was a basic training in communication with the opposite sex which I never learned at home, and feel I never have. At school this was to emerge in paralysing shyness with boys – for years I could hardly speak to them, at meals or in class. They were frightening aliens who spoke in some special language which I didn't understand.

A friend of mine always used to amuse me by talking of 'handling' men, as if they were horses, but that's really what I mean. Friendship with men has always been difficult because I misread the sexual stop-go signs, sometimes disastrously, and am quite unable to cope with the sort of reflex flirting which comes to some people as easily as breathing. This sounds frivolous, but isn't; I feel an awkwardness in all but the most familiar male presences which has affected most aspects of my life, from work to friendship.

That early relationship between father and daughter is a powerful sexual conditioning which all too often can go badly wrong, but like other forms of play (so long as that is what it is) it's potentially very valuable – by which I mean that you can learn a lot from play without getting damaged in the process. For the daughter, it's an essential stage in developing a sense of self-worth and confidence in relation to other people. Without a father's protectiveness and reassurance when you're becoming aware of yourself as a sexual being, you're likely to devalue yourself. As a result you base your sexual relationships on what other people think of you, without daring to rely on your own opinions. However caring the mother, this is one area in which she can't substitute.

Trying to define the effects of an *absence*, rather than a presence, is an elusive exercise. My own experience must be quite different from someone left with the aftermath of grief or bitterness from death or divorce, and whose father actually represented 'fatherhood' to them. For myself, it's as if there are various blind spots, gaps in understanding which stem from not having experienced *what the father stands for*; but aside from the crucial aspect of sexual development you could make out quite as strong an argument for the positive side of these effects as for the negative ones. I never had an image of masculine superiority to pitch myself against, or a sense of unfairness in being born a girl. My feminism was so instinctive that at first I found it hard to understand why other women had had to fight so hard – I couldn't see the opposition clearly. The universe, to me, was female.

One reason, for instance, why I could never work up any strong religious belief may well have been because I had no earthly figure of fatherhood on which to model my idea of a heavenly one. 'Our Father, Which Art in Heaven . . .' I can remember trying my hardest, willing myself to believe in God when I was small, and even convinced myself briefly that I should go out as a missionary to help the heathen abroad – but the central concept was blank. Try as I would, God remained a vacuum. Admittedly there wasn't much encouragement in this direction at home; my mother's bizarre religious education – at the age of ten she was sent to Belgium to board in a convent but when she showed signs of embracing the Faith was packed off to a Quaker school in Yorkshire – had left her determined that if Simon or I showed any signs of religious awakening it was for us to follow them up. But more than that, it seems to me that my inability to summon up any convincing image of God was connected to early attitudes towards Duty and Authority. As a child I learned to respond very strongly to the unspoken concept of Duty. That, associated with a deep loyalty and love for my mother and brother, was what the equation of our family relationship was based on, and has been a powerful – if often tiresome – governing force in many aspects of my life since.

Duty is a voluntary obligation, and to me (as to many other women) is all the stronger for being self-imposed. Authority is power, imposed from above. I see Authority as entirely masculine. Its ultimate image is God in his Judgement Seat, and the family equivalent is Dad. Even if the real flesh-and-blood father is far from an authoritative figure, he's used as one: 'If you do that again I'll have to tell your Father. . . .' Without

Authority to subdue us, fatal flaws will grow unchecked in us, like the wicked charmer Steerforth in *David Copperfield*. He knows too well what's wrong – it's all Mother's fault for indulging him. 'David, I wish to God I had had a judicious father these last twenty years!' he sighs, hurrying off to seduce Little Em'ly.

Authority, and fear or respect for it, was the last thing to motivate my family, and it can hardly be a coincidence that I distrust and respond badly to it – less in the sense of being in a state of constant rebellion against it, than in seeking out all possible ways to avoid confronting it. This takes various forms. I dislike the idea of holding authority over other people as much as of others exerting power over me. So, for instance, the thought of being in charge of other people at work, or equally of subordinating myself directly to an employer, I find equally unpleasant; on the other hand, I'm strongly motivated in working for myself at home, as a freelance journalist.

This attitude might help to explain a peculiar phase I went through at boarding school. Though I felt miserably out of place there I wasn't a noticeably mutinous child, but there were times when I was simply unable to respond to aspects of authority; it didn't seem to be *relevant*. During this phase, I got into serious trouble over a single petty rule, which was that during games anyone whose hair touched her collar should fasten it back. I decided this rule was pointless – though dozens of others were equally idiotic – and regularly disobeyed it, knowing perfectly well that punishment would follow every time. From having an unblemished record I sat stubbornly in detention every week for nearly two terms, until I was summoned to explain my behaviour to the headmistress in the presence of my perplexed mother, and threatened with being sent home. My mother's being there must have changed my attitude; some compromise was certainly reached, because a year or so later I was conforming to the extent of playing for the school hockey team.

Despite the fact that most of my teachers at school were men, that headmistress was the only member of staff who impressed me as someone to respect. The lack of positive masculine influence all during my upbringing was striking – or was it? I could probably have found such an influence if I'd looked hard enough for it. No, almost without exception I would respond more strongly to female than to male influence as I grew up, and afterwards – doubly conditioned by my absent father and my powerful mother. At university, tutors and lecturers (all men) remained distant. Without a doubt, the nearest I got to finding a father surrogate was in my husband Richard, whom I married when I was twenty-two.

There were eight years between us, but it seemed like more. He came from a highly patriarchal family, pulsating with tremendously strong if eccentric views; and I suspect that what intrigued me most about him was that he embodied all the *intellectual* qualities of masculine authority which I'd never experienced at home. One of my family's features was that we scarcely ever argued – it's still a shock to find that we don't always think alike. The result was that I'd grown up with the restricting assumption that disagreement was somehow dangerous. Richard's family was the reverse image of mine, and I was exhilarated and appalled by the vigorous arguments and power games which went on between his father and himself, and which they often seemed to *enjoy*. It was a revelation to find that arguing was an acceptable form of behaviour.

I relied on his approval a great deal, and when we separated by mutual agreement years later, I had a recurring anxiety dream, which depicted not scenes of violence but simply his icy rejection of me in public. These dreams, mild as they are compared with the conventional horrors of nightmares, left me exhausted and completely demoralised. For years after we separated, he would still be the person I most wanted to impress, and I was quite irrationally opposed to a divorce.

The past is another country, so they say – but how insidiously it directs the paths of choice and chance you take later. Except for my marriage, my close relationships with men have always mirrored my mother's in one striking respect: the conventional permanent commitment of living together has always been blocked for one reason or another. I can blame circumstances, but I also prefer it this way. There's a web of motivation to point to: a driving need to be on my own, in reaction to those hated years at boarding school; repetition of the pattern of relationships I saw at home as a child; or revenge on other men, for the father who never came back.

There was only one time I wept for David, and that was after my grandmother died, when I was fifteen or so. We'd gone to her house for the funeral and to sort out her belongings. Among all the papers, at once too personal to throw away and yet impossible for us to keep, was an entire set of letters from David to his mother: every one he had ever sent home in his life. That set was for my brother, and Granny had copied out each letter in longhand for me. With the two sets of letters were photographs, and a wartime copy of *Picture Post* with a cover picture of David in a tin hat at an air raid post. I saw, then, the waste of it: the quiet young man who'd embodied, then vaporised, the ambitions of his clever, beautiful, frustrated mother, and left my mother alone with their children, demanding in the fury of grief, "How *dare* he die and leave me alone like this?' But I cried for what they'd lost, not for what I'd missed myself.

58

The relative rank, the hierarchy, of the sexes is first brought to her attention in family life; little by little she realises that if the father's authority is not that which is most often felt in daily affairs, it is actually supreme; it only takes on more dignity from not being graded to daily use; and even if it is in fact the mother who rules as mistress of the household, she is commonly clever enough to see that the father's wishes come first in important matters, the mother demands, rewards and punishes in his name and through his authority.

Simone de Beauvoir, *The Second Sex*

'If, I say, you should ever be tempted to tricks like that, thinking to please some man, remember that they detest those tricks and see through them. They know they are traps, mean little chicane to bend them to woman's purpose. I was at Random's the other day. He let his little daughter climb over him and beg him for something he had refused. He gave in. It was a humiliating sight for me, and for the man. I could see her years later, because she is pretty, a warped, dishonest little creature, only thinking of making men do things for her.'

Andrew Hawkins to his daughter Teresa, in
Christina Stead, *For Love Alone*

Only once, in a very rare moment of confidence, have I ever heard him betray the slightest doubt. Seventeen years after his conversion (he was then fifty-three and I twenty-four) we managed for the first and only time, for the space of a few minutes, to talk naturally to each other on the subject of religion. He said that he was glad that he had become a Catholic but that if he found himself once again in the position of hesitating between alternatives, he was not sure that he would make the same choice. After that the shutters came down again completely between us and I was never able to talk frankly to him again.

Antonia White on her father, in
The Hound and the Falcon

OLIVIA HARRIS

Heavenly Father

I grew up in a large family that became even larger after my mother died and my stepmother and her two children came to live with us: six children within eight years of each other. Home resounded to footsteps running up and down the stairs; there was always something happening, older brothers and sisters to admire, listen to, try to copy, and a stepsister my own age to play with and fight with. But the surest form of communication for me was always through music. By the time cousins, aunts and uncles were added on it was a bit like the Trapp family and I loved it. My stepmother tells me I never said a word.

One by one we were all sent to boarding school; faced there with the need to survive, I suddenly broke into speech.

My desire to see England from outside has taken me across the English Channel, across the Atlantic, and especially in Bolivia where I spent some two years working as an anthropologist. In the middle of all this came feminism, first as an inspiration, later as a thorny instrument. At present I teach anthropology at Goldsmiths' College in south-east London.

In writing about fathers I have had the help of illuminating conversations with many friends and family. I am grateful for their sharing of memories and experiences with me.

I was born in 1948; in many ways the date is immaterial, since the time in which I became conscious of the world about me was family time, and the world scarcely extended to the bottom of the garden. The pulse of that world was not the newspaper flopping daily through the door, not 'Childrens' Favourites' on the wireless, but the flood tide of the Southern Region sweeping fathers, briefcases and harassed bowler hats out of every house at the appointed moment; and on the ebb leaving them washed up on suburban stations where their wives, poised between kitchen and childrens' bedroom, waited in rows like celluloid. Mysterious London, where fathers worked, a magnetic pole: we, the children of Surrey, surreptitiously within its gravitational pull. Its demands on fathers, and therefore on those they left behind, were inexorable. And every evening these same fathers must be welcomed home from London; in the face of his arrival, all our rhythms, all other periodicities were subordinate.

Perhaps English fathers are archetypally absent. In my family we grew up feeling that he was rarely there, kept away by work. What 'work' was remained a mystery for many years; I could see it involved a briefcase and interminable pieces of paper, but failed to understand why it was so tiring, or what was done with the paper, except that the secret could be explained in the 'office'. In retrospect I think it is the same sort of mystification as that felt about my 'work' by the Bolivian Indians among whom I lived for two and a half years, and whose lives I studied as an anthropologist. Endless writing, covering page after page, whose major reason for being taken seriously was that in spite of my apparent inactivity I earned through it an income beyond their wildest dreams.

Since he was mainly absent, Sundays were his time. He took us all to church, and would marshall us into the pew, deciding who was to sit next to whom, in full view of the rest of the congregation. And then in the evening there were family prayers, and special Sunday books like *Pilgrim's Progress* and *The Water Babies*. Monday and the rest of the week were completely different. And yet absent fathers are eternally present. In English culture men are masters of their homes in a way that seems not to be universally true. Whether or not the father is there, whether or not he takes an active part in domestic life, he is the undisputed source of authority. His absence as well as his presence structures the home; his position in it is sacred. For me to this day my father occupies a similar place in my dreams. The real man who exists and who reads this has changed almost beyond recognition, but the father still hovers on the edges of dreams, rarely intervening directly, but marking their confines, acting as an organising principle.

A Latin American friend commented to me recently how exotic she found English patriarchy. In her Bolivian world, mothers are the authority within the family, and rule the home, counterbalanced by the father's place in the outside world. In the English families she knew the father alone seemed to rule, with the mother acting as his lieutenant. By comparison with Latin American culture, where men's footing in their own households is somewhat insecure, English women seem extraordinarily self-effacing. Latin American men dwell in a public world, meet

61

their friends in public places, and the home is the woman's space, one with which men are scarcely familiar. In English homes, even where fathers take little interest in their children, the privileged place is kept for them; and when mothers openly take over the primary position of power in their children's lives they are thought deviant and suspect.

I talk of English culture because while the details of my experience may be unique, the world is surely a shared one. I am not even clear how much of my experience of the father is of my own unique father, and how much the salient features come from other sources, from books, from friends, school, and, importantly, from Anglican Christianity. A lot of it – but not all – is peculiar to the comfortable Evangelical professional classes from which my father's family came, and whose values were so crucial an element in the evolution of Victorian domestic culture.

What is certainly true is that although I went to school in post-war Britain, the events and characters that crowded my imagination came from books that were mostly written before the end of the nineteenth century. These were children's books that had been favourites of my father's childhood, and I think some of them the favourites of his mother's childhood too. The stories were vivid and terrifying, recounting the gory death of a child, the piety of another being rewarded, or a faceless monster that tore people from their homes. There must have been other books. I know that I read *Winnie the Pooh* and Enid Blyton like everybody else, and listened to the wireless occasionally, but those Victorian books were more than mere entertainment; they were the world we shared with our father, the driftwood of his childhood that we could rediscover together and a real point of contact between the generations. These and the hymns, sung into the recesses of my memory week in, week out, were real and resonant; they belonged to us in defiance of the world outside where things changed. In our world little girls were punished for their sins; in the Victorian twilight of Sunday evenings we sang,

> Lead us, Heavenly Father, lead us
> O'er the world's tempestuous sea.
> Guard us, guide us, keep us, feed us,
> For we have no help but Thee,
> Yet possessing every blessing
> If our God our Father be;

and the picture of Charles the First about to be executed, saying goodbye to his children, gazed nobly and discreetly from the pages of *The Nursery History of England*.

The objective time of historians corresponds very little to the generational time by which we are bound to those who gave us life. I feel my early childhood belonged at the end of the nineteenth century, not in the post-war baby boom of which I was objectively part. How is family mythology, family meaning, recreated in each generation? How far does the outside world impinge? I scarcely knew my grandmother directly, but I sense that whatever she suffered, imagined and desired in her youth she handed on to my father and he to me: an ironic chain of being in which we are entrusted with fighting the spectres that haunted people who died long ago, and of realising their dreams. Mother to son, father to daughter.

If family time obeys its own laws, my sense of place is also dislocated. The stockbroker belt in which I grew up was the other side of the railway tracks; on the side where we lived was the beginning of the country. Living on the edge of outer London, we hovered between worlds which were always exterior, and recognised differences which were never made explicit. And my father who to look at was indistinguishable from all those other hurrying dark suits, was different too – old-fashioned but unconventional, argumentative and charming.

My father came and went like the tide. My mother on the other hand was always there but faded away, ill, anxious, exhausted by her son and daughters until one day she died. My father's vitality and robustness in contrast are all the more deeply implanted in my consciousness. In my family, the father really *was* strong and the mother weak, and since she died when I was seven I am doubly his child. My sisters have sometimes said I was the favourite daughter. Whatever I was, it certainly did not mean any special privileges. Perhaps I showed most prospect of fulfilling certain of his own ambitions and hopes, and shared his passion for history and the past. Children offer fathers the possibility of treading roads they did not tread, and also evoke their longing for the past, for the ideal remembrance of the mother. I think I came closest to the image of my father's mother when I was young.

The dreams of fathers are hard. They want daughters in their own image, to embody masculine prowess, achievement, independence. For many women, to do 'well' in public terms is the only way they can hope to attract his attention. Life becomes an anxious struggle to live up to impossible, and often imaginary, standards, apparently the only means of communicating with a person who has no real sense of their lives, but wants a mirror for his own. But fathers also want ideal women, the perfect spouse, and that involves something quite different. Most of us find it hard to be both.

It could be called the Cordelia and Brünnhilde syndrome, since both of

these are 'favourite daughters'. Shakespeare and Wagner seem to recognise the situation and faithfully portray the rage of the all-powerful fathers when they find they have raised not a woman but a rival. The 'faults' of Cordelia and Brünnhilde were acts performed in the spirit of the father's own professed values, in the name of pleasing or obeying him. The punishment they suffer is because they have understood their fathers too well, not too little, and have competed with him on his own terrain. If Cordelia and Brünnhilde are thought unsatisfactory as dramatic heroines, it is because they mirror the obstinacy of the kings who sired them.

For how many women is it true that their whole energies seem spent in ever more complicated ways of pleasing him? How many have the feeling that their proudest moments of independence turn out to be a communication with their father? A friend who is a father described his seven-year-old daughter to me in tones of fervent admiration of her independence and spirit, in marked contrast to the slavish dependence, as he saw it, of his wife. He then admitted that her budding feminism was her way of pleasing *him* since he got on so badly with her mother. Some fathers desire a devoted and obedient slave, others a suffragette. In reality most probably want both at the same time – a fatal contradiction which daughters can spend most of their lives and ingenuity trying to resolve.

It is clear from much nineteenth- and twentieth-century writing that the father is the cornerstone of English morality. The place of the father is built on paradox; he is absent yet present, indeed the more present for his absence. His authority is unquestionable and yet rarely exercised directly; it is at the same time impersonal, concerned and selfish. For me, paradox brings a curious satisfaction. I remember vividly the place I was sitting in class when the history teacher first mentioned the term 'benevolent despot', how someone asked her how it was spelt and she wrote it on the blackboard. The phrase seemed instantly familiar. Remote control, benevolent despot – the words contradict, challenge and yet embrace each other.

Time – I cannot pretend to a completely Victorian childhood, nor one immune from outside influence, but the fragments I remember most and that evoke my childhood most powerfully are those that symbolise living in a very private world. Perhaps for this reason, when I went to school history was from the start my favourite subject. It nourished the seeds sown by Victorian story books, gave a means for constructing and recreating a world apart from the mundane world. And it did not entirely dislodge the myths already implanted. In *The Nursery History of England* which my father read to us when we were little it said: 'The little princess was older than her brother, and understood better what was going to happen, and she cried very much. King Charles was very sad but very brave, and when he walked out to have his head cut off in front of his palace at Whitehall, in London, he looked so good and beautiful that all the people were very sad.' Why did they kill him then? And why did they regret it? I learned in history lessons that this bloody and apparently meaningless act did after all have its reasons, and that not everybody was very sad. But the image of remorseful regicide, carried out in defiance of reason and of feeling, lurked in my consciousness for a long time.

One of the motivations that leads people to the study of anthropology is the need to understand contradictory, sometimes irreconcilable experiences: the sense of belonging and yet not belonging; the desire to find out whether our ways are best, indeed what other ways are possible. For me there was the increasing realisation that English culture was a distinct oddity in world perspective, and had managed to combine a morality of non-interference in personal relationships with a practice of massive interference in global terms.

Anthropology took me to a world where fathers just laughed when their children disobeyed them.

One of the early impulses to study 'savage societies' was to understand their family systems, their treatment of women, how marriage was organised and experienced. There was a fascination for reconstructing a mythological evolution of society from the earliest times of 'primitive promiscuity', or from the supposed brutality of 'marriage by capture' to the civilised restraint of Victorian monogamy. Overwhelmingly the early ethnological or anthropological texts which achieved the greatest popularity or notoriety among the reading public addressed these themes. That the patriarchal family was the pinnacle of civilised values was disputed by some, but even those who stressed the less aggressive, more generous qualities of matriarchal societies, or argued that the patriarchal family system relied fundamentally on an iniquitous structure of private property, generally agreed that, with all its shortcomings, it was a historical phenomenon essential to social evolution, and especially to the development of the state as the basis of political organisation.

In the early twentieth century, anthropological investigation shifted away from such grandiose attempts to reconstruct universal social evolution in order the devote its energies to detailed first-hand studies of so-called 'primitive' societies. The belief in a matriarchal stage at some prior moment in history, based on a mixture of observation, of archaeological discoveries, of sometimes wild conjecture on the evidence from classical texts, and sheer fantasy, gave way to the description of matrilineal societies still in existence. The concept of matriarchy had proposed that at some point women exercised real power; but the accounts of matrilineal organisation were more in line with Western sensibilities since, although descent and inheritance in such systems is traced through the female line, most anthropological accounts until recently have argued that power and control over property nonetheless remain firmly in the hands of men. Thus, children inherit not from their father but from their mother and more particularly from their mother's brother(s). They in turn will transmit family identity, the woman directly to her children, and her brothers also to her children rather than to their own. It is a system found in most areas of the world, in native cultures of Australia and the

Americas, Africa and South-East Asia. However women in matrilineal societies almost always have a greater degree of freedom and autonomy than in comparable patrilineal societies, and even if men ultimately occupy the positions of power, the role of the father is less stressed than in cultures where inheritance is through the male line.

In some examples, such as the famous Trobriand Islands off the coast of New Guinea, studied by Bronislaw Malinowski in the early years of this century, and more recently by Annette Weiner, the father appears as a nurturing and unthreatening figure, while the mother's brother occupies the position of authority for his nephews and nieces. In Malinowski's words:

the husband fully shares in the care of the children. He will fondle and carry a baby, clean and wash it, and give it the mashed vegetable food which it receives in addition to the mother's milk almost from birth. In fact, nursing the baby in the arms or holding on the knees, which is described by the native word *kopo'i*, is the special role and duty of the father (*tama*). It is said of children of unmarried women who, according to the native expression, are 'without a *tama*' . . . that they are 'unfortunate' or 'bad' because 'there is no one to nurse and hug them.' Again, if anyone inquires why children should have duties towards their father, who is a 'stranger' to them, the answer is invariably: 'because of the nursing' . . . 'because his hands have been soiled with the child's excrement and urine'.

The father performs his duties with genuine natural fondness: he will carry an infant about for hours, looking at it with eyes full of such love and pride as are seldom seen in those of a European father. Any praise of the baby goes directly to his heart, and he will never tire of talking about and exhibiting the virtues and achievements of his wife's offspring. *Sexual Life of Savages*, 1929, pp. 20–21

Trobriand society is matrilineal, and the father therefore has few long-term rights and obligations in his children. The picture that Malinowski paints, and which has been confirmed by more recent anthropological study, contrasts strikingly with the typical pattern of fatherhood in Malinowski's own time. Malinowski used the Trobriand Islanders, as anthropological accounts have so often been used, to argue forcibly that European family patterns were neither universally found, nor were self-evidently the best and most civilised. He disagreed particularly strongly with the Freudian assertion that the Oedipus complex was a universal feature of human development, and argued instead that each culture develops a distinct family form and pattern of socialisation in accord with other aspects of its economy and social system.

Not all matrilineal societies are alike then. Other accounts present a somewhat less idyllic picture than that painted by Malinowski. According to Mary Douglas, ethnographer of the West African Lele (Congo Brazzaville):

Lele honoured fatherhood. Boys were taught, 'Your father is like God. But for his begetting, where would you be? Therefore honour your father.' They were taught that the debt which they owed him for his care of them in infancy was unrepayable, immeasurable. It was very shameful for a man to show disrespect to his father. Fathers were expected to avoid their grown sons, so that the latter should not feel bowed down with the burden of respect. If a daughter disobeyed her father's wishes in respect of her marriage, he was supposed to be able to curse her fertility. . . . The father took the larger share of a girl's marriage payments, fifty cloths and an axe, against forty for her clan.   *The Lele of the Kasai*, 1963, p. 114

The overall impression given by Mary Douglas of Lele girls is a flirtatious independence; as is clear from the quotation, sons were more in awe of their fathers than daughters were. But the key point of daughters' subordination to their fathers was in the matter of marriage.

In most anthropological descriptions, the question of her marriage seems to overshadow the entire course of a girl's relationship with her father. Her early life is only of concern in so far as it is a preparation for her marriage: the training and education she receives, the virtues and values instilled in her, the work she does, all have a specific aim. Not only her father, and older brothers, but in many instances also the wider kin group has a lively interest in how its younger members marry. Even where there are negligible property interests, marriage is the relationship by which kinship is recreated from one generation to the next, and may thus be the means of reproducing class identity, ethnic identity, religious affiliation, family ethos. It is this fact which dominates a father's view of his daughters.

In some societies, women are directly and explicitly exchanged by their fathers and other male kin, in return for bride price, or in return for a wife for a male member of the family. But even in societies like ours where ostensibly women are free to choose their own husbands, looked at objectively there is a sense in which they are still 'exchanged' between their fathers and their future spouses ('Who giveth this woman to be married to this man?').Beatrice Webb in her early diary illustrates the point in a reflection on her father when she thought he was about to die:

He took his wife and all his children into his confidence: to each and all he showed the cards he held in his hand, described to you exactly the reason for each move, for his suspicions and calculations as to the cards of his opponents. And yet to see him with these men, to watch his sympathetic smile and apparent want of purpose in all he said and did, the natural way in which they themselves were made to suggest what he wished – the absolute unselfconsciousness of his effort – one felt one was in the presence of a born diplomatist. It flashed upon one: is he not handling his family in the same way? And certainly, judging by the results, he handled it effectually, for it was he who married seven headstrong self-willed women to men he thoroughly approved and considered suitable, and prevented, without forbidding, all other marriages.   *Diary*, Volume I, 1982, p. 309

It does not always require formal negotiation, then, between father and prospective husband, to establish a suitable match. While the Lele father exchanges his daughter explicitly against fifty cloths and an axe, in other cultural settings the exchange is symbolic, based on 'free choice'. 'Headstrong, self-willed women' are quite capable of doing what their fathers want without any direct intervention.

From the South Sea Islands to the eminently respectable liberal Victorian family of Beatrice Webb, the bond between father and daughter is premised on his giving her up, relinquishing her to another man. 'Daughters! What is the value of daughters? They are things to be given away!' one reads in one anthropological account after another. The meaning of a daughter lies in the future. Her early life is a prelude, a period of latent existence which is only given meaning by her subsequent marriage. She achieves social existence as a married woman.

I am the only daughter of my father whom he never led towards the altar to meet the waiting husband. Does this mean that there is unfinished business between us? How much difference would it make if I had ever been married? Beatrice Webb herself, who saw her father's concern in her sisters' marriages so clearly, refused to marry Sidney until after her father's death on the grounds that he would have been upset, and could not have understood why she was drawn to Sidney. But it is hard not to infer from her diaries that quite apart from her father's possible reactions she herself felt little need to marry until his death approached. Is there a sense then in which at the same time as being exchanged, daughters themselves exchange one man against another? In much anthropological theory, father, husband, even sons are indeed treated as virtually interchangeable. How far do women choose in their spouses, encourage in their sons, the ideal remembrance of the father? Am I, by not being married, refusing to exchange my father, or am I diffusing that chain of being?

There is a limit certainly to the interchangeability of male kin. In psychic history there is an order of precedence: the father is authority, not in a preliminary but in a primary sense. And in the Christian – particularly the Protestant – world, the authority of the individual father is generalised and incorporated into the transcendental image of God the Father.

Where I, in the aftermath of libertarian assertiveness, have been charmed by knowing a world where fathers lack coercive authority, my forebears would have been perplexed and scandalised. Missionaries in particular were preoccupied with family morality. Monogamy, paternity, proper attitudes towards the father were defining features of the religion exported to so-called savage societies. How could you be a proper Christian unless you also adopted Christian family morality? Malinowski makes the point clearly in cadences redolent of the post-Victorian world:

If we consider that the dogma of God the Father and God the Son, the Sacrifice of the only Son, the filial love of man to his Maker – that all this falls somewhat flat in a matrilineal society . . . we cannot wonder that Paternity must be the first new truth to be inculcated by proselyting [sic] Christians. Otherwise, the idea of the Trinity would have to be translated into matrilineal terms, and we would have to speak of a God-*kadala* (mother's brother) and a God-sister's son, and a divine *baloma* (spirit).

In another passage he is still more explicit:

The religion whose dogmatic essence is based on the sacredness of the Father to Son relationship, and whose morals stand or fall with a strong patriarchal family, must obviously proceed by making the paternal relation strong and firm, by first showing that it has a natural foundation. Thus I discovered – only during my third expedition to New Guinea – that the natives had been somewhat exasperated by having preached at them what seemed to them an absurdity.

While in these passages his particular concern is to explain the apparent ignorance of paternity in matrilineal Trobriand society, the description has obviously wider implications. Religious imagery uses family relationships as a primary metaphor; religious beliefs and family organisation are profoundly interdependent. The close connection between monotheism and patriarchal family forms has long been recognised. But if it is true that representations of deity owe much to their incarnation of idealised parent figures, the converse is equally true and its implications not so widely assimilated.

West African Lele children are taught 'your father is god'. In a world where religious and secular authority are increasingly distinguished this seems almost blasphemous, and yet similar sentiments are echoed through the centuries of Christianity. In the epistle to the Ephesians Saint Paul enjoins wives, children, and servants to obey the master of the house as they obey God. In English culture the relationship seems to have been even closer than this, particularly in the century of Puritanism, revolution and regicide. Christopher Hill argues that in seventeenth-century England the household was 'spiritualised' and its head to a great extent replaced the local priest as the representative of holy authority. God was the 'Great Householder' and the mortal householder correspondingly shared some aspects of divinity, regardless of his human failings. In a tract on 'Domesticall Duties' the Puritan William Gouge wrote, 'Though an husband in regard of evil qualities may carry the image of the devil, yet in regard of his place and office, he beareth the image of God.'

In Anglican religion the mother is virtually invisible. The imagery employed in Anglican worship is almost exclusively masculine; even qualities which might quite uncontroversially be thought of as maternal are in Protestant imagery monopolised by the Father and the Son. In nineteenth-century Anglicanism, beliefs associated with the Church of Rome, among them the veneration paid to the Virgin Mother, appear to have been considered not only effeminate but positively pernicious. In contrast the broad Church of England encouraged manliness, and God was an English gentlemen. The testimony of Charles Kingsley, author of *The Water Babies* and an influential Christian socialist of the mid-nineteenth century, is eloquent:

I only ask you to pause . . . while you consider whether you know what the Church of England is, what God's education of England has been, and whether the one or the other are consistent with each other. I say they are. I say that the Church of England is wonderfully and mysteriously fitted for the souls of a free Norse-Saxon race. . . . And I say that the element which you have partially introduced, and to drown yourself in which you must go to Rome, is a foreign element, unsuited to Englishmen and to God's purposes with England. How far it may be the best for the Italian or Spanish spirit I cannot judge. I can only believe that if they had been capable of anything higher, God would have given them something higher, I say, because the highest idea of man is to know his Father, and to look his Father in the face, in full assurance of faith and love; and that out of that springs all manful energy, self-respect, all self-restraint, all that the true Englishman has, and the Greek and the Spaniard have not . . . if anyone wishes to benefit the poor whom God has committed to their charge, they must do anything and everything rather than go to Rome – to a creed . . . [which will] make association and cooperation impossible to them, by substituting a Virgin Mary, who is to *nurse* them like infants, for a father in whom they are men and brothers. *Letters and Memories*, Volume I, 1877, pp. 252–3

The heritage of mysogyny which reached such extraordinary heights in the last century was not of course restricted to the Church, but religious teaching presses the point home.

Another distinguishing feature of Protestant Christianity is the absence of priestly confession as a means of absolving sin. Where the priest has a direct involvement in the intimate lives of his flock, and authority to punish and forgive, as in Catholic Christianity, the place of the household head must necessarily be different from that of a culture in which it is the father who has virtually undisputed moral authority. Some of the resistance to auricular confession by nineteenth-century Anglicans during the revival of ritualism stemmed from an indignation over its intrusion into family life, superceding as it did 'God's appointment of intimacy between husband and wife, father and children'. Whatever this latter 'intimacy' was, it was certainly quite different from that of the confessional. The father had the right, the obligation, to concern himself with the activities and states of mind of his family and to reprove or punish them as and when he saw fit, but children do not voluntarily confess their sins to their fathers. The intimacy was moreover a one-way, not a reciprocal relationship. What children should offer in return was respect, love and obedience.

The father's moral authority includes the duty to punish, but it is the cultivation of conscience that guarantees the authority. Introspection, the individual searching for sins she knows she must have committed, is as important as obedience; in fact it is the foundation of obedience. This finely tuned instrument accompanies us waking and sleeping, makes us doubt the words we utter. To live as an English person in another culture is to become suddenly aware of the obsessional finesse with which we apologise, even to the level of asking people's pardon before speaking to them. At the same time, English sensitivity to possible intrusions into other people's existential territory is the other face of a placid sense of superiority. There is something empty about the faculty of guilt; in Protestant faiths there is a disquieting desire always to be right, and the prospect of hell somehow lacks conviction.

If God the Father encourages us to become our own judge, the father correspondingly becomes more impersonal. If the daughter sins, it is not an offence against the father, but against morality. Punishment never arises from so base a motive as revenge, but is carried out in the name of a greater good – that of the punished. Since God is above personal motivation, so is the god-like father. In a sense under such a regime one is neither punished nor forgiven; punishment if it is good for you blends into all the other things that are good for you like cod liver oil.

One of the most unlikely, but to me curiously resonant, portraits of the English God is sketched by Dickens in *Bleak House*. John Jarndyce is a genial bachelor, kindly, cosy, remote from everyday passions, and never angry even when his ward, his surrogate son, betrays him. Dickens concedes to this figure the privilege of knowing more about everybody's lives and what is best for them than they themselves. The surrogate son suffers the consequences of his rebellion, and lives to feel remorse without Jarndyce ever uttering a word of reproach. But it is the other ward, Esther, sweet-tempered and unselfish, who perhaps best defines the god-like qualities of her guardian. He knows what is best for her even to the extent of arranging her marriage against her expressed wishes, and of course she admits that he was right. But through all their supposed affection and intimacy there is an overpowering sense that Jarndyce is far away. Even his genial, well-meaning smile maintains the distance.

In appearance, God seen through Victorian filters was not an elderly bachelor but of indeterminate middle age, handsome in an aristocratic English way: not unlike a Van Dyck portrait of Charles I in fact – noble, discreet, polite, but also detached. Patriarchal authority in the English culture in which I grew up was not Old Testament style wrath, but based on restraint and dignity.

Perhaps the English version of patriarchy is paternalism. Strictness was a virtue for parents: obedience and evasion a way of life for children. Open resistance was virtually unthinkable. Parents reinforce in each other an anxiety about spoiling their children. 'Spoiling' means ruining their characters by indulging their whims and demands, but also perhaps something more; spending too much time with the child, excessive contact. Hence the distrust of matriarchy, since it is supposed that mothers will spoil their children if there is no civilised restraining hand to stop them. The father's authority is the greater for his remoteness. The distance means a less personal interest in the child's behaviour, so that he can act both with objectivity, and a certain impartial magnanimity. Remote control, benevolent despotism. . . .

There comes a moment when you begin to detach the father from his moral camouflage, to realise that his displeasure is not always dis-interested, that even when he pretends otherwise he can be ordinarily angry, genuinely unfair. My older sisters grasped this long before I did, and I was confronted with the impossibility of reconciling their new grown-up perceptions with my own version of a person who was above merely human reproach.

And yet it is not simply a question of growing up. There are more immediate ways of mitigating the weight of paternalism. The other face of daughterly obedience is the person at whom and with whom we laugh. My thirteen-year-old niece and I were looking at birthday cards for fathers, discussing which one was most suitable for her father. There was 'To a Wonderful Father for his Birthday' accompanied by a Boeing 707 taking off; there was 'Special Birthday Greetings, Father' above a race between two speedboats (the one sporting a Union Jack was in the lead); and there was an old red car driving through a folksy village. But the card she chose without a moment's hesitation was of 'Dad' completely tangled up in his fishing line, the hook through his hat and the fish laughing at him. She said by way of explanation that it was just like him.

Whether or not it *is* like him, I can understand why she would choose the joke card rather than blatant images of power, or the suggestive sentimentality of the red car. Perhaps a son would have picked the speed-boat or the plane taking off. She reminded me that in the face of the solemnity of paternal authority daughters can also laugh, and the laughter says many things. The Incompetent Father is perhaps the necessary antiphon to God the Father. He is the alternative version of the paradox of the father, another juxtaposition of mutually contradictory elements. When I remember the laughter in my childhood and compare it with *real* Victorian memoirs, and then listen to my niece, I realise how far the ground has shifted.

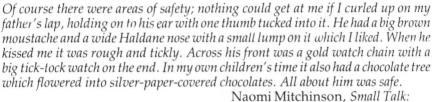

Of course there were areas of safety; nothing could get at me if I curled up on my father's lap, holding on to his ear with one thumb tucked into it. He had a big brown moustache and a wide Haldane nose with a small lump on it which I liked. When he kissed me it was rough and tickly. Across his front was a gold watch chain with a big tick-tock watch on the end. In my own children's time it also had a chocolate tree which flowered into silver-paper-covered chocolates. All about him was safe.

Naomi Mitchinson, *Small Talk:*
Memories of an Edwardian Childhood

KATE OWEN

My Dad

I was born in Oxford in 1970. I was adopted at ten days old and lived in Oxford for 6 months. Then we moved to London. My parents split up and now I see my mum in the week and my dad at the weekends. In 1982 I went to America with my dad and stepmum for 4 or 5 months. I loved America and I wish I could go back.

I have three dads, two of whom I see and one I don't. Dad number one lives in France and I don't know who he is because I am adopted. One of my other dads is a stepdad and the other one is real.

My real dad I see at the weekends and half the holidays. He has a wife who makes my third mum. They also have one boy called Ben who is my brother.

The first thing I remember about my dad is that when we were on holiday in Spain (I was one and a half) I ran away from where we were staying. There was a path which was very long to me at the time. It had hedges at either side. I can't quite remember why I wanted to run away but I suppose it was because I got angry with him. I ran down the path, out of the garden and on to the road. He was following me. This made me very angry because I thought I was being brave by running away. I went and sat in the middle of the road and he watched me from behind a telephone box. This made me *furious*. But he didn't let me stay there for long in case I got run down.

I thought he didn't like me because I got angry with him – and you're not supposed to like people when you're angry with them – but this shows he *did* care! My dad is kind and generous to everybody. He is very sympathetic when someone is ill but he doesn't pet them so they get to think that it's good to be ill. He got very angry when people were killed in the war in the Lebanon.

He objects to me fighting but I do, because I think it's very important when it comes to self-defence, which others, including my dad, may or may not agree with.

When my dad goes away to the Middle East I get worried in case he gets killed. In one place he was sitting on his balcony and it started to shake because there was a minor earthquake and there was shooting down below. But I wouldn't want to stop him from going to these places because I know he enjoys himself a lot. There was one time when I stayed with my dad for four months in America. This is the longest time I've been with him since my mum and dad got divorced. Staying with him in America was great fun. He changed a lot in America in the way that he went and bought different clothes like tank tops and casual trousers whereas at home he usually wears suits. I prefer that because they didn't make him look so businesslike. I like my dad more than my friends' dads, because one of my friends' dads won't let her out at all in case she gets beaten up; another because he shouts at her when she makes the slightest noise; and another because he's SDP! My dad is not like any of these.

The only thing I don't like about my dad is that he is keen on early bed times which I think is fuddy-duddy.

My dad doesn't put pressure on me to do what he wants me to do because he thinks that I should be what I want to be. This is why I love him.

PS. I love my mum just as much too.

It is well known that there are many women who have a strong attachment to their father; nor need they be in any way neurotic. It is upon such women that I have made the observations which I propose to report here and which have led me to adopt a particular view of female sexuality. I was struck, above all, by two facts. The first was that where the woman's attachment to her father was particularly intense, analysis showed that it had been preceded by a phase of exclusive attachment to her mother which had been equally intense and passionate. Except for the change of her love-object, the second phase had scarcely added any new feature to her erotic life.

Sigmund Freud, *On Sexuality*

Women who have not idealized their fathers usually have no urge to create, because creation implies the projection of one's narcissism onto an ideal image which can be attained only through creative work.

Janine Chasseguet Smirgel,
'Feminine Guilt and the Oedipus Complex', in
Female Sexuality

'I can make porridge, but I can never quite make it for her the same as Daddy can!'
Window cleaner's wife, from John and Elizabeth Newson,
Four Years Old in an Urban Community

DORIS LESSING

What Good Times We All Had Then

I was born in Kermanshah, Iran, an ancient town on a high brown plateau surrounded by snowcapped mountains. A flash of memory: I am sitting in front of my father on a tall horse, going down a long avenue of trees to a white gate. Although artificial legs were then clumsy and heavy, he insisted on trying to do everything he used to before he lost his leg. From Teheran where the family moved when I was two and a half, my memories are many. Of my father, a strong abrasive presence. Of my mother with whom I was quarrelling even at that age. This piece is about my father, but the older I get the more I admire my mother's courage in putting up with so many trials, not the smallest of which was her daughter, the opposite of everything she would have chosen.

My memories of being in England at the age of five for six months are strong and powerful. It was a wet grey grimy place full of dingy railway stations and sorrowfully shrieking trains, of dirty windows that streamed rain, of nasty neat little gardens, of white slabs that stuck out everywhere into streets where poor lobsters crawled among white limp stinking bits of fish. An atmosphere of irritable respectability. 1924. Places where one has spent a week, or a day can provide thicker crops of memories than those where one lived for years. How about that month spent on the farm that took paying guests with my brother and the governess while my parents went off, leaving us, while they chose a farm. I was in a rage of despair, lied, stole, ran away, cut up my mother's dresses with scissors. A month? – an eternity! About the farm, in Lomagundi, the old Southern Rhodesia, I have written enough. Salisbury as I knew it is in the Martha Quest books, *The Golden Notebook*, short stories.

When I came back to England, or rather, London, in 1949, the England of my memories had vanished, though it was grey, dank and chilly, and unpainted because of the war. The difference? I was grown-up and in charge of myself. All my childhood, every minute, I waited to be grown-up. I have made a hundred mistakes, but coming to England, or London, was not one of them. The most sensible thing I ever did. People grumble and complain, disparage London. Are they mad, I wonder? The place is a cornucopia.

We use our parents like recurring dreams, to be entered into when needed; they are always there for love or for hate; but it occurs to me that I was not always there for my father. I've written about him before, but novels, stories, don't have to be 'true'. Writing this article is difficult because it has to be 'true'. I knew him when his best years were over.

There are photographs of him. The largest is of an officer in the 1914–18 war. A new uniform – buttoned, badged, strapped, tabbed – confines a handsome, dark young man who holds himself stiffly to confront what he certainly thought of as his duty. His eyes are steady, serious, and responsible, and show no signs of what he became later. A photograph at sixteen is of a dark, introspective youth with the same intent eyes. But it is his mouth you notice – a heavily jutting upper lip contradicts the rest of a regular face. His moustache was to hide it: 'Had to do something – a damned fleshy mouth. Always made me uncomfortable, that mouth of mine.'

Earlier a baby (eyes already alert) appears in a lace waterfall that cascades from the pillowy bosom of a fat, plain woman to her feet. It is the face of a head cook. 'Lord, but my mother was a practical female – almost as bad as you!' as he used to say, or throw at my mother in moments of exasperation. Beside her stands, or droops, arms dangling, his father, the source of the dark, arresting eyes, but otherwise masked by a long beard.

The birth certificate says: Born 3rd August, 1886, Walton Villa, Creffield Road, S. Mary at the Wall, RSD. Name, Alfred Cook. Name and surname of Father: Alfred Cook Tayler. Name and maiden name of Mother: Caroline May Batley. Rank or Profession: Bank Clerk. Colchester, Essex.

They were very poor. Clothes and boots were a problem. They 'made their own amusements'. Books were mostly the Bible and *The Pilgrim's Progress*. Every Saturday night they bathed in a hip-bath in front of the kitchen fire. No servants. Church three time on Sundays. 'Lord, when I think of those Sundays! I dreaded them all week, like a nightmare coming at you full tilt and no escape.' But he rabbited with ferrets along the lanes and fields, bird-nested, stole fruit, picked nuts and mushrooms, paid visits to the blacksmith and the mill and rode a farmer's carthorse.

They ate economically, but when he got diabetes in his forties and subsisted on lean meat and lettuce leaves, he remembered suet puddings, treacle puddings, raisin and currant puddings, steak and kidney pud-

dings, bread and butter pudding, 'batter cooked in the gravy with the meat', potato cake, plum cake, butter cake, porridge with treacle, fruit tarts and pies, brawn, pig's trotters and pig's cheek and home-smoked ham and sausages. And 'lashings of fresh butter and cream and eggs'. He wondered if this diet had produced the diabetes, but said it was worth it.

There was an elder brother described by my father as: 'Too damned clever by half. One of those quick, clever brains. Now I've always had a slow brain, but I get there in the end, damn it!'

The brothers went to a local school and the elder did well, but my father was beaten for being slow. They both became bank clerks in, I think, the Westminster Bank, and one must have found it congenial, for he became a manager, the 'rich brother', who had cars and even a yacht. But my father did not like it, though he was conscientious. For instance, he changed his writing, letter by letter, because a senior criticised it. I never saw his unregenerate hand, but the one he created was elegant, spiky, careful. Did this mean he created a new personality for himself, hiding one he did not like, as he hid his 'damned fleshy mouth'? I don't know.

Nor do I know when he left home to live in Luton or why. He found family life too narrow? A safe guess – he found everything too narrow. His mother was too down-to-earth? He had to get away from his clever elder brother?

Being a young man in Luton was the best part of his life. It ended in 1914, so he had a decade of happiness. His reminiscences of it were all of pleasure, the delight of physical movement, of dancing in particular. All his girls were 'a beautiful dancer, light as a feather'. He played billiards and ping-pong (both for his county); he swam, boated, played cricket and football, went to picnics and horse races, sang at musical evenings. One family of a mother and two daughters treated him 'like a son only better. I didn't know whether I was in love with the mother or the daughters, but oh I did love going there; we had such good times.' He was engaged to one daughter, then, for a time, to the other. An engagement was broken off because she was rude to a waiter. 'I could not marry a woman who allowed herself to insult someone who was defenceless.' He used to say to my wryly smiling mother: 'Just as well I didn't marry either of *them*; they would never have stuck it out the way you have, old girl.'

Just before he died he told me he had dreamed he was standing in a kitchen on a very high mountain holding X in his arms. 'Ah, yes, that's what I've missed in my life. Now don't you let yourself be cheated out of life by the old dears. They take all the colour out of everything if you let them.'

But in that decade – 'I'd walk ten, fifteen miles to a dance two or three times a week and think nothing of it. Then I'd dance every dance and walk home again over the fields. Sometimes it was moonlight, but I liked the snow best, all crisp and fresh. I loved walking back and getting into my digs just as the sun was rising. My little dog was so happy to see me, and I'd feed her, and make myself porridge and tea, then I'd wash and shave and go off to work.'

The boy who was beaten at school, who went too much to church, who carried the fear of poverty all his life, but who nevertheless was filled with the memories of country pleasures; the young bank clerk who worked such long hours for so little money, but who danced, sang, played, flirted – this naturally vigorous, sensuous being was killed in 1914, 1915, 1916. I think the best of my father died in that war, that his spirit was crippled by it. The people I've met, particularly the women, who knew him young, speak of his high spirits, his energy, his enjoyment of life. Also of his kindness, his compassion and – a word that keeps recurring – his wisdom. 'Even when he was just a boy he understood things that you'd think even an old man would find it easy to condemn.' I do not think these people would have easily recognised the ill, irritable, abstracted, hypochondriac man I knew.

He 'joined up' as an ordinary soldier out of a characteristically quirky scruple: it wasn't right to enjoy officers' privileges when the Tommies had such a bad time. But he could not stick the communal latrines, the obligatory drinking, the collective visits to brothels, the jokes about girls. So next time he was offered a commission he took it.

His childhood and young man's memories, kept fluid, were added to, grew, as living memories do. But his war memories were congealed in stories that he told again and again, with the same words and gestures, in stereotyped phrases. They were anonymous, general, as if they had come out of a communal war memoir. He met a German in no-man's-land, but both slowly lowered their rifles and smiled and walked away. The Tommies were the salt of the earth, the British fighting men the best in the world. He had never known such comradeship. A certain brutal officer was shot in a sortie by his men, but the other officers, recognising rough justice, said nothing. He had known men intimately who saw the Angels at Mons. He wished he could force all the generals on both sides into the trenches for just one day, to see what the common soldiers endured – *that* would have ended the war at once.

There was an undercurrent of memories, dreams, and emotions much deeper, more personal. This dark region in him, fate-ruled, where nothing was true but horror, was expressed inarticulately, in brief, bitter exclamations or phrases of rage, incredulity, betrayal. The men who went to fight in that war believed it when they said it was to end war. My father believed it. And he was never able to reconcile his belief in his country with his anger at the cynicism of its leaders. And the anger, the sense of betrayal, strengthened as he grew old and ill.

But in 1914 he was naïve, the German atrocities in Belgium inflamed him, and he enlisted out of idealism, although he knew he would have a hard time. He knew because a fortune-teller told him. (He could be described as uncritically superstitious or as psychically gifted.) He would be in great danger twice, yet not die – he was being protected by a famous soldier who was his ancestor. 'And sure enough, later I heard from the Little Aunties that the church records showed we were descended the

83

backstairs way from the Duke of Wellington, or was it Marlborough? Damn it, I forget. But one of them would be beside me all through the war, she said.' (He was romantic, not only about this solicitous ghost, but also about being a descendant of the Huguenots, on the strength of the 'e' in Tayler; and about 'the wild blood' in his veins from a great uncle who, sent unjustly to prison for smuggling, came out of a ten-year sentence and earned it, very efficiently, along the coasts of Cornwall until he died.)

The luckiest thing that ever happened to my father, he said, was getting his leg shattered by shrapnel ten days before Passchendaele. His whole company was killed. He knew he was going to be wounded because of the fortune-teller, who had said he would. 'I did not understand what she meant, but both times in the trenches, first when my appendix burst and I nearly died, and then just before Passchendaele, I felt for some days as if a thick, black velvet pall was settled over me. I can't tell you what it was like. Oh, it was awful, awful, and the second time it was so bad I wrote to the old people and told them I was going to be killed.'

His leg was cut off at mid-thigh, he was shell-shocked, he was very ill for many months, with a prolonged depression afterwards. 'You should always remember that sometimes people are all seething underneath. You don't know what terrible things people have to fight against. You should look at a person's eyes, that's how you tell. . . . When I was like that, after I lost my leg, I went to a nice doctor man and said I was going mad, but he said, don't worry, everyone locks up things like that. You don't know – horrible, horrible, awful things. I was afraid of myself, of what I used to dream. I wasn't myself at all.'

In the Royal Free Hospital was my mother, Sister McVeagh. He married his nurse which, as they both said often enough (though in different tones of voice), was just as well. That was 1919. He could not face being a bank clerk in England, he said, not after the trenches. Besides, England was too narrow and conventional. Besides, the civilians did not know what the soldiers had suffered, they didn't want to know, and now it wasn't done even to remember 'The Great Unmentionable'. He went off to the Imperial Bank of Persia, in which country I was born.

The house was beautiful, with great stone-floored high-ceilinged rooms whose windows showed ranges of snow-streaked mountains. The gardens were full of roses, jasmine, pomegranates, walnuts. Kermanshah he spoke of with liking, but soon they went to Teheran, populous with 'Embassy people', and my gregarious mother created a lively social life about which he was irritable even in recollection.

Irritableness – that note was first struck here, about Persia. He did not like, he said, 'the graft and the corruption'. But here it is time to try and describe something difficult – how a man's good qualities can also be his bad ones, or if not bad, a danger to him.

My father was honourable – he always knew exactly what that word meant. He had integrity. His 'one does not do that sort of thing', his 'no, it is *not* right', sounded throughout my childhood and were final for all of us. I am sure it was true he wanted to leave Persia because of 'the corruption'. But it was also because he was already unconsciously longing for something freer, because as a bank official he could not let go into the dream-logged personality that was waiting for him. And later in Rhodesia, too, what was best in him was also what prevented him from shaking away the shadows: it was always in the name of honesty or decency that he refused to take this step or that out of the slow decay of the family's fortunes.

In 1925 there was leave from Persia. That year in London there was an Empire Exhibition, and on the Southern Rhodesian stand some very fine maize cobs and a poster saying that fortunes could be made on maize at 25/- a bag. So on an impulse, turning his back forever on England, washing his hands of the corruption of the East, my father collected all his capital, £800, I think, while my mother packed curtains from Liberty's, clothes from Harrods, visiting cards, a piano, Persian rugs, a governess and two small children.

Soon, there was my father in a cigar-shaped house of thatch and mud on the top of a kopje that overlooked in all directions a great system of mountains, rivers, valleys, while overhead the sky arched from horizon to empty horizon. This was a couple of hundred miles south from the Zambesi, a hundred or so west from Mozambique, in the district of Banket, so called because certain of its reefs were of the same formation as those called *banket* on the Rand. Lomagundi – gold country, tobacco country, maize country – wild, almost empty. (The Africans had been turned off it into reserves.) Our neighbours were four, five, seven miles off. In front of the house . . . no neighbours, nothing; no farms, just wild bush with two rivers but no fences to the mountains seven miles away. And beyond these mountains and bush again to the Portuguese border, over which 'our boys' used to escape when wanted by the police for pass or other offences.

And then? There was bad luck. For instance, the price of maize dropped from 25/- to 9/- a bag. The seasons were bad, prices bad, crops failed. This was the sort of thing that made it impossible for him ever to 'get off the farm', which, he agreed with my mother, was what he most wanted to do.

It was an absurd country, he said. A man could 'own' a farm for years that was totally mortgaged to the Government and run from the Land

Bank, meanwhile employing half-a-hundred Africans at 12/- a month and none of them knew how to do a day's work. Why, two farm labourers from Europe could do in a day what twenty of these ignorant black savages would take a week to do. (Yet he was proud that he had a name as a just employer, that he gave 'a square deal'.) Things got worse. A fortune-teller had told him that her heart ached when she saw the misery ahead for my father: this was the misery.

But it was my mother who suffered. After a period of neurotic illness, which was a protest against her situation, she became brave and resourceful. But she never saw that her husband was not living in a real world, that he had made a captive of her common sense. We were always about to 'get off the farm'. A miracle would do it – a sweepstake, a goldmine, a legacy. And then? What a question! We would go to England where life would be normal with people coming in for musical evenings and nice supper parties at the Trocadero after a show. Poor woman, for the twenty years we were on the farm, she waited for when life would begin for her and for her children, for she never understood that what was a calamity for her was for them a blessing.

Meanwhile my father sank towards his death (at sixty-one). Everything changed in him. He had been a dandy and fastidious, now he hated to change out of shabby khaki. He had been sociable, now he was misanthropic. His body's disorders – soon diabetes and all kinds of stomach ailments – dominated him. He was brave about his wooden leg, and even went down mine shafts and climbed trees with it, but he walked clumsily and it irked him badly. He greyed fast, and slept more in the day, but would be awake half the night pondering about. . . .

It could be gold divining. For ten years he experimented on private theories to do with the attractions and repulsions of metals. His whole soul went into it but his theories were wrong or he was *unlucky* – after all, if he had found a mine he would have had to leave the farm. It could be the relation between the minerals of the earth and of the moon; his decision to make infusions of all the plants on the farm and drink them himself in the interests of science; the criminal folly of the British Government in not realising that the Germans and the Russians were conspiring as Anti-Christ to . . . the inevitability of war because no one would listen to Churchill, but it would be all right because God (by then he was a British Israelite) had destined Britain to rule the world; a prophecy said ten million dead would surround Jerusalem – how would the corpses be cleared away?; people who wished to abolish flogging should be flogged; the natives understood nothing but a good beating; hanging must not be abolished because the Old Testament said 'an eye for an eye and a tooth for a tooth. . . .'

Yet, as this side of him darkened, so that it seemed all his thoughts were of violence, illness, war, still no one dared to make an unkind comment in his presence or to gossip. Criticism of people, particularly of women, made him more and more uncomfortable till at last he burst out with: 'It's all very well, but no one has the right to say that about another person.'

In Africa, when the sun goes down, the stars spring up, all of them in their expected places, glittering and moving. In the rainy season, the sky flashed and thundered. In the dry season, the great dark hollow of night was lit by veld fires: the mountains burned through September and October in chains of red fire. Every night my father took out his chair to watch the sky and the mountains, smoking, silent, a thin shabby fly-away figure under the stars. 'Makes you think – there are so many worlds up there, wouldn't really matter if we did blow ourselves up – plenty more where we came from.'

The Second World War, so long foreseen by him, was a bad time. His son was in the Navy and in danger, and his daughter a sorrow to him. He became very ill. More and more often it was necessary to drive him into

Salisbury with him in a coma, or in danger of one, on the back seat. My mother moved him into a pretty little suburban house in town near the hospitals, where he took to his bed and a couple of years later died. For the most part he was unconscious under drugs. When awake he talked obsessively (a tongue licking a nagging sore place) about 'the old war'. Or he remembered his youth. 'I've been dreaming – Lord, to see those horses come lickety-split down the course with their necks stretched out and the sun on their coats and everyone shouting.houting. . . . I've been dreaming how I walked along the river in the mist as the sun was rising. . . . Lord, lord, lord, what a time that was, what good times we all had then, before the old war.'

Her father must be taken care of first. He was the one Yahweh had trifled with. She would make him smile his whistling smile, he would whistle for her bright in the new morning, whistle the mill song and strop his razor. She loved his hands and his cuffs on which he had written the name of every lamb. She had named all the lambs and he had remembered them. She would make him a blue handkerchief with a great J which would be like life springs to him. He would vault over the great gate with one hand and when the bull charged on the tree he would spring to one side.

Emily Holmes Coleman, *The Shutter of Snow*

A father can be not there enough, which leads a girl to idealize her father and men, or to endow them with immensely sadistic or punitive characteristics – or can be there too much (be too possessive, seductive, or identified with their daughter), requiring her to develop defensive measures against involvement with him and with men. Fathers . . . must be able to make themselves available as a heterosexual love object and to offer affection without being seduced by their daughters' fantasies or seducing them with their own.

Marjorie Leonard, 'Fathers and Daughters',
International Journal of Psychoanalysis

When she saw his eyes and the fear crouched there she knew that she should have said nothing – for it was like shattering his life. A fierce protectiveness welled in her. She knew suddenly that she had to lull him with lies. Slowly she raised her hand to calm him and said softly, 'I . . . I'm . . . sorry, Daddy . . . I didn't mean . . . to scare you . . . It was . . . nothing.

Paule Marshall, *Brown Girl, Brownstones*

DINAH BROOKE

An Obsession Revisited

1936   Born.
1950–54   Cheltenham Ladies' College. Couldn't stand it. Left at sixteen to go to Paris and live romantic life à la Cocteau/Juliette Greco. Very naïve. Studied sculpture and Greek. Went slightly mad. Spent many solitary afternoons in the cinema. Developed wonderful French accent. Came back not much less naïve. London crammers to get into Oxford. Failed the regular colleges but accepted by St Clare's. Had a great time, parties, champagne, theatre, the Bodleian – got an Eng. Lit. degree.
London Film School. Made a movie about a mad girl and discovered sex.
Started out to be a dynamic young writer/director in small documentary film company, ended up after two years licking stamps and tying parcels. Decided I was more cut out for the solitary life. Went to Cold Cure Centre and started novel.
Year in Greenwich Village, New York, being a Writer, living out much more satisfactory version of bohemian fantasies (never discovered hippies).
1965   Back to London with actor Frank Dux, got married, had twins (1966).
1970–75   Four novels published, two plays produced. Became ardent feminist, then ardent encounter groupie. Turned house into commune. Husband left.
1975   Took sannyas, given new name by Bhagwan Shree Rajneesh, Ma Prem Pankaja, Panky for short, moved to Poona, India, to live in his ashram. Twins didn't like it and came back to live with their Dad.
I lived in the ashram for six years; work included making and selling clothes, cleaning toilets, acting in Shakespearean plays, making soap and face cream.
1981   Bhagwan went to America, I came back to London. Ran a market stall, met Derek, now Mahabodh. Work as temp. sec. and freelance journalist. Tomorrow?

I was obsessed with my Dad for twenty years. You could almost say I made a career out of him – or out of the lack of him. Do people whose fathers are more present in their lives become so obsessed? I never lived with him after I was three, hardly saw him between the ages of seven and twenty-five, yet the amount of energy I focused on him was phenomenal.

It would be hard not to describe his life as a failure. He started off all right. He was the second of four sons, the fifth and youngest child was the only girl. While the children were still small, his father became managing director of Lysachts Steel Works, in Scunthorpe, and built a large, comfortable house near the works, with a rose garden, kitchen garden, orchard, Chinese water garden, tennis courts, everything that the prosperous middle classes could think of to make life enjoyable in the golden years before the First World War. The family grew up untouched by that war – all it did was increase the demand for steel. Their mother was gay, fat and eccentric; they had loyal servants, delicious food, endless parties, dances, concerts, charades – to me it always sounded like the perfect idyll of family life. The boys all went to public school, Charter-house, and then two of them went on to Oxford, but Joe, fascinated by steel-making, went straight into the works, and started to learn the business from the bottom up.

I was fascinated by steel-making too, when I used to visit Scunthorpe as a child. At the bottom of the garden were rows of conical slag heaps like miniature Japanese volcanoes, glowing scarlet at the top as fresh slag was poured on; and by the side of the road as you biked downhill were the huge, elegant shapes of the three cooling towers, so close that you could put out your hand and touch them. Sometimes my Dad would take me, when I was five or six, holding my hand tightly, to see the molten steel being poured, in an immense dark building like a cathedral. We climbed up hundreds of steps and walked along the narrow gantry, with people being very polite because my Dad was the boss, and then a sort of crane with an enormous dipper on top trundled with a great roar up to our end of the cathedral and tipped a stream of molten steel into the mould far below. The blast of heat would hit me thirty feet away, I'd gasp and have to shut my eyes. The stream of blinding heat and light poured down and showers of sparks bounced up like golden rain; two or three more times the crane trundled back into the darkness, and then the last glorious moment was over, and it was time to go home for lunch. Even as a child I saw why people feel they have put their heart and soul into steel-making. My Dad felt that way.

He only had one hobby, flying aeroplanes, which came in useful during the war. He always promised he would teach me to fly when my legs were long enough to reach the rudder bar; but by that time his life had started to fall apart somewhat. He joined the air force as an instructor; he was too old to be a pilot. With my mother, who had TB, and should have been in a sanatorium, I followed him round England from one air-force base to the other during the first two years of the war, one ghastly lot of digs, one horrible new school after another. My mother got sicker and sicker, and I don't remember seeing Joe at all. But he ended up as a Wing Commander flying bombing raids over France – until they recalled him to Scunthorpe. The need for steel was getting desperate, and they wanted someone who could treble production in a year; apparently he did.

Those were the days, when he was back at the works at the end of the war, when his London address was the Savoy. He took me there once, but I have a feeling it was when the good times were already over. Somehow, during the nationalisation of the industry after the war, he got shuffled out. He and my mother got divorced; my mother went back into the sanatorium; I went to boarding school; Joe married the widow of an air-force pal, and emigrated to Kenya.

Things didn't work out in Kenya either. He became an alcoholic, went mad, and spent most of the rest of his life in asylums of varying degrees of Dickensian horror. Actually the horrific ones were the ones he preferred. They added a rich touch of realism to his paranoia when they kept him with fifty other men in a locked, evil-smelling ward; but when they moved him to a room with chintz curtains and his own armchair the security of his world began to shake. If he could have that, why not the Savoy as he had been used to? His madness began to lose its sharp, sustaining edge. But he did have his moment of glory. He played possum for a whole year, being the good, obedient patient, until he was allowed to go for walks in the garden. One day he simply strolled through the main gate and set out for London (the hospital was in Bristol). On the way he stole a car, and when he arrived went straight to Scotland Yard to report the theft, so that he could be charged, and the issue of his sanity brought up in a court of law. Nobody got the point at all, stupid fools, they didn't even appreciate the joke; and they locked him up again for several more years.

As for me, I couldn't hate him, or blame him for not living up to my expectations of what a proper father should be. He had removed himself neatly from any possibility of hatred or revenge – all I could do was try to save him, and take out my rage and frustration on the world which had treated him so badly; which, translated, means myself and my nearest and dearest. Our relationship was one of intense passion, devotion, rage, hatred, anguish, desire, disgust, but it was all on my side. I don't know what he felt about me. He read the book I wrote about his life, but made no comment. Whenever I made an emotional demand on him he retired rapidly into his madness; otherwise he was polite, humorous and amenable.

Melanie Klein described the genesis of a work of art as the desire to make reparation; to give back to the parent the gifts they have offered in defective form – the good breast that is not always good. Infantile anger and consequent guilt fuels the shaping of a work of art – and that, goddammit, *is* perfect.

I mean look, a book, printed pages, hard covers, shiny pictures. Just look at you, see what a mess you made of your life? You're much better like this. Neat, full of good things, fixed, appreciated. You really fucked it up didn't you, you silly old man, but don't worry, I'll make it OK. I'll rewrite your life for you, not improving things much – playing around with the facts a bit, yes; putting you into the army instead of the air force so I can have some nice games with Monty at El Alamein, but not papering over the cracks; not trying to make you appear better, more successful, a better father. You were a disaster as a father by any standards at all – and pretty much of a disaster as a human being, except that there you were, alive, yourself. That's what always floored me. And why couldn't other people see it the way I did? Why did they want to lock you up in an asylum because you were mad? Deprive you of All That Makes Life Worth Living, and condemn you to the Worst Fate a human being can imagine – bastards, unthinking brutes – you were innocent of course, and I would rescue you – be the knight on a white charger – oh, you did provide me with some good roles. As your next of kin I became your legal guardian when I was twenty-five, when the new Mental Health Act came in. I hadn't seen you for ten years, and there you were, toothless, scabby, filthy, stinking, incarcerated – and innocent! And you didn't even sound that mad, either.

For years you were my crusade, and trying to get you released was my reason for being alive. The doctors simply said, 'No, he's chronic, he'll be here till he dies.' Then one year, while I was living in the States I came over to take you away on holiday, and when we got back to the hospital after a fortnight in Ireland they said, 'Oh, didn't you get our letter? He's been released into your care.' There you were, on my lap, a great big Christmas present – all my dreams come true. Teach me to have dreams. My American lover, Frank, stayed in England and married me, and we forgot all about our flat and possessions and lives in New York.

The shock of freedom was too much for you, Joe. Dreams coming true again. What the hell do you do then? They're never quite what you expect. You walked under a car – by mistake of course, then moved into our two-room summer rental near Charing Cross with a broken arm, a broken leg, two cracked ribs and a cracked head. It made a good excuse. We used to take you round to visit friends and dare them not to be truly warm and accepting. But it was all still a dream world. No one was quite living in the real world. Where is the bastard anyway? The longer I live the more I realise how hard it is to find the real world. Yes, I know it's here all the time; but finding it, or rather recognising it – that's the problem. When, years later, my recreated You came out between hard covers, I took you along to the Arts Council launch, expecting somewhere, somehow, that all these literary characters would stand up and cheer – and give you back all that you thought you had lost. No one would have known you were a loony; I was quite proud of you. But they were all busy hustling as usual, and nobody realised what an event your presence was. You thought they were a tough bunch, tougher than the iron and steel magnates you used to play with. No wonder you went mad. I don't think I'll compete any more either, thank you very much. Sense of anticlimax. But I was really hooked on fathers; I wrote another book – deep stuff this – incorporating the father. A suicidal daughter pursues her father through the horrors of war-torn Vietnam, and finally, in the heat of the afternoon, she makes love to him, and as he comes he has a heart attack and dies. Thank goodness I've finished with that little lot. Burned out.

What's left? An old man; a senile wreck; a shell. Where are you in all this, Joe? Were you ever there? You were just a screen for me to have mad daughterly fantasies about; for me to act out all my frustrated rages and passions and Joan of Arc and Mother Teresa roles.

When I last saw you you were living in an old folks' home. Nice, not very different from the better sort of loony bin; your own room, wireless, TV, good food, lots of care. You'd been on your deathbed again. You were an expert at deathbeds – loved them. Innocent, of course; your sort of going mad relieved you of all responsibility. You just went to the pub, got pissed, fell over and broke another bone – or got pneumonia – and bingo! another deathbed scene. My mother and I went to the first one together, though you'd been divorced for twenty years. I think she felt responsible for landing me with a father like you. She kept on taking over when my fantasies landed me in trouble. She'd remove you, look after you, find somewhere for you to live outside the hospital; eventually took you in herself when her second husband died, until you broke your ankle and couldn't get to the loo, and she'd had enough. I'd escaped to India by then. I did suggest that you come along too, but you didn't fancy that idea, thank God. Anyway the last time I saw you, several deathbeds later, you wheezed so much you could hardly breathe, and had to piss every three minutes. You shuffled half in half out of the door of your room; three steps in three steps out; should you go to the toilet again, or try to stay and be polite? Who were these two women? You could no longer go down to the pub so chocolate had become your passion – you could hardly wait to tear the silver paper off the bar of Fry's Turkish Delight before stuffing it into your sunken mouth. Your eyes were huge and blue, and it seemed to me when I looked into them that they were full of terror. You'd been dragged back from death so often – what was so bad about it that they wouldn't let you go? In the end you had a heart attack while sitting down to lunch. I only heard about it casually. My daughter wrote saying I suppose you heard that Joe died a few months ago.

You'd given it all up years before, I think. And so had I. I wasn't sad when you died; I didn't miss you. I don't think anyone did. The person that we might have loved, or missed, seemed to have disappeared a long time ago. I never really knew you. I was never your little girl who could come to you for comfort and cuddles. I was the strong one. You even called me the Boss. You seem to have finished with your own life twenty-five years before you died. It took me another fifteen. Then I had finished with you too. All the emotions had been played out. There was nothing left.

And yet perhaps I failed to see you completely. Obsessed with you for years, but blind – seeing only the huge holes you had left in my life, and not you at all.

Looking at photos of you on your wedding day, and holding me on your lap when I was a baby, there is such a tender, sweet expression on your face. You were handsome, dashing, all the local girls were in love with you before you disappointed them and married my beautiful, independent mother, who was an artist, and must have appeared infinitely exotic to you. You were the reliable, hard-working son, who took it upon himself to keep everything together, the works, the family, the steel industry. You had a highly developed sense of responsibility. You were also a very shy man; you never looked directly at the camera, but gazed with utterly naïve love and pride at your wife or your daughter. But even then you were living in a world of dreams and definitions that left them out. My mother said you always used to find someone to blame when things went wrong, and brooded and sulked for days. Not one to look at yourself and think maybe you did it wrong, and try again. Or forget about the past, drop it and put all your energy into today. No, you preferred to brood and sulk until it was all the fault of the Russians, who read your letters as soon as they dropped through the slot in the pillar box and had managed to implant into your broken arm a microphone, which

could pick up not only your conversation but your thoughts. Clever chaps, those Russians.

I wanted you to love me so much, and I can see from your expression as I sat on your lap, aged one, that you did – you loved me like any other father loves his daughter, after his own fashion, as much as you could manage. You drove down to my school, Cheltenham Ladies' College, in a hired Daimler when I was about fifteen, and took me out to tea, though you were up to your ears in debt and working as a labourer at the time. You told me about Africa. You had recently come back from Kenya in circumstances not of your own choosing, and we talked about buying a Land-Rover and driving from the Cape to Cairo. People have these fantasies. Some people act on them. We didn't. I didn't really think we would. I can just about count them on one hand, the times I remember being with you in my childhood. There was one Christmas at Scunthorpe; my mother was in the sanatorium, I must have been six or seven. You were sitting at the end of the polished mahogany table, surrounded by brothers and sisters and cousins and nephews and nieces, all our rations combined to make a feast, and I kept climbing onto your lap to suck your ear lobe, which embarrassed you no end. And you'd rashly made one of those resolutions to give up smoking because of your horrible, permanent cough, but someone had given you a box of Havana cigars, precious as gold. Overexcited by the festivities, I seized the box, and threatened to hold them under the tap. You didn't believe me, but horrible little creature, I did! You were caught in the trap of your own logic, but for a moment you were really angry.

And then there was the time you went to have a drink with some air-force cronies in a pub, and I had to sit outside in the car. You brought me some orange squash, and had one of your coughing fits when your face went a deep purple, and you brought up horrifying noises and substances from the very depths of your bowels, or that's what it sounded like, and you went on and on and on, and I sat and watched, forgetting all about the orange squash, waiting for you to choke to death. And then the time when you had shaved off your air-force handlebar moustache and asked me if I noticed anything different, and I didn't.

I could rake up a few more instances – like the time when you took me on a bike ride past the cooling towers and told me you and my mum were getting a divorce, and I fell off my bike; and the time I asked you if you loved me best of all the children (my cousins), and you said you loved us all the same. Threadbare relationship; mingy little threads to weave into fatherhood; there's still a taste of bitterness in my mouth. Love, warmth, cuddles, kisses, guidance – you knew the sort of things a father is meant to do, and you tried. But circumstances and your other preoccupations made it impossible. Once, when my own children, your grandchildren, were five, they went down to stay with you in the farmhouse in the country where you were living. It was Mrs Selway's idea, the farmer's wife. She and her husband gave them rides on the tractor, and had their photograph taken, and showed them the animals; but you didn't take any notice of them. You had other things on your mind. Another of your characteristic poses in photographs is you with your hands on your hips – legs spread wide, gazing over one shoulder into the middle distance. Even if we had lived together I don't suppose you would have noticed me much.

You were a charming and entertaining man in your own way, so long as no one expected too much of you. Perhaps that was the best time in our relationship, the time when you'd been let out of the asylum, and because you'd been run over and had a broken arm and leg the embarrassing question of where you had been for the last fifteen years did not need to arise, and it was perfectly clear why you weren't working. You were the focus of my life. All my friends were judged by how they reacted to you. Frank and I had this secret agreement that people could only pass – be accepted into the fellowship of the truly human – if they could not only accept you but follow the convolutions of your fantasy, which pedestrian and unimaginative doctors had labelled paranoia.

A middle-aged man, about five foot ten, sparse grey hair combed back very neatly – your hair had always been sleek and smooth – good solid features, a rather severe expression, grey toothbrush moustache. Nothing there to give you away. And you were always neatly dressed.

Cheap clothes, bought by your daughter at Marks and Spencer, no more going to Savile Row – but always neat. And you were good company a lot of the time, with a fund of stories you didn't repeat any more often than other old men; and even your paranoid fantasies were quite entertaining if you weren't too pissed. Chinese coffins was your favourite; your signature tune, as it were. Solve the problem of overproduction in the steel industry and make friends with China at the same time by manufacturing stainless steel enamelled coffins with pictures of Chairman Mao on them for sale to the Confucian Chinese. Everybody knows that the Confucian Chinese are willing to spend more on their coffins than they are on their houses, and you can't get better quality than stainless steel. We might not have been able to figure out what Chairman Mao was doing in there, and where to find Confucian Chinese these days, but you could.

You did have a few little habits though, which spelled out Institution. You always used to clean your nails with matchsticks, and file them with the striking edge of the matchbox. (You don't get files and nail scissors in a mental hospital.) And you'd collect dog-ends from the ashtrays and use the tobacco to make roll-ups. It was agony for you to let a dog-end lie. The same with people's unfinished glasses of beer and wine. Before leaving the dinner table, and before going to bed at night, muttering some casual excuse about 'waste not, want not' – you had a developed sense of correct social behaviour – you would swig down the dregs, one after the other, eyes darting from side to side as your head went back, to see if anyone had noticed. Then it was the turn of any bottles which were open, but not empty. You were very good at the little start of surprise, 'Oh,' addressed to the wall, 'might as well finish this up,' with another quick look round to see that no one, especially me, was within earshot. I quickly developed a nasty habit, when you were staying with us, of locking bottles up. You also had a wonderfully guilty expression when caught, lower lip sucked in, upper lip right down to your chin, covering up the evidence, eyes round as egg cups. Just William, about ten years old. But that expression didn't come from madness, it came from school and the nursery. I can do it pretty well myself.

Trouble was when you first came out of the mental hospital, with the whole glorious world of London at your feet – even though one of the said feet was in a plaster cast – what were you going to do with it? London, I mean. There were still connections to be made. You went along to the Savoy to see if there was anyone there you recognised; there wasn't, but you tipped the doorman a fiver for old times' sake. It wasn't the same doorman that you used to tip a pound in the thirties, but he was very polite. Trouble was, that was your old age pension gone for the week.

And then there was the time you bought several hundred pounds worth of pictures. You disappeared all day, and about eight o'clock in the evening we got a call from a young man called Bob, an unemployed trapeze artiste. You had met Bob, and a very nice man called Max, in a pub in Sloane Square at lunchtime, and after a few drinks had gone round to Max's place to have a look at his pictures, and you thought they were great, and after a few more drinks decided to buy the lot, but unfortunately you didn't have your cheque book on you, so you were just ringing your daughter who would come round with the money. Oh. She wouldn't? Um . . . Bob, the trapeze artiste, came back on the line. He wasn't surprised, he'd been expecting something like this. Max could turn nasty – but Bob would explain things to him, and bring Joe home himself. They left, Joe promising fulsomely to send a cheque.

Frank and I decided that what we needed was not so much a baby-sitter as a father sitter – who could go to pubs with Joe and see that he didn't get too pissed and have a chat with him, and listen to his stories, and then bring him home. We were trying to earn a living, and didn't much like pubs anyway. Bob, who brought Joe back, good as his word, and stayed to supper, thought this was a very good idea, and would have done it himself, but he had a job next week, back on the high wire. He liked Joe; they'd had a fine time together, and swapped some good jokes.

Joe, while I'm writing about you I feel as if I'm pushing something uphill. Making a tremendous effort, as if I have to act both parts at once, the parent and the child. I did so want you to be a father to me. I did so want someone to be a father to me. You did the best you could. It wasn't a lot. The desire was there, but the execution was feeble.

When I became a sannyasin in 1975 and went to live in Poona, at the ashram of Bhagwan Shree Rajneesh, my last novel, about your life, had just come out. When Bhagwan read it he sent a message back saying, 'You don't need to do Primal.' Primal was a group that many people did when they first came to the ashram, to give them some insight into the life patterns that had been set up in their early childhood. I had been wallowing in the pains of my childhood for too long already; I was imprisoned by my own pain, and the ego's involvement with making art out of it. If you want to let go of the pain you have to let go of the goodies you can get out of it as well. Bhagwan kept on talking about 'dropping negativity', and I was furious. Where would I be without my negativity?

What would I be? The essence of Bhagwan's teaching is, perhaps, that in order to experience God the ego must be dropped; the ego is only an illusion anyway, just our fantasies about who we are, not who we really are, and the ego makes us miserable. I saw it. But I only saw it after having wallowed for thirty years in the misery I created out of the events of my childhood – and through meeting Bhagwan, living near him, sitting in his presence every day, I began to have a glimpse – just a faint glimpse – of the possibility of being happy, not only happy but overflowing with joy, for no reason, not because a book has been accepted, praised, a movie made of it – I have become rich and famous, appearing on TV chat shows, ever-present fantasies – but just sitting, cleaning – cleaning? – dancing – help! – I'm a serious woman, an intellectual, a Great Talent, a 'Female Hemingway'.

I shaved all my hair off and wrote my obituary as I would like to see it. Full of purple passages, 'literary genius', 'turning Agony into Art', and 'because you didn't appreciate her enough, you rotten sods, she's killed herself, so there'. I almost sent it off, that obituary, really pretended that I was dead. But it was because of you, dear Joe, that I had to stay unappreciated, just as it was because of you that I couldn't handle being loved. I had never learned any behaviour patterns that fitted in with being loved and appreciated. But I'd learned to like it that way. What do you write about if you haven't got a tortured soul? My soul was so used to being tortured it didn't know what to do with itself without a good dose of anguish. And when a man told me he loved me my reaction was not pleasure, but rage and terror. It was so extreme that I went to see Bhagwan about it in Darshan, an evening meeting for maybe twenty sannyasins. When I had calmed down a bit he told me that I was like a child who had been hungry for so long that when her mother finally offers her food it is too humiliating to accept, and she hits the cup away in a rage.

A lot of my psychoanalytically oriented friends think that a guru is a sort of father figure, and that the reason I went to Poona is because of my obsessive 'fatherlessness'. They may be right; I mean that may be the reason that I was lucky enough to find my way to Bhagwan. He's an En-lightened Master – someone who has dropped his ego, so when you come into contact with him you can project anything you like on to him, and he can fulfil all your needs because he is simply mirroring you – reflecting your contortions, not judging or condemning you, accepting you totally and yet not taking you seriously. Whatever image is reflected perfectly in the still waters of a lake is beautiful. He is a lake, and his stillness is perfect. All the frenzy is my own. If my frenzy is the desire for a father, it is there, reflected. Because of his stillness I can, occasionally, be still.

Maybe in some way Bhagwan was a father for me in that he loved me and allowed me to grow. But the love of a Master is very different from any other sort of love – it is at the same time more personal – he loves every part of me, there is nothing that is hidden from him, I am more totally myself in his presence than in the presence of the most tender parent or passionate lover – and yet less personal because it is not limited to me; it is undirected; the waters of the lake are simply there for anyone who wants to come.

Have I forgiven you, Joe, for not being the sort of father I would like you to have been? Have I learnt anything? That your life is yours, and mine is mine, and we are not responsible for each other. That it was my free choice to torture myself because of you? Am I still scratching away at those old wounds? Probably, from time to time, when I'm in a bad mood, or Mercury is travelling backwards in the heavens, or just before my period.

Yours seems a life to be pitied, to be condoled with. What a tragedy, what a waste. But you never saw it like that. You seemed to have chosen it very deliberately, to preserve your innocence. And who knows what was happening in those last years of your life? Who knows what is happening in the soul of someone who appears mad or senile? Were you acting out some penance? Were you perhaps removing yourself to just the right distance so that your daughter could spend thirty years tying herself in knots about your absence? What were you doing, Joe? Why were you doing it? I don't believe in wasted lives. It must have fulfilled some purpose for you, taught you some lesson you were too stubborn to learn any other way. Was that it? Did you ever learn that lesson? What have I learned from your absence? The strength of my own need for love, my destructiveness when that need is thwarted – I learned very well how to cut off my nose to spite my face – and the painful process of accepting the rage, the anger, the destructiveness, the pain, the need, the emptiness – and finding that love is all around if I could only see it. I was a bitch to my mother for years because I couldn't accept her love. I wanted it the way I wanted it, the shape and size I wanted it, now. All right. Enough. No – take it away, it's the wrong sort, I'd rather starve, thank you. Most people are bad at expressing love. You were, Joe. Hopeless. Any emotional demand and you took to the bottle as quick as you could. Perhaps that was why you went mad – so no one would be able to make any demands on you. But looking at your expression as you gazed at my mother on your wedding day, or so proudly at your pudgy little one-year-old daughter, there was love in your heart, tears in your eyes, probably. Tears in mine too. Sentimental cow.

101

The smell of tobacco, ink and old leather which made up the permanent atmosphere of the study oppressed her like a drug. She felt her arms and legs growing thick and heavy and her eyes stiffening in their sockets. But why, she kept asking herself, should she be in such a state simply because she was alone with the person she cared for more than anyone in the world? Only a few months ago they had been companions and conspirators; her greatest delight had been to steal half an hour with him when her mother was not there. She had even wished that something terrible would happen to him so that she could prove how much she loved him. Now it had come and she felt nothing but terror and distaste. She glanced at his tired face, bent over the prose he was so methodically correcting. Why could she not get up this minute, go over and put her arms round him and say the perfect comforting words?

Antonia White, *The Lost Traveller*

Quite different are the effects of the castration complex in the female. She acknowledges the fact of her castration, and with it, too, the superiority of the male and her own inferiority; but she rebels against this unwelcome state of affairs. From this divided attitude three lines of development open up. The first leads to a general revulsion from sexuality. . . . The second line leads her to cling with defiant self-assertiveness to her threatened masculinity. . . . and the phantasy of being a man in spite of everything often persists as a formative factor over long periods. . . . Only if her development follows the third, very circuitous, path does she reach the final normal female attitude, in which she takes her father as her object and so finds her way to the feminine form of the Oedipus complex.

Sigmund Freud, *On Sexuality*

Our egos are born delicate. Bestowing pleasure upon a beloved father is much easier than discovering the joys of solitary achievements. It was easy for me to please my father; and this ease bred in me a desire to please men – a desire for the rewards of a good girl. They are by no means inconsiderable: safety and approval, the warm, incomparable atmosphere created when one pleases a man who has vowed, in his turn, to keep the wolf from the door.

But who is the wolf?

He is strangers. He is the risk of one's own judgements, one's own work.

Mary Gordon, *The Writer on Her Work*

MICHELE ROBERTS

Outside My Father's House

I was born of a French mother and an English father and live and work in London. I have co-authored several poetry collections, the most recent of which is *Touch Papers* (Allison & Busby, 1982), and a short story collection, *Tales I Tell My Mother* (Journeyman Press, 1978). My first novel was *A Piece of the Night* (Women's Press, 1978) and my second *The Visitation* (Women's Press, 1983). At the moment I'm working on a third novel and a new collection of poetry. I teach part-time in adult education, am one of the London Borough of Bromley's writers-in-residence in schools, and also edit the poetry column in *City Limits* magazine. I'm a member of the Greater London Arts Association Literature Panel.

Break the silence, I tell myself, break the taboo. I'm struggling against feelings of betrayal and disloyalty involved in attempting to write an article in which my father, and my feeling for him, will appear, however invented, however transformed or veiled. We've had a passionate and troubled history together. He's still alive, contentedly retired now, though it's taken him several years to come to terms with being made forcibly redundant. Now he paints, sings in the church choir, serves on the local parish council and in the Conservative Association, plays squash and tennis, has more time to spend with my mother, helps look after my sister's two children on visits. Shouldn't I leave him in peace?

Writing about the *image* of the father is a literary strategy for dealing with the problem. It also opens up a way of exploring the distinction between my 'real' father (whose life continues independent of mine, who has his own private interior life, whom I am still getting to know) and my shifting perceptions of him, my 'imaginary' father. From an early age I projected these images into the father-daughter relationships I found described in novels.

Aged twelve, newly a recipient of pocket money, I began setting up a personal library on the shelf above my bed. It contained already the books I'd been given for Christmas over successive years. One favourite was stories of the Knights of King Arthur, over which I wept copiously: Gawain, Tristram, Percival were my heroes. I couldn't bear it when the book revealed that the fellowship of the Round Table came to an end through the involuntary agency of a woman, Guinevere. The first book that I bought with my saved-up pocket money was *Pride and Prejudice* by Jane Austen.

Puberty marked me as female in a way I hadn't had to deal with before, named me as daughter to my father: previously I'd imagined myself as either sexless or male; my father passionately desired a son and was delighted when my younger brother was born. If I had to be daughter, I wanted to be my father's favourite daughter and there were three of us. I wanted my father to be my companion, to praise me for wit and intelligence as Mr Bennet praised Lizzy. Their fictional relationship compensated for what I felt I lacked in real life: I wasn't pretty and sparkling as Eliza Bennet was, did not know how to tease men as she teased Mr Darcy for pompousness, rarely spent time with my father or talked to him as father. He was a distant hero, an ideal I created; my favourite film stars at this time were older men like Rex Harrison and Cary Grant, and I flirted with my father when I felt bold enough to do so, telling him he looked like a film star. I was impressed by Eliza Bennet's ability to criticise her father as well as love him, since I was too far away from mine to know him well. I took refuge in unconscious fantasies of intimacy, which I didn't understand or recognise until years later.

One summer, aged about fourteen, I accompanied my parents on a trip to the south of France. We stayed in Avignon during the August festival. My father commented on the beauty of so many of the young French women, their slim bodies, their long dark hair swept up with combs, their dark eyes. I felt jealous and depressed: I was plump, with short curly hair and a tendency to spottiness. We halted in the main square to watch a group of North African men dancing, their women watching from the sidelines. Suddenly I leapt into the middle of the group of men and began dancing with them. They were amused, clapping me and calling out, 'Come on, English miss.' I danced for my father; he laughed and clapped too. Twenty years later, this scene repeated itself: last summer I stood in exactly the same spot outside the Palace of the Popes in Avignon, remembering the earlier incident, and then saw my father coming towards me. Astonished, we hugged each other, laughing, while next to us a group of young people played guitar music. I'd known my parents were visiting relatives in Provence, but had never dreamed that there we would be, running towards each other in that great square, meeting by chance. This time I felt joyful, no longer ugly; this time I felt close to my father, glad to introduce him to the friends I was with.

By the age of sixteen I'd become hooked on the historical romances of Georgette Heyer. For a long time my favourite was *Regency Buck*: one summer I read it ten times. On the death of her father, the heroine, beautiful, spirited, wayward Judith, comes to London, only to discover that her guardian, the handsome, tough, cynical Earl of Worth, is determined to curtail her freedom within conventional bounds. The power struggles between the daughter and the surrogate father both express and conceal the sexual attachment between the two: at crucial moments in their arguments Lord Worth taunts Judith with how he kissed her when they first met, before he realised that she was his ward (you can kiss a servant with impunity, less so a lady). At the end of the novel he rescues Judith from being kidnapped by a fortune hunter into a fate worse than death, and proposes to her next day: it is her twenty-first birthday and he can now, legally released from his guardianship, seek her hand in marriage. Thus the novel neatly deals with the dangers of incestuous attachment between father and daughter while relying on it for excitement. Of course I didn't see this at the time; I was simply gripped by the elegant Austenish narrative, the hints of sex and violence, the suggestions of sado-masochism as Judith is gradually tamed by her keeper-father Worth, kissed into melting submission on the last page. I myself longed to yield to the power of sexuality and at the same time was terrified of doing so. *Regency Buck* described and resolved these fears and conflicts: I could enjoy incestuous fantasies without conscious guilt, and also imagine a transition away from them towards a lover of my own.

Aged eighteen, I did what my father hadn't been able to do: went to university. He'd had to leave school at fourteen and go out to find work, and wanted us to have the chances he'd missed. I identified strongly with Dorothy Sayers' novel-writing heroine, Harriet Vane, and worked out that the women's college described in *Gaudy Night* was Somerville College, Oxford. I wanted to be a writer: to Somerville, therefore, I would go, and they accepted me. Of course there was also the cachet of the Establishment institution and my father's dreams of glamorous Oxford life gleaned from novels such as *Mr Verdant Green* and *Brideshead Revisited*.

The contradictions of being a woman at Oxford were neatly summed up when my father came to visit me. He wanted to dine in a college hall, a real hall, a men's hall, not a women's one. So one of my men friends took Dad off to dine in his own college; I couldn't go because ladies were not allowed in. Dad returned disappointed. 'They ate fish and chips, they gobbled it down in ten minutes flat,' he complained, 'there was no witty conversation, no sconcing, no Latin grace.' I felt I'd let him down.

I began to oppose my father. I became an ardent feminist, and then a socialist. I joined a communal household, cut my hair off, participated in the plays and actions of the Women's Liberation Street Theatre Group, argued ferociously with Dad whenever we met. This struggle to break away, to leave home in the psychic sense, continued all through my twenties. I wanted my father to recognise my autonomy and independence, yet needed and sought his approval. Of course I didn't get it.

We fought passionately over politics; my mother passed on his other messages: 'Tell Mimi she should wear a bra.' Even when I wrote a novel about a lesbian relationship, his only comment was: 'Beautifully written. Good English.' He didn't comment, either, on the fact that for three years I chose to have lesbian relationships. Only when I began to have relationships with men again did he tell me what he thought. 'Men need to have sexual experience before marriage,' he explained, 'in order not to hurt their wives on their wedding nights.' 'These days,' I taunted him, 'women are sexually experienced too. The double standard is irrelevant.' 'You talk like a whore,' was his reply. Recently I read that it's common for fathers to say this when their daughters are becoming personally and sexually independent. At the time, I felt tremendously guilty, and it redoubled my aggression; our fights escalated.

I found and read Antonia White's sequence of novels, *Frost in May, The Lost Traveller, The Sugar House, Beyond the Glass*, which were a source of comfort. Her heroine, Clara, struggles in a sticky web of guilt and ambivalence; her father Claude is the spider luring her back to this unsatisfactory home. Her impossible attempts to combine dutiful daughter with independent woman mirrored mine; I identified with her desire to be a writer, her romanticism, her solutions that were often as painful as the situations she sought to escape from. I understood Clara's breakdown, in the fourth novel, to be the inevitable result of the conflict between her guilty and unconsciously incestuous attachment to her father Claude and her desire to have a full sexual life of her own. I didn't have a breakdown in the same way, but I certainly, for several years, repressed my longing to love men. I began to face up to my own unconscious feelings for my own father. They ceased to terrify me, and I began to forgive myself, and him. My love for women survived the ups and downs that are part of friendships and the wider political network of the women's movement; it began to seem possible to acknowledge love, not solely fear and anger, for men too.

I went back to the nineteenth-century novels I'd first read as a teenager, rediscovering Mrs Gaskell's work. I reread and reread *North and South*, *Wives and Daughters*. The father-daughter relationships in both novels are characterised by deep mutual affection and respect and are subsequently flawed, for the daughter, by her forced recognition of her father's imperfections: Mr Hale, in *North and South*, undergoes a spiritual crisis and rejects his calling as a Church of England clergyman; Mr Gibson, in *Wives and Daughters*, remarries unwisely and none too happily. Margaret, in the first novel, is plunged into poverty as a result of her father's decision; Molly, in the second, has to cope with feeling jealous, misunderstood and unwanted. Mrs Gaskell is such a heart-warming moralist: both her heroines bravely face up to misery and crisis, grow up, and are rewarded with loving husbands. Both ardently question the wisdom of their fathers' decisions; neither falters in her love for him. That love is shown less as a consequence of familial duty enjoined by the Church than as a result of mutual knowledge gained through emotional and spiritual intimacy.

In my childhood God was the Christian God the Father. Feminism enabled me to understand that God was just as much Mother. Now I can say that if we choose to understand 'God' in human terms, we simply end up with all we're capable of expressing in words: God as the expression of opposites and conflicts and their integration: good and bad; light and dark; masculine and feminine; creative and receptive; and so on. God for me no longer represents the patriarchy. My father is no longer God to judge and punish me.

I remember standing with my father at a family Christmas party some years ago, both of us looking at my mother across the room. I was about thirty at the time. My father suddenly turned to me and remarked: 'You're like your mother, aren't you? Passionate and independent, loving your friends.' From this point on we began to value each other, to get to know each other. He was painting, I was writing; we were able sometimes to share our worries about blocks, wanting to do it better, how to learn. I'd go out into the garden and chat to him while he worked in his vegetable plot. We accepted our political differences with a little more grace; he began to say: 'I don't want to be an old patriarch, laying down the law.'

He and I have won through to some sort of peace, to a late and pleased recognition of love and respect between us. The struggle to achieve this has left its mark on me, has helped shape my personality. Schooled by Catholicism (not my father's religion) into total, unquestioning obedience, I relinquished my independence into the hands of God the Father, my own father, who, like the priests, represented an authority not to be

argued with. During all those years when my emotional and sexual feelings for my father were interwoven with an acceptance of him as Patriarch, as Law-Giver and Judge, I was vulnerable to the critical words he punished me with: mad; foolish; whore; ignorant; bad; immature. I couldn't be indifferent to these words: I allowed my father to represent my conscience, and then fought back, angry and despairing and hurt.

Even when I began to reject this way of relating to him, I continued, for some time, to accept the patriarchal and Catholic morality which divides women into madonnas and whores, good married women and bad sexually free women.

It's taken me a long time to learn to think for myself without experiencing enormous guilt. The way out of this impasse was provided by three separate but related practices, during my twenties and thirties: facing and then exploring the guilt in years of psychotherapy with a sympathetic and wise woman; becoming a writer and starting to state my own versions of reality, waking and dreaming, in novels and poems; exploring pre-Christian systems of imagery whose myths named women as whole and integrated, not split and damaged.

I felt sustained and encouraged in these years by novels which dealt with women as writers: Doris Lessing's *The Golden Notebook*, Cora Sandel's trilogy of *Alberta* novels, Colette's *La Vagabonde*. None of these novels represented blueprints, since all delineated personal struggles, conflicts and confusions; but all of them helped and help me keep going. They help me see struggle and conflict as the root of art; that what matters is to seize the struggle, accept it, explore it. Myth to me doesn't represent a negation and glossing over of conflict (this way of viewing myth is a hangover from nineteenth-century dualism splitting art from science, illusion from measurable truth, dream from reality, ideology from theory – I reject these dualisms as unhelpful) but simply a temporary solution. Each novel I write is a myth, a solution. The moment I've finished one, and solved, for the time being, one conflict, another erupts and demands to be dealt with. But it's astonishingly helpful to feel I inherit a tradition of women struggling to sort things out, from Margery Kempe in the fourteenth century feeling impelled to leave husband and children, go on pilgrimage and write a book about it (an early novel if you like), through Aphra Behn coping with the seventeenth-century double standard and despite it earning a living as playwright and novelist, to those of us in the late twentieth century exploring the breakdown of syntax/psyche/notions of self/old moralities.

Fiction, along with poetry, now represents for me the most fruitful medium (if words are to be used) for thought. I don't despise intellectual thought – far from it – but find it limited in usefulness, especially when it's placed in either an antagonistic or a superior relationship to imagistic, intuitive thought. I've needed both kinds of thinking, both kinds of language, in order to understand my relationship to my father; yet I've chosen to express this search mainly through fiction and poetry. Much of Freud's theoretical writing on women, for example, reproduces for me 'common-sense', i.e. patriarchal, notions current in his time about women as deformed versions of men. It's ironic and marvellous that he derived the concepts of the unconscious and hysterical neurosis from his experience of listening to women patients talk about how they needed to repress both their sexuality and their anger in a culture dominated by men and by the double standard. At least fiction and poetry don't pretend to be *the truth*. I'm wary about *truths*: they're too often used to beat other people over the head with. Of course I believe passionately in the truths I discover (invent meaning to find) through writing poetry and novels; but what I'm giving you here, as elsewhere, is temporary and partial. There's always a deeper truth (perhaps a joke) to go on to find. I could now, for example, characterise my writing as being on one level concerned with spiritual quest.

One book, not a novel, more an exploration of images of femininity, Nor Hall's *The Moon and the Virgin* helped me particularly: it proposes that women can be seen in the light of at least four aspects: mother, sibyl, amazon and hetaira. Few women, the book suggests, can live out all four aspects at once; our culture makes it difficult. The image of the hetaira erupted for me with peculiar force, offered me a way of validating my life as a single working woman who is not a spinster, not a virgin, not a whore. Patriarchy offers, of course, only corrupt versions of these archetypes. The spinner originally represented power, an aspect of the moon goddess spinning our fate; the virgin originally represented the sexual woman who is not married; the whore originally represented the independent woman who is a companion to men. In our culture, the whore is despised and exploited according to the double standard. The ancient meaning lingers on: independent women, feminists, are often called 'whore' by men. I think it means she-who-goes-away-and-comes-back, the inverse of the perfect mother men want, who stays around all the time and whom they fear. To escape from the double bind of mother-whore provided by patriarchy, I put up the flag of hetaira.

It was only when I began accepting myself as hetaira, rather than as the patriarchal definition of the whore, that my father's attitude towards me really changed. He sensed my recent discovery of self-respect. The wounds which were part of my shape as a person began to heal; their scars are now part of me.

A dream summed up the change. On the night that I split up with my lover, whom I'd been with for two years, I dreamed that I flew up into the air and danced and was joined by a dark young man with whom I made love in the air. This symbolised for me a recognition of the part of myself which was like men, liked and understood them as well as resenting and fighting them. I woke up filled with joy, newly conscious of my love for my men friends, of my affection for the men I worked with. I began to believe that men could know, understand and like me just as I could know, understand and like them. The word *friend* entrenched itself firmly in my vocabulary for men.

This allowed me to see and understand and like my father in some kind of new way. He became *my father* in reality, in a way he had never done before. We began to find out about each other in earnest. When I told my father on the telephone how I'd broken up with my lover, Dad said: 'Look, you're a woman of the world, you've made your mark in the world, you can look anyone in the eye. You don't have to be in a rush. Choose the best person you can see.' Then he said, 'And when are you coming down to look at my paintings? There's a self-portrait I want you to see, and one of your mother, and one of you.'

I love my father so dearly. I regret it's taken me so long to recognise and accept my need for him. My relationship with him has helped make me who I am. How could I regret it? I might as well chop my foot off. The pain and repression and chaos of it have forced me into explorations I would never otherwise have made. I have never felt that a close and loving and open relationship with a father was mine by birthright, I went through loss and grief to end up cherishing the beginning we have made. I hope we have plenty of years left.

memories of trees

our confusion, to make men sound like gods:
unnatural woman, you are a tree
fixated, lost, with a deep gash
to be rained upon, rubbed up against
hidden in, struck down
sold, and burnt, your ashes
worthless

I plead, I can twist like metaphor
I approximate, I sway kneedeep
in ferns, I am cultivated, lovely
my bark is a thick plait

I rear myself near a woman lover
we are the hedges around farms
the milking-stool, the cradle
we furnish ships, and boxes
brooms, coffins, desks, and paper
we are your floors, your windows

111

our roots nourish us, twinned
labyrinthine memories, between us
passages, and gaps, and halts
the darkness wet beneath
the perplexed canopy of our hair

my father carves his name
on each in the plantation
clears our flowers, strips us
in a single word
I have stooped for years
I have smiled around him
now, when I fall upon him
crushing, still
he protests
you are my tree, only a tree

I too have words now, I have words
I am a woman in the city, I transform
nature, I survive
tempests; but my dreams
flower with him

the forest is long ago, is
deep coal
now
I pace the labyrinth
following the gold plait, thick, and knotted
when I find her, I am not only
heroine, but also
minotaur, she too

memories of trees
who never suffered pain
or yelled
or wept
or went away

Michèle Roberts

Her face grew solemn. 'It's true,' she said slowly. 'I shall be a frostbitten virgin. I'm doomed. My father won't ever let me marry.'

'You infinitely childish one!' he cried, becoming angry. 'When it is well known that all fathers wish to get rid of all daughters.'

'You don't understand. It's different. My father – why,' she broke out, 'I used to dose myself secretly with cod liver oil so as to keep up to his level. He's wonderful. When he praised me I usedn't to sleep. And if he scolded me it seemed to send me lame.'

Herr Dremmel sawed her hand up and down in his irritation.

'What is this irrelevant talk?' he said. 'I offer you marriage, and you respond with information about cod liver oil. I do not believe the father obstacle. I do not recognise my honest little friend of these last days. It is waste of time, not being open. Would you, then, if it were not for your father marry me?'

'But,' Ingeborg flashed round at him, swept off her feet as she so often was by an impulse of utter truth, 'it's because *of him that I would.'*

And the instant she had said it she was shocked.

She stared at Herr Dremmel wide-eyed with contrition. The disloyalty of it. The ugliness of telling a stranger – and a stranger with hair like fur – anything at all about those closely related persons she had been taught to describe to herself as her dear ones.

Elizabeth Von Arnim, *The Pastor's Wife*

BARBARA TAYLOR

Freud: Father – a poem in three parts

Saskatchewan, where I spent the first twenty-one years of my life, is a province in the Canadian wheat belt with a strong tradition of socialist populism. Both my parents (my father an immigrant from the Welsh mining valleys; my mother a Canadian Jew) had been Communists in the thirties and forties. By the time I was in school, in the late fifties, they were both left-wing lawyers and our life style gradually shifted from the relatively austere to the casual affluence of the North American professional class.

I took my first university degree locally. I had always been a 'good' student, but a restless one – a restlessness which, combined with my familial–political background, drew me into the student movement and, after 1969, into feminism. But by 1971 even energetic politicking wasn't enough; I needed to leave. I arrived in London that autumn to do postgraduate work at the London School of Economics. My academic career developed in fits and starts, culminating in a D.Phil. for the University of Sussex on the history of early socialist feminism (now published by Virago as *Eve and the New Jerusalem: Socialism and Feminism in the Nineteenth Century*, 1983). My deepening involvement in feminist theory and history – as well as in the practical politics of the women's movement – brought me into the British left. It also brought me into my life as a writer – of feminist theory and history, of children's books, of review essays for feminist and socialist journals. In 1979 I joined the editorial collective of *History Workshop Journal*: in 1980 I became a lecturer in history at a college of higher education. I am single; childless. The poems which make up 'Freud: Father' are the first I have published.

Freud: Father

'Freud is dead now, and believe me, the genuine Freud was really a great man. I am particularly sorry for you that you didn't know him better.' Freud, aged sixty-eight, to a pupil.

I

'We will now turn our interest on to the single question of what it is that brings this powerful attachment of the girl to her mother to an end. This, as we know, is its usual fate: it is destined to make room for an attachment to her father.' Sigmund Freud, 'Femininity' (*New Introductory Lectures on Psychoanalysis*)

'It must be grand to have a father one can love and esteem, and when the Fourth Commandment does not confront one like a terrifying spectre with its "Thou shalt—".' Karen Horney, aged 15 (*The Adolescent Diaries of Karen Horney*)

*   *   *

Looking past my mother in the mirror
I saw him enter from behind
Us.
The door was ajar.

I ducked my head so that I would not see
His face.
But he told me to 'Look'. So
Looking past my mother in the mirror
I saw him enter.

The mirror held us: all. But 'Turn and look' he said.
My reflection held my mother's face but at his look we faded.
'Mother, look!' I could have, should have wept to see her look.
But she had turned, the mirror had turned, the room had turned.
I had turned
To see that in his hand he held some thing precious, precise, beyond
    price.
Beyond recall.

'Tell me' he said. So I told him. For what were words compared to that
    which the mirror had not shown me, which the mirror had
    withheld from me, which my mother's reflection had hidden
    from me?

115

But words were not enough to open his hand.

And Father, I have given you
So many words.

Freud with his daughter Sophie

II

'. . . *you can get anything you like out of your father.*'   Freud to 'Dora' (*Fragment of an Analysis of a Case of Hysteria*)

'. . . *she was about to tear herself free from her father . . .*'   Freud of 'Dora'.

I have been in this country before.
The stiff, feathery trees by the crusted lake;
The still air, the smoke
Of the cigarette rolled for me
Before he spoke
Of me – or rather of his desire for one
Whose name I bear
Whose clothes I wear
Whose father is his friend
Whose love is her father's whore
Whose whoredom was in his eyes and mouth
And in the reek
Of stale cigarette smoke;
Of the rest I cannot speak.

Nothing is rightly named.
Names slide, like smoke, behind our speech
And make words a cacophony
Of lonely, phoney mystery.
The smoke carried my name away from me;
Drew the meaning out of me;
Sucked the still centre from me;
Until I was left, as you found me,
Voiceless
On the blank horizon of an ancient land, that oblique
Shoreline on which we now stand.
Of the rest I must not speak.

I am a meaning men give to one another.
An adjective whose qualifications
Speak across my soul, beyond my speech, beyond my self, and
Beyond this cold country to which I am brought
First by one man, then another:
One called me daughter; the other, lover.
And now you, Professor, accompany me here too
To see what you can do
For a little girl who knew that talk could kill.

117

Papa, Herr K., Professor: now you see how little can be had from me.
I have shown you the woodland, the lake, the smoke which lingers still
In the landscape which you seek.
Enter it without me.
Of the rest I will not speak.

III

'The Professor said, "The trouble is – I am an old man – you do not think it
worth your while to love me." . . . *I said nothing. What did he expect me to
say?'* H.D. (*Tribute to Freud*)

*' "This is my favourite," he said. He held the object toward me . . . It was a little
bronze statue, helmeted, clothed to the foot in carved robe with the upper incised
chiton or peplum. One hand was extended as if holding a staff or rod. "She is
perfect," he said, "only she has lost her spear." I did not say anything.'* H.D., (*Tribute to Freud*)

> I too was a favourite daughter once.
> Conceived through my father's speech, my mother's silence:
> I grew.
> A sly little Minerva
> Armed with all the weapons fathers bestow.
> Possessed of all the powers father allow.
> Just enough of a warrior to be a woman;
> Enough of a woman to be a daughter;
> Enough of my father's daughter to know
> That famous old men can have too many sons.
>
> > Sons stalk their dreams,
> > Steal their schemes,
> > Devour their means.
> > Daughters are a better bet.
>
> But Antigone is dead.
> And imperfect as she is
> This daughter breeds words as well as men.
> Spear-less as she seems,
> This warrior has the woman's art
> Of spinning curses in her webs;
> Weaving symbols through men's souls;
> And, hearing old men speaking through her voice,
> Chokes them with the fullness of a woman's tears.
> Sweet, savage tears for a dying god.

'Power!' she said suddenly, smiling her little hand upon the rail. 'Yes, we have power; and since we are not to expend it in tunnelling mountains, nor healing diseases, nor making laws, nor money, nor on any extraneous object, we expend it on you. You are our goods, our merchandise, our material for operating on. . . . We are not to study law, nor science, nor art; so we study you. There is never a nerve or fibre in your man's nature but we know it.'

Olive Schreiner, *The Story of An African Farm*

The point is less that Margaret's father wished she were a boy than that he treated her with as much seriousness as if she were one. . . . He asked of Margaret not feminine grace and imprecision but masculine fidelity to fact, to 'common sense.' In an age when women were taught to appropriate a special language of politeness and complaisance, Mr Fuller forbade Margaret the use of phrases like 'I am mistaken' and 'it may be so'.

Ann Douglas, on Margaret Fuller and her father, in *The Feminisation of American Culture*

JULIA O'FAOLAIN

Sean at Eighty

Since I am a fiction-writer like my father, reviewers sometimes describe me as 'the daughter' and it is quite likely that if I had lived my life in Ireland, this label would have become as inescapable as a Russian's patronymic. Odious comparisons might have been made. Luckily, I left when I was twenty and have spent the decades since then moving between Italy, France, California and London. My few shreds of nationality – thin moss on a rolling stone – are that parochial mix, Irish/English. It is a description easily understood in these islands, puzzling to people as close as the French, a paradox to North Americans and can be meaningless elsewhere. I discovered this when some rural South American Indians asked me whether I belonged to the First or Third World. They had never heard of Europe. Well, I said, mine was in some ways a Third-World country. They 'looked crooked' at me exactly as Irish peasants would have done, and I read their minds: I was a liar, trying, as outsiders always do try, to establish unreal kinship. And yes, I am a sort of liar: a fiction-writer and the daughter of a fiction-writer. Facts are metaphors for me and I prefer to supply few here because, as used to happen with the old Celts, they have a way of shifting shape in my hands. This may have been the shape-shifters' way to escape the bonds of a small, tight country – and my way of dealing with that label, 'the daughter'. Yet everything I have written about Sean is perfectly true.

My books include Women in the Wall (to be reissued by Virago in 1985), *No Country For Young Men*, (Penguin, 1981) *The Obedient Wife*, (Penguin, 1983), *Daughters of Passion* (Penguin, 1982). I was co-editor, with Lauro Martines, of *Not in God's Image* (Virago, 1979), a documentary history of women.

In my earliest image of him he is playful, moody and, of course, tall: a captivating father figure with a shimmy of sepia hair flopping onto a high forehead and – in one silky streak of memory – a moustache. In the Sixties,

young men started looking like him again and shrunken reincarnations of his early self would approach me on London or Los Angeles streets only to turn, at close range, into strangers. He had always been elusive.

As a child, I yearned to be on his side if only I could locate it. I knew sides had been drawn because our house crackled with secrets and talk was apt to slip into unguessable Gaelic. Once, he was sued by a bishop and I had an adversary to hate but such occasions were rare. Even this one was not wholly clear for it was hard to tell who supported whom. I have, for instance, a blurred recollection of being out walking about then with my mother Eileen and running into two priests who, amidst shy guarded laughter, sent encouraging messages back to Sean. The bishop was a tartar and the Church less monolithic than it seemed. Even my school nuns could be roused to flutters of skittishness, as if Sean's presence had shaken them from the comfort of their moral certitudes. Perhaps it had? In the forties, he became the gadfly of an Ireland which had turned itself into a sanctuary for nineteenth-century authoritarianism. Seconded by a very few liberals, Sean pitted himself against an alliance of patriot prigs whose ideal society was to be protected from free speech or foreign ideas. This was de Valera's fantasy and for a while economic protectionism, isolationism and the war masked the folly of its ostrich stance. The roll call of Sean's targets has an oddly antiquated ring: flogging school masters, bigots, clerical bullies, toadies, censors, they might all be escapees from some novel of Gogol's written a hundred years before. Ireland is hospitable to Russian literary ghosts.

'How much of an outsider were you in those years, Sean?' I ask him now. 'Were you shunned?'

He gives me a lazy half-shrug. *'By some,'* he says. *'They thought I was a sourpuss. I was washing Irish dirty linen in public. That was letting the country down. It was a timid time and you were expected to cover up national failings. Others, mind you, urged me on. "You're doing a great job," they'd say. "We'd be right there with you if it wasn't for the wife and kids!"'* He smiles. *'You know the refrain?'*

'Bishops controlled jobs?'

'Oh indeed! Support, however, came from unexpected quarters. There were surprises, contradictions . . .'

Contradiction is an Irish climate and I am reminded that Sean's own signals could be hard to read. Take privacy. He clung to it like a badger, doing his writing in a hut at one end of our garden which turned its blind side to the house and its windows to a field containing bog plants and one haughty, stilt-legged heron. Here he wrote fiction out of a life which must have started turning in on itself the day he stopped being Publicity Director for the Republicans during the Irish Civil War.

That war had fizzled out in an erosion of hope which brought him his second disillusion with public promises. The first had been with the British Empire in whose values he, like all Irishmen of his day, had been brought up to believe.

'After all,' he says, *'I was born in 1900 in a place which didn't exist. That is to say in Ireland, which was just not there. All that there was, was a bastard piece of the British Empire. So I believed in that and was proud of belonging to it. I gloried in its trappings. I can tell you that when the Irish rebellion of 1916 presented us with a country whose birth was supposed to wipe out the social values I had been absorbing for my first sixteen years, I suffered a trauma. You see I had been a great reader of the school stories published in boys' papers like* The Gem *and* The Magnet. *My boyhood heroes were Gordon of Khartoum, characters from Kipling. . . . Besides, just then, I was beginning to read and love English literature too. Disowning that was a trauma.'*

He was to suffer a second one when his new heroes let him down.

122

Swearing never to accept less than a thirty-two-county Irish Republic, de Valera's Republicans led their followers – Sean and Eileen among them – into a civil war, lost it, then accepted the compromise they could have had in the first place. Judged by the standards of Gordon of Khartoum, this lacked style.

'I began life,' says Sean, *'as a dreaming, romantic revolutionary and fell flat on my ass, betrayed both by Ireland and the Empire, both of which I had been prepared, at different periods, to adore.'*

To look at that another way:

Sean tells me that an old schoolteacher of his remembered him years later as 'a nice boy but quite mad' and I wonder was that teacher a very innocent man? Sean must have been a born trouble-maker; the sort you get in every class who is intent on stirring things up. To say that the Empire and the Republicans let him down is to say that *he* was ready for a new reality sooner than *they* were, wanted the next swing of the pendulum and was ready to give it a push. Bolshie, a bit of a scrapper, as soon as everyone was settled with their books open, he'd start complaining that the books were boring and that what they said should maybe be turned on its head: 'Can we discuss that, Sir? No? But what about free speech, pleasure principles, tolerance and . . .' Naturally, authorities tried to shut him up and he threw inky squibs at them. My mother thought him a great tease. On their first meeting, he sat behind her at an Irish-language class and stuck her pigtail into an inkwell. In the days of Gordon of Khartoum, such restless youths went out to the colonies. Sean was lucky, in 1926, to get a fellowship to Harvard.

He spent the next three years in Boston where Eileen joined and married him. They went to New Mexico on their honeymoon, considered going to China to teach, then went instead to London where Edward Garnett, at Cape, published Sean's first book of stories and advised him to return to Ireland and write about it. That is how, at the time of my first clear memories, he came to be living on the top of Killiney Hill, working in that hut next to that boggy field and attempting to live within the confines of his imagination. The *Who's Who* of the day listed his hobby as 'day-dreaming'.

'I'm a bit of a loner,' he claims. *'Loneliness – being alone – is important to me. I have to be able to close the door – sometimes for no reason, just to rest. Sometimes to start articulating my feelings through the medium of other, imaginary people.'*

'In your fiction?'

'Yes.'

In his hut, I am reminded, there *was* a phone, but calls were monitored at the house and even our charwoman grew skilled at protecting Sean's solitude. Then, in 1941, he breached it himself. He began running a magazine, *The Bell* – a Russian echo: *Kolokol, The Bell*, was a nineteenth-century Russian émigré magazine – which stated that its aim was to help the Irish, whose neutrality had finally cut them off from the old British yardstick, determine who and where they were. Irish society, Sean had discovered, was one which offered no hold to the social novelist.

'Garnett,' he recalls, *'said to me: "Now you must be the Balzac of Ireland," and I thought: "All right, I must." But I was barmy and so was he. Balzac was writing about a highly reticulated society and no such situation existed in Ireland. There was no social framework once the old Anglo-Irish one broke down – at least none that we could observe at the time.'*

In the Ireland to which Sean and Eileen had returned in 1933, criteria for distinguishing fact from fantasy had been deliberately mislaid. The Republican Party – Sean's old comrades – had now come to power and, finding themselves unable to implement old promises, chose to pretend that they *were* implementing them. Faced with a society of mummers, a writer could reasonably feel that before starting to write fiction it would be well to establish some facts.

It was partly as a writer then that Sean felt the need to make sense of the Irish experience. But as editor of *The Bell*, he was also performing a social service when he tried to cut through the prevailing rhetoric to where, as he wrote in his first editorial: *'Among the briars and the brambles there stands the reality which generations died to reach – not, you notice, the Ideal . . .'* Readers were encouraged to turn writer and tell about whatever patch of Irish life they knew at first hand: *'if you look through the first number,'* the editor invited, *'you will see several things whose merit is not chiefly Art but Truth. . . .'* *The Bell* was asking ordinary Irish people to help *'stir ourselves to a vivid awareness of . . . what we are becoming, what we are'*.

Odd for a literary magazine to eschew ideals in that wartime era of agitprop? Yes and no. After the long social struggle with its surfeit of hope, truth in the land of blarney was in noticeably short supply. Mistrust, not only of absolutes but of the objective world itself, shows up in the Irish writing of those years. Flann O'Brien and Beckett were already writing what critics now call 'metafiction' – fictions about fiction; Frank O'Connor's stories display the same bifocal vision as those Camus was to publish in 1957, during another civil war, and a perennial Irish tradition of romancing pointed to that preference for taking hold of experience with the tongs of metaphor which prevails where reality is untractable or hard to find.

Sean was moving counter to this trend when he gave up his daydreaming to tangle with the phenomena around him and with the values of the new oligarchs. 'If,' Sartre was to write four years later in 1945, 'a society sees itself, and especially if it sees itself being *seen*, its regime and established values are ipso facto challenged: the writer, by presenting it with its own image, calls on it either to acknowledge this or change it and . . . in this way . . . endows society with an unhappy consciousness. . . .'

Unsurprisingly, in the small towns of Ireland, *The Bell* was often sold from under the counter with a furtiveness usually associated with pornographic magazines. I ask Sean if this made him feel more alienated than ever.

'*Not at all. No. In the days of* The Bell *I was fully integrated because I was on the attack. I had accepted responsibility as a citizen and thought of myself as speaking for a great silent majority.*'

'Were you? Did you find them?'

'*I found a silent minority which in time became more numerous. Life in Ireland has changed completely since those days – not, to be sure, because of liberals like myself but, inevitably, with the changing quality of life, the coming of radio and television which swept Ireland into the bosom of the twentieth century. Those were the forces which won the battle for us – as we had always known they would. By then, however, I had given up. I grew tired of the fight. I wanted to get back to myself and my writing. I wanted to be a private person again.*'

He could never keep completely out of the fight. In the forties, he single-handedly founded an artists' trade union called WAAMA (Writers, Actors, Artists, and Musicians Association) which foundered but paved the way for an Irish branch of Equity. In 1945 he was a founding member and Vice President of Irish Civil Liberties and though he gave up the editorship of *The Bell* in 1946, he was always apt to return for a Parthian penpointing at some fresh impropriety, as when the bishops, in 1951, torpedoed a public health project by intriguing with cabinet members behind parliament's back. This, Sean pointed out, was an example of a non-elected power using its ghostly sanctions to manipulate an elected one. The citizen in Sean was at odds with the writer who preferred personal relationships, privacy and art. He has always been protean and, mark, I don't say 'chameleon'. A chameleon blends into its background. Sean stood out. On a greenish tartan, he glows pinkly. Faced with a red flag, his eye will suffuse with a tincture of true blue individualism.

What he achieved in *The Bell* was, I think, to clear the ground of myths so that people could start to think. Myths do prevent thought. Think of Dostoevesky's character who says 'if God does not exist, then all is permitted' and kills himself in despair. Locked into a belief that only divine retribution stood between mankind and savagery, he could not conceive of a social conscience. Neither would the Irish Church allow for

one in 1951. You need lay moralists to elaborate a social code and Sean –
moved by the civic spirit absorbed from his boyhood reading of English
schoolboy papers? – took up the challenge.

Civic but not gregarious, he remained the most private of Irishmen, for
he went rarely to pubs and almost never to literary ones: a snub. 'How's
yer aul' Jansenist Da?' I was asked when I started going to them myself.
Defused and emptied like an old cartridge case, his own word was thrown
back at him. By then he had been fighting the Jansenist rigours of the Irish
Church for two decades.

Or am I unfair? Perhaps the drinkers had caught that ascetic quality in
Sean? He can be convivial but is choosy about whom he is convivial with,
and backscratching is beyond him. His inability to accept patronage
seems to me typified by the story of the stag. This happened during or just
after the war, when someone who had venison in his gift bethought
himself of Sean, the struggling writer and of his family who might
perhaps be starving. A stag was delivered to our door: furred, horned,
hooved and very dead. How turn it into meat? Sean and Eileen consulted
several hunting-and-shooting Anglo-Irish gents who lived nearby.
Perhaps they had never shot anything bigger than a snipe? 'Hang it by the
horns until it falls,' was their advice. 'Always hang game.' So it was hung
in the turf shed and poked daily, like Hansel being poked by the witch,
until one day someone noticed that it had turned into a moving mass of
maggots and it had to be buried in the yard. The romantic gift, like Sean's
romantic ideals, took badly to Time's test.

Yet it was place rather than time at which he seemed to chafe. He often
talked of leaving Ireland and, in fact, he left it often. Even in the forties he
was one of the few who managed to get out of the war-sealed country to
do jobs for the BBC. Later, he taught on American campuses, toured Italy,
wrote two books about it, and took innumerable trips to Paris and
Provence.

'Would you have been a different sort of man if you'd left for good?' I
ask.

'Certainly. I'd have been less of an outsider.'

But would he have liked that? An outsider, knowing just where he is, is
open to change. What more static, on the other hand, than to be an exile
like Joyce stuck in the frozen memory of a bygone Dublin and the arrested
time of expatriot communities? Sean was too mercurial for that. I suspect
that leaving appealed too much for him ever to leave totally. Dublin was a
good base, a perfect airstrip for departures and, wisely, he did not get too
chummy with the personnel.

Neither did he settle elsewhere. Though he can fit in anywhere, and I have swathes of images of him bringing off appearances at places as diverse as the Gauss Seminar at Princeton and a Playboy Writers' gathering in Chicago, he has a trooper's urge to press on. An emblematic snapshot shows him driving a tinker's horse caravan he hired one year to tour West Cork – to the alarm of local people who wondered to which tribe he might belong and hid their hens. Horse caravanning was not the done thing at the time but Sean was playing a game with his own sensibility. The tour was a *retour*, for the villages he passed were those where he had been on the run during the Civil War.

'Why do you write?'

He laughs. He has agreed to let me interview him but his answers are too pat and we both know this. Moreover, his way of presenting himself is oblique and deprecating while my urge is to pin things down. While we spar a little, it becomes clear – as it mightn't to strangers – that our interests only seem to be the same. He, as always, wants to give a good performance, I, this time, would like to get behind it, see how it's done and with what. But why should he let me? The only way to tell the dancer from the dance is to trip him up.

'Writing,' he decides to say, '*is an experiment in human relations. You put people in motion then wait and see what happens. You're never sure. That's where the excitement comes in. You say to yourself: now what would happen if such and such were so. Characters do take on an autonomy of their own . . .*'

We smile. He's said it before. What did I expect?

'Is your new novel an experiment?'

'*Absolutely, very much so.*'

And Again?, his thirtieth book published in his eightieth year, is a fable about an old man who is picked at random to be the guinea pig of some gods who are curious about the ways of humans. *They* are conducting an experiment and, in the course of this, the man's life trajectory is reversed so that it runs backwards through middle age and youth towards infancy and annihilation. Bob Younger, the younging protagonist, lives his second chance at life as a series of passionate and treacherous love affairs – necessarily treacherous since he must conceal what is happening to him while Time whirls him and the women he loves in opposite directions. The gods' gift is poisoned. Sean, the old campaigner, who would take on the British Empire, the puritan Irish Republicans and Church prelates, is fighting now with Time, extracting pleasures from its grasp, observing and dissecting its ways as a writer always does with his targets, distancing and controlling it through fiction – except that, it strikes me suddenly, fictional forces *do take on an autonomy of their own . . .*

'All literary discoveries,' Mauriac wrote, 'are made on our own flesh.'

For a moment I am appalled at the self-surgery writing can entail and no questions seem possible. But apparently, I have asked one already about why Younger's second life should be so purely private and erotic and have no social dimension to it at all. Sean is answering this tranquilly and fluently, falling into familiar phrases which suddenly no longer seem like the camouflage I had expected, but shockingly revelatory.

'Well,' he says, 'one wants a coming together of people and if you take them on the level of sex and passion then the social element can seem to disappear – it never does, of course. It's there in the pressures. But the social carapace can be burned away by a great force like love. . . .'

Or Time? Age? Doubt?

'You get to the essence of man, what Yeats calls the "personality", meaning what is left when all the dross of "character" and place, all the social trappings, fall away and leave the naked nucleus of self.'

Something, the phrase 'social trappings' perhaps or my desire to dodge 'the naked nucleus of self' – I am sorry now that I wanted to get behind Sean's smooth performance – brings back a sharp memory of the Fifties. I am waltzing with Sean; he is wearing tails which move outwards with the speed of his pirouettes and someone remarks as we return to our table that Sean O'Faolain has been round the ballroom six times for everyone else's one. The implication is that certain restless characters should be quieted down for other people's mental comfort. Another dressed-up occasion pushes into the front of my mind. We are at the old, plushy, New York Met to hear Renata Tebaldi sing *Manon*. Her art melts scepticism about her physical rightness for the role and Manon's worthiness as a heroine. Sean, who is teaching the novel at Princeton that year, talks about being flummoxed by the students' dismissal of Manon as someone too dishonest and trivial to get her act together. Their lack of tolerance taxes his.

Coming back to our interview, I ask if he is still a romantic and he bursts out:

'Of course I am! Still and always. You're born a romantic, no matter how you wrestle with it. The whole point of this new novel of mine is that destiny is hanging over it. You're born a certain way and no matter if you lived ten times over, you'd still be the same bloke and kismet is there. Mektoub. It's decided once and for all. That's what I was writing about. I had a notion of using as epigraph Valery's 'La mer, la mer toujours recomencée'. Man is like the sea, the ever-renewing sea . . .'

His eye gleams blue as ever. He is alert, alive, pursuing his prey down the phantom highways of his parallel life. In this one, old age is sneakily trailing him like a car in the blind spot just out of range of the rear-view mirror. Even now, at eighty, neither he nor I can be sure it's there. He is so youthful still, so gaily game to drive to the West of Ireland and back with me or to come to the theatre in London with my husband and myself, then to a late Soho dinner followed by that nervous search for taxis around Piccadilly in the rain. Can he do it? Should we expect him to? Coax him out? Enliven or coddle him? In contrast, Eileen has long ago accepted old age and expertise in those two old people's subjects: health and money. It annoys her that he should be innocent about both to the point of foolishly climbing apple trees and getting heart palpitations which put her own heart across her. She is right in her sensible way but *he* is being true to his balky, vital relationship to the way things are. His novel is a half snook cocked at time – only a half one because the old man who grows young does not find perfection. Its frozen forms could hardly appeal to Sean for whom perfection must, paradoxically, be process. What he does find are tenderness, irony, more yearnings and a great deal of betrayal. The protean man betrays. The romantic, hung up on the excitement of change, is condemned to dislike its outcome.

'*I'm rather pleased with it,*' says Sean of the novel, '*as a model of how the Irish curse-gift can successfully deal with the despotism of fact in art. We're not so good at this in terms of social consensus. . . . As to my being a romantic – I know it. Everything I write is. But I know too that I have to put in – that my only hope of sanity and balance is to put in – irony. Irony is the one element that saves me from being soppy.*'

Curse-gift? To hear Sean, his romanticism might be biological: an act of God. 'Destiny,' he says, but I think of history and of Fernand Braudel's remark that change comes late to the peoples of islands and high mountains. Ireland has indeed often been late in getting rid of old influences and the romantic mode flourishes in its social climate. Like farce, romance thrives where safety valves are required – think of Feydeau and Labiche, Verdi and Puccini. In the godly, hardworking heyday of the modern middle class, outlets everywhere were intense and ritual and this made for hyperbole in art. In Ireland rigid moral corseting lingered late and provoked iconoclastic humour and a feeling for operatic gesture. Artists in restrictive societies luxuriate in counter-images of rich and risky passion. As Yeats preached:

> Those men that in their writings are most wise
> Own nothing but their blind stupefied hearts.

Perhaps, to be fair, I should turn my scrutiny briefly on myself and on how all this affected me while I was growing up. The moment I do, I see that the primal influence wasn't Sean's at all but my mother's. Eileen wrote children's books: an act of piety and thrift. Like the jars in which she pickled the produce of our acre of garden, her stories salvaged some of the excitement she and Sean had found in the West Cork mountains, where they spent the summers of their late teens learning Gaelic, singing ballads and dancing at ceilidhs. Their youth became entwined with a disappearing oral culture and later, when they looked back, the charge of nostalgia was immense. Since Eileen's stories were partly based on folk tales heard during those enchanted holidays, it must have been hard for her to judge them. Yet if she was to market them, she must try them on an unbiased consumer: me. Like the viewers who supply the Nielsen ratings for American TV, I was needed at home and Eileen kept me there until I was eight, teaching me to read and telling me so many tales of pookas, leprachauns, magic coaches, fairy forts, and the like that these phenomena were far more real to me than the angels and demons in which the nuns expected me to believe when I finally arrived in school. It was embarrassing to find myself among classmates whose belief in fairies had been shed three years earlier on leaving kindergarten. Having incautiously revealed my own credulity, I felt disgraced, determined not to be caught out again and started casting a cold eye on the devils and angels too. Gradually, as I grew older and became obscurely conscious of Sean's being at odds with Church and State, I developed a habit of sly, universal, vigilant mistrust. He and Eileen, a pair of reluctantly disillusioned romantics, made romanticism impossible for me. They bequeathed an appetite for magic together with an inability to believe in it. The flick of a conjuror's handkerchief alerts me, not to the pleasure I might prefer, but to the sleight of hand which procures it and often, like Molière's miser, I find that the hand robbing me is my own.

Sean, by contrast, still manages his pleasures with easy nonchalance.

Snapshot memories of him in recent years find him frequently with a hat over his face stretched flat on a wall in Volterra or a bench in Arles taking a quick, sly siesta. He winds up to a pitch of genial garrulity, bobbing out of taxis when he visits us in London with bottles of airport gin and a fizz of chat about everything from God to gossip, then, three martinis later, slips upstairs for one of those brief, restoring naps. By dinner time he is down again, unfolding fresh samples of bright, aphoristic talk so that my son and husband limply wilt and are astounded by his stamina. Routines are calendered by expectation, holidays funpunctuated, conversations prepared like flambé puddings. The Edwardian effect is in keeping with his colour which has grown higher. I think of him in grey-green tweeds or – when abroad – cream linen and a rust silk tie. His ruddy complexion sharpens the blue of his eyes. Alert and inquisitive, he puts his all into the first hour of a party and, surprisingly from one who had seemed intent on his own performance, turns out to have noticed everything. Shamelessly, he will read other people's letters if he comes on them, open bathroom cupboards and go through handbags found abandoned under chairs. Magpie tidbits may turn up later reshuffled in stories: the stuff of realism, ballast for that ballooning romance.

The end of the cassette we made together has got twisted or somehow slowed. At first I could make out that it was an argument against realism. Wilde is mentioned and Alain Fournier. I catch the names Faust and Cervantes and then there is only rumble. Playing it hopefully through once more, I become aware that there is something arrestingly familiar in the gobbledygook. What? I play it louder. Sean's voice surges and bellows like the sea or wind and suddenly I have the memory: he sounds as if he were speaking Gaelic. His voice is like the deep, damp, feathery voices of men in those West Cork villages where he courted my mother and, later, went on the run. Like a ghost in the machine, a voice older than his own – a Gaelic-speaking ancestor's or his own voice of sixty years back? – booms out at me and I can make nothing of it.

Ellean is so different from — most women; I don't believe a purer creature exists out of heaven. . . . What is to be her future? It is in my hands; what am I to do? When I remember how Ellean comes to me, from another world I always think, when I realise the charge that's laid on me, I find myself wishing, in a sort of terror, that my child were safe under the ground!

Aubrey Tanqueray on his daughter, in Arthur Wing Pinero's *The Second Mrs Tanqueray*

Papa Love Baby

My mother was a romantic girl
So she had to marry a man with his hair in curl
Who subsequently became my unrespected papa,
But that was a long time ago now.

What folly it is that daughters are always supposed to be
In love with papa. It wasn't the case with me
I couldn't take to him at all
But he took to me
What a sad fate to befall
A child of three.

I sat upright in my baby carriage
And wished mama hadn't made such a foolish marriage.
I tried to hide it, but it showed in my eyes unfortunately
And a fortnight later papa ran away to sea.

He used to come home on leave
It was always the same
I could not grieve
But I think I was somewhat to blame.

Stevie Smith, *Collected Poems*

CORA KAPLAN

❧

Wicked Fathers: A Family Romance

Every émigré has a snapshot of home. Mine is a double exposure, in which the Berkshire hills surrounding the Connecticut Valley town where I grew up blurs and merges with the dirty thrilling streets of Manhattan where I was born in April 1940 and where I spent two exciting years in my early twenties trying – and failing – to be an actress. The eldest child and only daughter of two second-generation New York Jewish Marxists, I grew up in Northampton, Massachusetts, where my parents' post-war flight from the city ended. There my father began a depression and war deferred vocation as an academic; he is an eminent historian and cultural critic of the Black experience of white America. There my mother put one successful career as an urban social worker behind her and began another as a reference librarian. I went to public high school in Northampton during the bitter McCarthyite years, and eventually, in the same town to Smith College where I read English and Drama. My passion for the theatre, lit when I was cast in a play at ten, dominated the fourteen years that followed, but gave way reluctantly in my mid-twenties to practical and psychological need for stable employment. A year at Newnham College, Cambridge in 1963–64 renewed and extended for me the love-affair with England that my father had begun during the war and transmitted to me through passionate anecdote. In 1966 after two years as a postgraduate at Harvard and Brandeis I returned to England to marry, mother, separate and work. America was the scene of my political education and youthful activism in the civil rights, student and anti-war movements, but England is where feminism has transformed my personal, political and intellectual life. I have been teaching since 1969 at Sussex University, increasingly on questions of gender in history and culture, the subject of my writing these last ten years. I teach also in adult education, am active in my union, in various corners of the women's movement; this year I joined the Labour Party. I live in Brighton with my fifteen-year-old son, Jacob, and others, but am itching to move to London. As anyone can see I have moved three thousand miles to remain, in many respects, profoundly my father's daughter.

133

'Whether one has killed one's father or has abstained from doing so is not really the decisive thing. One is bound to feel guilty in either case. . . . So long as the community assumes no other form than that of the family, the conflict is bound to express itself in the Oedipus complex, to establish the conscience and to create the first sense of guilt.' Sigmund Freud, *Civilisation and its Discontents*

'But what you do *not* see, what you *cannot* see, is the deep tender affection behind and below all those patriarchal ideas of governing grown-up children. . . . The evil is in the system – and he simply takes it to be his duty to rule . . . like the Kings of Christendom, by divine right.' Elizabeth Barrett to Robert Browning, August 1845

This essay was begun as a brief feminist reprise of an historic parent–child encounter which has achieved modern mythic status. I started out by thinking I could integrate my own experience as a daughter with that of Elizabeth Barrett Browning, for I have always prided myself on my ability to let my own life stand as one example of the road women take to feminism. But after writing a page or two about myself and my father I realised how deeply – and irrationally – I felt such a public exposure of our embattled but loving history to be an attack, a betrayal. It is with some chagrin that I acknowledge that there are quite ordinary areas of my personal history which I can not yet transform into public prose. This revelation has led me back to enquire how this problem was met by the subject of my piece. I had thought, at first, that I would concentrate on discovering how such a 'wicked father' came into being in cultural and psychological terms. Instead I have centred more fully on the daughter, exploring the oblique and fragmented ways in which she constructed the meaning of paternal authority in her autobiographical and imaginative writings, placing the 'private' personal texts of her youth against the great feminist achievement of her maturity, the novel-poem, *Aurora Leigh*, in which she draws us the portrait of the poet as a young woman. In following her struggle to understand and come to terms with the complex meanings which fathers hold for daughters as they can and cannot be represented in writing, I have made some sense of my own inhibition, my own father-daughter history. I hope this exploration will be as enlightening for others has it has been for me.

Literary legend

Elizabeth Barrett Browning's name is remembered today less as the major nineteenth-century poet she was than as the defiant daughter, semi-invalid, turned forty, who, in September 1846, fled her father's oppressive household with a younger, penniless and unknown poet, Robert Browning. Given our culture's consuming reductive interest in the life stories of women writers in preference, often, to their work, it is not surprising that Elizabeth is best known for this romantic biographical fragment, sentimentally framed by her love poems to Browning, *Sonnets from the Portuguese*. In fact we might never have known under what circumstances Browning acquired a wife had she not been one of the most well-known poets of her day. It is that, in the end, which makes her courtship and elopement visible and immortalised her tyrannical parent Edward Barrett Moulton Barrett. There he stands on our mantelpiece, propped up next to his fictional contemporary, Dickens's Paul Dombey, senior, one of the two most wicked fathers in Victorian culture.

Selective popular memory has been helped along by the 1930 play by Rudolph Besier, *The Barretts of Wimpole Street*, adapted in turn for screen and television. Besier gave the story a post-Freudian twist, and a new tang for the twentieth century, by exposing Edward Barrett's paternal cruelty as barely disguised incestuous desire. 'My father is not like other men,' Elizabeth is made to cry in terror and disgust as she grabs her spaniel Flush and exits from Wimpole Street for ever, closely followed by her loyal servant Wilson staggering under the weight of Victorian impedimenta. The unveiling of an incest motif (which to be fair to Besier lies embedded though slumbering in the contemporary letters and accounts) serves to weaken the feminist implications of Elizabeth Barrett's actions. By emphasising the normal and feminine in the daughter and the pathological and villainous in the father Besier suppressed the ways in which Edward was precisely 'like other men' and his poet daughter something more than a nice girl protecting her person from a nasty, over-age seducer.

Besier's melodrama toys with the potentially subversive notion that resistance to tyranny begins at home, and with the women of the family, only to draw back from such dangerous interpretation. Instead the play roots Edward's perverted investment in the illness and celibacy of his talented child back in his own sexually unsatisfying marriage to a terrified but compliant woman. Like a Hitchcock film or Ross MacDonald thriller the play constructs a crude family psychohistory, an outrageous trauma in the closet, as the reason for skewed and oppressive family relations in

the present. In order for Elizabeth to be the heroine of Besier's story she must be carefully absolved of any collusion with her lecherous jailer, beyond of course the formal obedience that supposedly came naturally to a resigned Christian daughter of the period. By spicing the story up, Besier masks its more interesting textures and flavours. His version covers up the passionate and tormented affection Elizabeth bore her unforgiving father for the rest of her life; it denies the complex interaction between them that led to their final impasse. If wicked fathers and their surrogates were not, often, also loved and living figures; if their female children bore them only the just measure of hatred due to abstract tyranny then they would not pose the kinds of problems that they do for feminism.

What evidence has come down to us, in an adolescent autobiography and a recently discovered diary kept for a crucial year in her mid-twenties, points towards a more contradictory and interesting narrative than Besier's highly coloured popularisation allows. If we read these personal accounts together with Elizabeth's poetic transformation of them we can begin to see the boundaries within which a mid-nineteenth-century middle-class woman could enact and imagine her liberation from patriarchal structures.

It is sometimes forgotten that Edward Moulton Barrett's eccentric ban on marriage extended to all ten of his surviving children of whom seven were male. Only Elizabeth, the eldest, had an independent income; she alone could afford to defy her father's prohibition, which was so rooted and fixed that Browning was persuaded by his fiancée that to ask for her hand would mean his instant banishment from the house. Yet, in spite of the extreme peculiarity of Barrett's stance, to marry without parental consent was almost, as Elizabeth noted wryly in the months following her elopement, to cohabit without benefit of clergy. To marry *so*, in middle age, and then to marry poorer and younger was, if one was female, to add insult to injury. It offered other restless daughters of the bourgeoisie a dangerous and dangerously attractive precedent of filial ingratitude, romantic excess and economic recklessness. As she had foreseen, Elizabeth's social circle took sides after the event with the most unqualified support coming from those older men who stood in quasi-paternal relationship to her – her cousin John Kenyon and the blind Greek scholar Hugh Stuart Boyd. Her sisters and her younger women friends were quickly reconciled, but her brothers and many other friends were only reluctantly persuaded. Although the Brownings visited England several times in the years following their flight, these visits were always somewhat clouded for her. While Elizabeth lived, the couple made their permanent home abroad.

As the scandal first entered the public domain in 1846 it intersected and merged with a wide range of contemporary representations about the meaning of family, childhood and marriage, as well as a very particular debate about gender which ran under the heading of 'the woman question'. Fiction and poetry were seen as perfectly appropriate mediums for such debates and both Tennyson's *The Princess*, a pantomime in verse about an all-woman's university, written while Robert and Elizabeth were courting, as well as the darker vision of Dickens's *Dombey and Son*, serialised in the months after the Brownings' emigration, were read as serious contributions to these public discussions. Indeed Florence Dombey's flight from *her* father's house in chapter forty-seven reads spookily like an inner narration of Elizabeth's last months in Wimpole Street:

She looked at him, and a cry of desolation issued from her heart. For as she looked, she saw him murdering that fond idea to which she had held in spite of him. She saw his cruelty, neglect and hatred dominant above it, and stamping it down. She saw she had no father upon earth, and ran out orphaned, from his house.

To these popular images of father-daughter relations, Elizabeth would, in 1856, add her own comment through her widely acclaimed novel-poem *Aurora Leigh*. Here she would rewrite in more bearable terms the emotional and artistic genesis of a woman poet, reaching back into the 1840s to rethink the debates on marriage, feminism, class warfare, art and love. A year after its publication Edward Barrett died without acknowledging his daughter's marriage, marking a bleak end to their long estrangement. 'So it is all over now,' Browning wrote helplesslessly to a family friend, 'all hope of better things or a kind answer to entreaties such as I have seen Ba write in the bitterness of her heart. There must have been something in the organisation, or education, at least that would account for and extenuate all this. . . .' Elizabeth grieving wrote to the same friend of her bitterness, 'and some recoil against myself. . . . Strange, that what I called "unkindness" for so many years, in departing should have left me such a sudden desolation. And yet, it is not strange perhaps.'

Family history

The father. The daughter. The family. How far, and at what width of angle does one rewind from that moment of departure, well enough imitated on stage and screen? Elizabeth left behind not only the father she still 'tenderly loved' but nine other intimate companions, forty years of her life torn through by an act of disobedience. 'Remember that I shall be killed – it will be so infinitely worse than you can have an idea,' she wrote to Browning a day or two after their secret wedding while she still lived at home. Her last hours at Wimpole Street were filled with 'agitation and deepest anguish'. 'It is dreadful . . . dreadful . . . to have to give pain here by a voluntary act – for the first time in my life.' A murder. A sacrifice. In Elizabeth's last letters to Browning in the week before the elopement it is hard to tell who is being killed, who doing the killing.

'Something in the organisation, or education . . .' – Browning's question is ours, but like him we are not quite sure whose organisation or education we need most to understand. About Edward Moulton Barrett's we know very little, except that it was ostensibly for his education that his mother and grandparents brought him and his younger brother home to England from their West Indian properties which he would one day inherit. The boys' father had run off when they were infants. There is no evidence that this 'difficult, insensitive, self-willed and isolated young man' did much more than have his name registered at Harrow and Trinity College, Cambridge. Eager to end his childhood he was married before his twentieth birthday to Mary Graham-Clarke, an heiress six years his elder. Edward was just twenty-one when the first of his twelve children, Elizabeth, was born. More insistently perhaps than most men of his time, fatherless Edward made a career of fatherhood.

His inheritance secured, he went looking for a country estate of his own, and found it at Hope End, Herefordshire. 'The more I see of the property the more I like it and the more I think I shall have it in my power to make yourself, Brother and Sister and dear Mama happy,' he wrote to his infant daughter. The power of money; the power of paternity. It seems unlikely that 'dear Mama' recovering from the birth of a third child in three years was consulted about the decision.

In later life, Elizabeth would see her overextended childhood at Hope End as too secluded, too tranquil. Yet they seem on the whole to have been happy years for the young father and his children. It was a strictly religious household but not a sombre one; if Edward was often autocratic, moody and stern, he was also by all accounts witty, playful and merry in the bosom of his family. He was the children's intimate and master, a typical, loving, patriarchal figure. The children, girls included, were allowed space and leisure to develop individual interests. 'Books and dreams were what I lived in – and domestic life only seemed to buzz gently around, like bees about the grass,' Elizabeth remembered. For its time it sounds a child-centred, relaxed regime.

What tensions there were in these early years surface especially in Elizabeth's clouded descriptions of her mother – 'very tender . . . of a nature harrowed up into some furrows by the pressure of circumstances . . . A sweet, gentle, nature, which the thunder a little turned from its sweetness. . . .' Elsewhere the daughter speaks of her as 'one of those women who can never resist, but in submitting and bowing themselves, make a mark, a plait, within – a sign of suffering'. The thunder, the forces not resisted but submitted to and suffered, these are never exactly named. Mary Barrett died in 1828 when Elizabeth was twenty-two, worn out one might guess, though no one says so, with bearing twelve children in eighteen years.

Elizabeth's adult portrait of her mother is of a woman so distinct from herself that she might be another species. This disavowal of her mother's way of being began young. It is certainly explicit in the manuscript autobiography 'Glimpses into My Own Life and Literary Character' written when she was fourteen. In this manifesto of personal and artistic identity, she traces her passionate, active temperament back to early childhood:

I was always of a determined and if thwarted violent disposition. My actions and temper were infinitely more inflexible at three years than now at fourteen. At an early age I can remember reigning in the Nursery and being renowned amongst the servants for self-love and excessive passion.

The author is transparently pleased and barely apologetic about this shocking self-portrait, and returns a few pages later to the irresistible subject of her unchanged, unregenerate character which was 'still as proud, as wilful, as impatient of control, as impetuous', although now 'thanks be to God it is restrained.' The 'habitual' command of herself is represented as a social cover, not a moral necessity, a surface 'revolution' of disposition that might fool her friends, 'But to myself it is well known that the same violent inclinations are in my inmost heart. . . .'

Violence, energy and impetuosity of character were assets and their impenitent owner looked 'upon that tranquillity which I cannot enjoy with a feeling rather like contempt as precluding in great measure the intellectual faculties of the human mind!' Poor Mary Barrett! While Elizabeth defiantly embraced a romantic definition of creative intellect infused with passion she was careful to distinguish it from the kind of feminine excess criticised by both Mary Wollstonecraft and Jane Austen – 'nothing is so odious in my eyes as a damsel famed in story for a superabundance of sensibility'. In spite of her assurance that she has mastered techniques of self-control, it is her 'good heart' and its right to acute feeling which had value and positive meaning for her that the essay defends against the invisible accuser, surely not just her gentle mother, who might think her 'vain, deceitful or vindictive', 'envious or obstinate'.

Near the end of the essay, conscious that she has throughout boldly presented a self almost wholly at odds with contemporary ideologies of the feminine, an 'I' modelled on a full-blooded male romanticism, Elizabeth confronts the issue directly.

My mind is naturally independant and spurns that subserviency of opinion which is generally considered necessary to feminine softness. . . . I feel within me an almost proud consciousness of independance which prompts me to defend my opinions and to yield them only to conviction!!!!!!!

The seven exclamation points marks out this passage as the climax of the piece, and its moment of greatest anxiety.

'Glimpses' is addressed to her younger brother by a year Edward, 'Bro' whose lessons and play she had always shared, and who remained her favorite sibling until his tragic death by drowning in 1840. 'Glimpses' was written soon after Bro was sent to Charterhouse school, and this inevitable separation, through which Elizabeth lost both her loved companion and the male tutor who could assist her progress in classical studies, brought home to her with shattering clarity the social meaning of sexual difference. Bro was an ordinary boy of no special intellectual gifts; yet the classical and literary education for which the precocious Elizabeth yearned was his by right. The expressive rage of 'Glimpses' suggests that it was triggered by some particular domestic conflict which we cannot identify, but we can guess that it involved her father. In this detailed review of her intellectual progress from infancy to adolescence 'Papa' appears only once, as the donor of a ten-shilling prize addressed to the 'Poet Laureat of Hope End' for a six-year-old effort on the subject of virtue. The pages of the autobiography burn with an angry silent denial of his influence and aid. Whether Edward Moulton Barrett read his daughter's broadside is not known. Had he done so, and noted her warning that she could never love those she could not 'admire, respect and venerate', her ultimate defection might not have come as a surprise.

Yet the father, whose minimal presence in 'Glimpses' already marks out an area of resistance and rebellion in the daughter, was, in quite straightforward ways, responsible for his daughter's intellectual progress and literary ambitions. Her precocity was consistently approved and rewarded throughout her childhood. She had almost the free run of his library which was extensive for a man of little formal education and no special intellectual interests. At four she was reading fairy tales; at eleven she had given up novels for philosophy. In spite of his devout belief, Edward Moulton Barrett's library was stocked with radical texts. Elizabeth read Tom Paine's *Age of Reason*, Voltaire's *Philosophical Dictionary*, Hume's essays – as well as Goethe, Rousseau and Wollstonecraft, all this before she was fifteen. Only a few books – Gibbon and *Tom Jones* are the ones she mentions – were considered too blasphemous or obscene for her scrutiny. From the age of twelve she was allowed to sit in on her brother's lessons with his tutor Mr McSwinney; these helped with classical and modern languages although she was mostly self-taught. More than this casual permission most nineteenth-century daughters could not expect to receive. In the year of 'Glimpses' her father had her juvenile 'epic' in four books, *The Battle of Marathon*, written when she was twelve, privately printed. It is suitably dedicated 'to the father, whose never-failing kindness, whose unwearied affection I never can repay' but the poem's intellectual parent, Byron, is also recognised. One of her first adult poems accepted by the *London Globe and Traveller* in 1824 'Stanzas on the Death of Lord Byron' pleased both parents and *An Essay on Mind, with Other Poems* (1826) was highly commended by her proud father. Edward Barrett's support for his daughter's aspiration was constrained but not wholly bound by contemporary prejudice. His kindness, affection and encouragement, his expressive pleasure in her efforts stood behind the arrogant energetic and independent mind of 'Glimpses'. Until Bro's elevation to Charterhouse showed Elizabeth where her gender marked the limit of parental indulgence, it might be said that Edward Barrett was rather the pattern for a feminist father than the model of paternal tyranny.

Her mind 'a turmoil of conflicting passions, not so much influenced by exterior forces as by internal reflection and impetuousity', Elizabeth spent her childhood at Hope End in study and dreams. 'Glimpses' records, with some humour, a twenty-four-hour religious crisis when she was twelve, but there is nothing but the evidence of the autobiography itself to predict the severe and mysterious illness that struck her at fifteen, and which kept her bedridden for almost eighteen months. It was preceded by a riding injury to her spine which would later prove more serious, but its character is clearly that of an hysterical illness, of the kind which would, at the end of the century, give Freud his first clues to the working of the unconscious. The nerve specialist, Dr Coker, kept a detailed account of the symptoms, which started with weeks of headache, then shifted to attacks of severe pain in 'various parts of the body'.

The suffering is agony – and the paroxysms continue from a quarter of an hour to an hour and upwards – accompanied by convulsive twitches of the muscles, in which the diaphragm is particularly concerned – The attack seems gradually to approach its acme and then suddenly ceases – During its progress the mind is for the most part conscious of surrounding objects but towards its close, there is generally some, and occasionally very considerable confusion produced by it – There are generally three attacks in the day and none during the night . . . Opium at one time relieved the spasms but it has ceased to have that effect . . .

Hysteria, Freud wrote, frequently affects 'people of the clearest intellect, strongest will, greatest character and highest critical power'; things that cannot be put into words – fantasies and feelings psychically and socially unacceptable – are spoken instead through the physical symptom. Elizabeth herself seems to predict her illness in 'Glimpses' warning that 'were I once to loose the rigid rein I might again be hurled with Phaeton far from every thing human . . . everything reasonable!' The illness should be read as another expressive text whose 'subject' was, probably, the powerful set of emotionally conflictful stakes set out in her autobiography. She was paying a high price for her restraint and control. Perhaps too, the 'independance' she desired was harder to enact, femininity a more pressing psychic obligation than she was willing to admit. How closely after the onset of menstruation her illness followed is not recorded, but she would herself in *Aurora Leigh* call daring attention to the importance of the menarche in emotional development, especially the traumatic changes it could trigger in father-daughter relations.

Aurora Leigh traces the growth of a woman poet from infancy to maturity, an adult epic version of 'Glimpses'. In this reimagined life, the girl poet is raised by her widower father, an 'austere Englishman' transformed from a 'common man' by his passionate love for his Florentine wife. In his grief he retreats with his daughter to a remote mountain hideaway where he gives her a liberal education in the fallibility of patriarchal knowledge – 'out of books/He taught me all the ignorance of men. . . .' After nine years this isolated childhood and idyllic relationship is shattered. 'I was just thirteen,/Still growing like the plants from unseen roots/In tongue-tied Springs, – and suddenly awoke/To full life and life's needs and agonies/With an intense, strong, struggling heart beside/A stone-dead father. Life struck sharp on death,/Makes awful lightening.' Menstruation and the death of the father. For Elizabeth, physical puberty was closely tied to the emergence of the 'intense, strong, struggling heart' so vividly evoked in the autobiography. In *Aurora Leigh* the fictional father enjoins his daughter to 'love' and then, providentially, removes himself as potent and potentially taboo love object – 'Ere I answered he was gone,/And none was left to love in all the world.' Aurora's nurturant born-again father, whose new creed was love, was created in the fruitful middle years of the Brownings' marriage against the background of Edward Moulton Barrett's 'unkind' silence. But the poem reaches back perhaps to the unclouded prepubescent years at Hope End. Female adolescence and the death of the loving father are made coincident, their conjunction a bolt from heaven. The symbolic parallel to Elizabeth's history continues as the grieving Aurora's suffering mirrors, in part, the period of her illness.

> There, ended childhood. What succeeded next
> I recollect as, after fevers, men
> Thread back the passage of delirium,
> Missing the turn still, baffled by the door;
> Smooth endless days, notched here and there with knives,
> A weary, wormy darkness, spurred i' the flank
> With flame that it should eat and end itself
> Like some tormented scorpion.

Elizabeth's illness weakened her permanently. Although she would walk and ride again, after it she tired quickly, cried easily, was subject to fainting fits and bouts of nerves – all external marks of the feminine sensibility she despised. Illness of various kinds became both a burden and a form of defence against a fully social public existence, a response to crises and conflicts which she could not always confront or resolve through action. By 1824 this initial serious illness had played itself out, and she was on her feet and writing again. The first major crisis had been negotiated.

Thoughts of the heart

One more episode from Elizabeth's youth, opened up to us through her single successful attempt to keep a diary, suggests how difficult it is to isolate the father-daughter relationship from the wider resistance to patriarchal culture in Elizabeth's demand for recognition as an independent, creative woman.

The period 1827–32 were harsh years for the Barrett ménage. Mary Barrett died in 1828 after a year's illness. By 1831 Edward Barrett's financial affairs were in such disarray that it became necessary to sell Hope End. Absorbed in his business troubles, Edward was frequently absent. Fortunately for Elizabeth the publication in 1826 of *An Essay on Mind* brought her to the attention of a new neighbour, the forty-five-year-old blind Greek scholar, Hugh Stuart Boyd. His 'quenched' sight, his age, and the fact that he was respectably flanked by a wife and daughter made him an ideal candidate for platonic intellectual friendship. Even so, Barrett warned his daughter that it would be improper for her as a 'young female' to make the first call. Once begun, the acquaintance thrived on their mutual need for intellectual companionship, respect and admiration. Boyd, in fact, had a stable of young female protégées who served as readers and amanuenses, among whom Elizabeth had a somewhat perilous position as favourite. We can see Boyd as Elizabeth herself would do in maturity, as a cranky and rather narrow pedant. In the years of their confidential friendship – 'no confidence, no friendship', Boyd decreed – Elizabeth used him to explore her capacity for strong feeling outside the family. Impeded by their different temperaments, the jealous interference of both families and Elizabeth's fragile health their connection had some of the character of a love affair, and gave Elizabeth a taste of her father's growing exclusiveness towards his children.

In March 1831, when Elizabeth began the diary, her relationship with Boyd was at fever pitch and suspense about the fate of Hope End was also rising. The diary shows the whole family hanging on Edward's letters and moods for clues to their future. Barrett had instructed brother Sam to 'say nothing on the subject of removal to the girls'. His proud silence about the impending loss of his kingdom emphasised his unqualified power within the family.

Like 'Glimpses', the diary was a place to record 'the thoughts of my heart as well as my head', and the long episodic opening entry was written in the wake of a real and inner thunderstorm which provoked 'hot & cold' anxiety for 'myself & everybody near me & many bodies not near me; viz for Papa and Bro who were out – for Mr Boyd who is at Malvern where the storm was travelling. Arabel dreamt last night that *he* was dead, & that I was laughing! Foolish dream –'. The *he* of Arabel's becomes through Elizabeth's associations all the men she loved – and hated. Then entry descends into a gloomy review of her friendship with Boyd – 'I suspect that his regard for me is dependent on his literary estimation of me & is not great enough for me to lose any part of it.' This negative assessment of her worth in the eyes of men is implicit in the last fragment of the entry, a seemingly cheery report at Edward Barrett's pleasure at Bro's reported success as an after-dinner speaker – 'Dear Papa! dear Bro!' The discontinuous 'bits' make up a revealing associative narrative of anxiety, anger, longing and threatened loss, with her sexual and her creative selves as uncertain protagonists. No wonder she was worried that her 'very exacting & exclusive & eager & headlong & *strong*' mind would produce thoughts that she could not 'bear to look on . . . after they were written'. The sexualised element of these thoughts were part of their terror and attraction: 'Adam made fig leaves for the mind, as well as for the body.'

Near the end of the diary Elizabeth records a dream which maps out and summarises her year of distress. 'Dreamt about Adolphe & Endymion, & a lady who was by turns Emily and Amalthea & of her murdering Endymion whose soul was infused into Adolphe. Papa reproached her. But she held up her beautiful face, & said, 'I am yet very fair.' 'Clay Walls,' said Papa!' The condensed mythic-romantic figures marry the classical world Elizabeth and Boyd shared with her 'modern' imaginative life. Endymion/Adolphe – Greek youth merged with Constant's Byronic hero – is assassinated by two notable daughters, Amalthea, child of the King of Crete and Zeus' nurse, and Emily, heroine of Ann Radcliffe's *Mysteries of Udolpho*, which Elizabeth had read the summer before. Radcliffe's novel spoke to Elizabeth's fears, for the orphaned Emily sees her safe country home broken up and becomes the prey of lecherous Gothic villains. In the dream this composite daughter murders desire in the shape of its popularly conceived object, a handsome young man. Perhaps the murder also represents the seduction it was designed to avert; perhaps too, it is a killing off of the romantic hero in the dreamer. Certainly all the passive/ active identities belong to the dreamer-transgressor, whose seductive self-justification is met with paternal rejection – the blind indifference of a clay death mask to the daughter with clay feet. One of many possible interpretations, this reading of the dream emphasises the frustration of these critical months when Elizabeth's future as artist, woman and daughter seemed to depend completely on the words and looks of two withholding, possessive men, both sexually barred to her.

In *Aurora Leigh* women's tendency to emotional and artistic dependence on the commendation 'of some one friend' is bitterly detailed and finally rejected in a brilliant passage which ends 'Must I work in vain,/ Without the approbation of a man?/It cannot be; it shall not.' But the diary, another trying out of the meanings of independence, proved too painfully revealing of this gendered, unrewarding dependence. After a year it was broken off in 'self-disgust'.

Family Romance

The opening lines of 'Family Romances', one of Sigmund Freud's most tantalising short essays, reminds us how general was the task our romantic heroine faced. Freud believed that the 'liberation of an individual, as he grows up, from the authority of his parents is one of the most necessary though one of the most painful results brought about by the course of his development . . . the whole progress of society rests upon the opposition between successive generations'. Persons who failed in that task, generally men, in Freud's therapeutic experience, were likely to entertain a typical neurotic fantasy, in which the real-life father is found to be an impostor, and is replaced by a more socially exalted and loving parent. A flexible fantasy, capable of endless elaboration, its narrative can turn siblings into lovers by removing the blood tie – the plot and characters in the subject's family history can be rewritten to fulfil a variety of impossible wishes. Born of the child's sense of being inadequately loved and recognised, and of the guilt engendered by its overtly hostile feelings, family romance stems as much from the overvaluation of the despised parent as from hostility to him. In the fantasy replacement, qualities of the original parent can always be discerned. The 'family romance' of a woman will always be deeply marked by femininity, the inner and outer construction of sexual difference. Femininity insists that women remain somewhat enchilded throughout adult life, deferential to the authority of all males of their own social class and higher. Women do not always choose to confront paternal authority directly, for they are not of the sex which must compete with it or indeed replace it. The demands of adult life allow them, often, to continue in dependent roles; liberation from their fathers often means no more than the passage from paternal to marital household. But femininity is neither an essential attribute of gender nor a very stable psychosocial structure. The adult identity that Elizabeth desired was in some but not all respects at odds with psychic and social femininity, and her experience illustrates just how violent the acquisition of 'normal' femininity can be, and how culturally asymmetrical its terms.

It may be that Edward Moulton Barrett did more than he could have known to set up the conditions of Elizabeth's ultimate resistance. By treating her in infancy in a way more culturally appropriate to an elder son – his confiding letter to her about his ambitions for Hope End suggests something of this – he reinforced the infant self will that reigned in nursery and below stairs. Elizabeth never let go of her right to that heady sovereignty, which she pinpoints in 'Glimpses' at around three, an age before the full psychic and social implications of sexual difference are clear to a child. The fourteen-year-old-girl clung obstinately to that pre-Oedipal moment of autonomy, agency and passion, for she understood with peculiar prescience that it was the constituent moment of her self-formation, as romantic artist. By encouraging her precocious intelligence and rewarding her poetic efforts, by identifying, as parents sometimes do, with her gifts, Edward inadvertently allowed her to develop unimpeded her vision of herself as 'Poet Laureat' (in 'Glimpses' she leaves out the final feminising 'e'). For the father it was a gentle joke; for the daughter, even before she understood the title, it was deadly serious.

As she moved in her reading from fairy tales to novels, from novels to classical literature, philosophy and modern poetry the image of herself as romantic poet gathered definition. As an eldest child, living in relative social isolation she was freer than most female children to imagine a world which would let her be that poet – and a woman. The model of the romantic poet was male; it insisted on authority, autonomy and the expression of strong feeling. Emotion expressed by women, as the fourteen-year-old Elizabeth knew from reading and experience, symbolised to others their weakness, inferiority and dependence. The contradictory uses of the word 'control' in 'Glimpses' – control of self, control of meaning – signal the impasse; what made her vulnerable to other people was internally, for her creative self, a necessary strength. When Bro was sent off to school, leaving Elizabeth lonely and tutorless, the hard realities of being a daughter and not a son were brought home to her. 'Glimpses' is a *cri de coeur* against the terminal condition of femininity, her illness a year later an equally expressive text of the violent conflicts she could not reconcile. The Hope End diary was another attempt to make sense through writing of this senseless social and spiritual contradiction.

By the time Elizabeth was in her twenties the pathological contours of her father's character were becoming clearly visible. The loss of Hope End was a drastic blow to his image of himself as father; even ten years later the name could not be mentioned in his presence. No other part of his paternal power would be eroded if he could help it; he could use his will and his considerable remaining resources to govern absolutely the lives in his little monarchy. His daughter could win whatever laurels she liked in the cultural community as long as she remained physically dependent upon him.

Elizabeth accepted these unspoken terms for many years, although her recurrent, debilitating illnesses say something about their cost. Two coincident events helped her to break free. In 1845 Browning introduced himself to her through an impassioned, admiring letter which began, 'I love your verses with all my heart, dear Miss Barrett,' and went on to praise 'the fresh strange music, the fluent language, the exquisite pathos and true new brave thought . . . my feeling rises altogether. I do, as I say, love these books with all my heart – and I love you too.' Meetings only deepened his infatuation and stirred her affection. How could she resist this late confirmation of her art and her femininity? At the same time her doctors advised her that she must escape south during the cruel English winters if she wished to live much longer. It was her father's unwillingness to bless her reasonable plans to winter abroad with suitable companions that finally moved her to action. With Browning to support and encourage her she found the strength to resist. Edward Barrett's love was not, after all, the kind she was prepared to die for. After years of living out the most disabling aspects of femininity while preserving an inner strength of will, she was offered a position where she might redefine the former, keep the latter. Browning's age, status, poverty and gentle nature were all in his favour. In personal terms the price of overvaluing male authority figures had been excessive. Thereafter it was only political patriarchs that she was prepared to venerate; her fascination with strong men still needed an outlet. And venerate them she did, from Cavour to the awful Louis Napoleon, Browning's dismay notwithstanding. They became part of her political romance with Italy.

But in *Aurora Leigh* she memorialised her own troubled history and the men who figured in it, in a pattern which very closely follows that of family romance. The loving, liberal, English father of Book I is certainly the father of her early childhood at Hope End who set his daughter free in his library, traced on top of Emily's idealistic, indulgent daddy from *Mysteries of Udolpho*. In Aurora's cousin and future husband, Romney Leigh, the trinity of important male relationships of her youth, Papa, Bro, Boyd, are all remembered, grafted on to later models. True to the narrative structure of family romance, Romney shares her surname, marking him out as the relative to whom she can at last have sexual access. Like father, brother and Boyd, the young Romney admires the young Aurora's gifts, lending her books without really acknowledging her right to an independent creative identity. And in the sadder-but-wiser older Romney, 'mulcted' of his sight but not of his desire for his cousin, the erotic element in the relationship with Boyd is tenderly acknowledged. There are much less benign fragments too in this collage cousin-lover; Romney's tragic flirtation with 'abstract' radical politics articulates a distaste for radical theory learned at the knee of her father who was a liberal in politics and an unreconstructed despot at home.

The plot and characters of *Aurora Leigh* nowhere explicitly recalls the unforgiving old man, still alive during its composition, but the still embittered author denies any role and influence to the father in the life of the adult poet, by writing him out of the narrative. Chaste, hardworking and independent, young Aurora lives on her own in London through her twenties, the most self-contained and successful female orphan in Victorian fiction. Yet further facets of Barrett senior and his domestic history, as they were transformed by Elizabeth's fantasies, are clearly recognisable. During Romney's picaresque career as a socialist he plans a loveless political marriage with a pure, devoted, dependent working-class girl, Marian Earle, whose character and Christian name recall gentle, passive Mary Barrett whose real social position is signalled by her fictional surname. Through this doomed cross-class mésalliance, Elizabeth sketches out a critique of her parents' unequal emotional union, substituting, perhaps, Romney's politically instrumental courtship for Edward's supposed economic one. In Elizabeth's family romance only true and equal love binds; in winning Romney from Marian, Aurora achieves that perfect union, and her creator, the once usurping daughter, wins her loved despotic parent from her only serious rival. Yet Marian is a saint-like portrait, and the passage near the end of the poem when she, her bastard son and Aurora live happily together in Italy render in idyllic transformation the years when Mary and Elizabeth presided over the half-grown, mostly male Barrett brood. In the harmonious household of her imagination, where all loves are permitted, the poet-daughter reigned supreme.

The family romance woven through *Aurora Leigh* is only one strand of this rich poem, the first and greatest imaginative celebration in English of woman's creative potential. Women's fictions, especially their utopian writing, are central texts for feminism; for they remap the terrain political feminism hopes to alter. In *Aurora Leigh* Elizabeth Barrett Browning tries to reimagine the making of a woman poet without the arbitrary parent who ruled her first forty years, the years of her own making as an artist. Up to a point she succeeds, but as I have suggested Papa is clearly visible through the disguises of the fictional father and cousin-lover, his bad and good qualities dispersed through the narrative, his love and desire captured in the last pages. Nor do I read this return of the father in *Aurora Leigh* as an element which weakens its feminist intent or message. On the contrary, it poses the problem of fathers, not just wicked ones, in its severest, most demanding form. Women's utopias are often character-ised by the absence or dispersal of paternal authority – a banishment which is in itself an important imaginative reshaping of the landscape of our lives. Yet the shadow father still lingers within us, as well as in Elizabeth's poem, constituent of the terms through which both our femininity and our feminism is constructed and lived. Do we want to depose him altogether? Elizabeth's life and work as read through her public and private writing suggests how imperfect is the fit between the social and the psychic father, between the official despot who ruled by 'divine right' and the father whose 'deep tender affection' both fuelled and foiled his daughter's desires. Can we depose the first without sacrificing the second, the loved, loving, imperfect parent from whom we must, as both children and women, struggle free?

When I tried to write about my father and myself I could only catch at the ebb and flow of our struggles. I could not, significantly, recall the text or pretext of a single one of our painful skirmishes, so closely strung from my fifth to my twenty-first year, when I left home. Twenty-one years past that break those desperate battles to establish autonomy seem no more – but no less – important than my father's extraordinary influence, exam-ple, support and affection, which have shaped my life in positive ways. Strong-minded daughters of dominating men will inevitably find them a site of 'all those patriarchal ideas' with which our culture is saturated, will, often, cut their political teeth in opposing their sanctions however mild, will, almost certainly, imagine a gentler, more loving father. I cannot remember my father literally denying me any access to the world I asked for, but his very existence symbolised the way I was to be denied. Elizabeth's story, which I too first encountered in Besier's play, had an instant resonance for me, as it has I am sure for many women, for it places the burden of guilt and illegitimate desire with which father-daughter relations are mutually drenched firmly on the shoulder of the male, where some feminists will say it belongs. My exploration of Elizabeth's life, and my reflections on my own history, suggest a more complex scenario in which love, anger, guilt and desire are orchestrated as a duet, not a baritone solo, in which daughters cannot be constructed wholly as social and psychic victims of their fathers or their fathers as wholly unregenerate villains. Because they include both social and psychological reality, binding together the worlds of material and imaginative possibility, literary texts express this contradictory relation more fully and accurately than most other discourses. Nowhere is it more poignantly and densely worked through than in the life and writing of Elizabeth Barrett Browning.

Patriarchy is the power of the fathers: a familial-social, ideological, political system in which men — by force, direct pressure, or through ritual, tradition, law, and language, customs, etiquette, education, and the division of labour, determine what part women shall or shall not play, and in which the female is everywhere subsumed under the male. . . . . The power of the fathers had been difficult to grasp because it permeates everything, even the language in which we try to describe it. It is diffuse and concrete; symbolic and literal; universal, and expressed with local variations which obscure its universality. Under patriarchy, I may live in purdah *or drive a truck; I may raise my children on a* kibbutz *or be the sole breadwinner for a fatherless family or participate in a demonstration against abortion legislation with my baby on my back; I may work as a 'barefoot doctor' in a village commune in the People's Republic of China, or make my life on a lesbian commune in New England; I may become a hereditary or elected head of state or wash the underwear of a millionaire's wife; I may serve my husband his early-morning coffee within the clay walls of a Berber village or march in an academic procession; whatever my status or situation, my derived economic class, or my sexual preference, I live under the power of the fathers, and I have access only to so much of privilege or influence as the patriarchy is willing to accede to me, and only for so long as I will pay the price for male approval.*

Adrienne Rich, *Of Woman Born*

ROSE
RIDER

Pater Familias

Rose Rider's just a cog in the wheel. Well, lexicographer to be precise. I work on a *Great Illustrated Dictionary*: construct neat modern definitions, predict semantic shifts, pronounce myself a rose by any other name. . . . The etymology is harder though. Word derivation seems a simple one-way road, leading from then to now. But meanings lie in wraps, miss a beat, or even double back. And so will I.

Riches from rags – a disappointed graduate, twenty-three, turned cross temp typist; sweating alcoholic boss spots spelling corrections she's rashly made on copy in a fit of rage. She's called in to Sir who notes she suits his swish new electronic typewriter. Soon it's c.v.s, Os, As, B.A.s, 'I see's, and she can even pronounce P/A with her little finger crooked.

Look back to same old disappointed graduate, twenty-two now, running a mail-order knitwear business; applies to train – solicitor, osteopath, Girl Friday peanut sampler in Sri Lanka, even civil servant (Cheltenham – hush-hush).

Back then to the Polish diploma, 'Language and Politics', 1980 – a wasted year academically, but nice chocolate cakes from Warsaw. Next to the Russian degree, slipped in after university entrance, Latin and Greek. Childhood, nomadic. India, land of my birth: the baby's rushed to nearest shrine, a Buddhist holy man intones . . . I am to die 'by the sword' at sixty-seven . . . I am the reincarnation of a little dog. How did I make it from dog to woman, all in one leap? And what was I before dog? Temp typist?

On the few occasions I bother to remember my father, I see two images: one near and recent yet unreal, the other vivid from my early childhood. They sit like snapshots in a dirty wallet, a sepia and a colour instamatic reversed in time.

The technicolour man appears now only in nightmares, rapidly snapping little children's fingers or slicing their faces off. He comes after me, a giant swarm of eyes on an empty escalator narrowing to a blank corner with no one by to hear the scream I can't produce. I clutch at my own throat to wake myself, but tangled hair drags my head down with it into the claybanks of a tepid sea – the mattress smothers me, I cannot wake, I cannot die.

I had long hair, long and golden, and my father loved me for that. It earned me praise and presents for a good little girl; he stroked it reverently, blowing it dry as I perched after my bath in a white wicker chair; he wound it tightly round his hand and dragged me with it to the floor.

His earliest attempts at fatherhood were unsophisticated, feet and hands the only weapons in his grasp. With time he learnt to extend his big stick repertoire: a cane here, a wet towel there, improvisation in the countryside with an old oak branch.

He sired three earlier children and abandoned them; our own brood were the lucky ones who had a father to protect us. For him, the four of us were a constant new reminder that he had parental status, head of the house, head of the table, head of the bed. Our presence also showed that he was no longer a child: as an adult, he must fend for himself and take responsibilities for others. Fathers commonly cannot accept the loss of child-husband privileges they formerly enjoyed. Mine was a normal man in this respect. He was crusading on a one-man invasion of the mother–children bond, raring to charge forward on the battlefield of women's bodies, minds and lives.

Which tactic was the worse, his violence or his gentleness? Perhaps they are two sides of the same coin he paid me with. Our Father too is cruel and kind, but I dismissed theodicy at the age of thirteen with the lock on a bathroom door gradually wrenched away under the pounding weight of a grown man and myself cold, wet, pressed at the far end against the frosted windows with Victorian nursery bars, shrieking out to God in the sky and a seven-floor drop to the ground below.

My rage now is for those cool town houses beyond the bars, those walls and doors and windows with their silent citizens inside, ignoring the cries of women and children and stifling those of their own.

In a café recently I saw a man repeatedly punch his five-year-old child. 'Shut your face,' he told her, 'or 1983 will be the worse for you.' There again, clear as through a sheet of glass, I saw my father's stone eyes stare from the face of this man, I saw the muscles in his arms twitch as his fists champed the bit under the table. Two women in the whole café took notice of this scene; we knew what that girl had in store for 1983, '4, '5 and so on till the day he died. We caught his eye: 'We know you, child molester; we are your child and her anger.' His reply: 'This glass is unbreakable, my power is unshakeable.' His wife's eyes were permanently downcast, glazed beyond our reach.

So much for violence; but gentleness from such a man is truly violation. This is how my father entered my nightmares, as gently as he sneaked into my sleep before. Those sensitive lovers, delicate poetic men, smile suavely savouring ladies like a fine wine: 'A beautiful girl under one of us is like a Stradivarius in the hands of a virtuoso.' . . . I knew, as I lay Jackfrosted on that tepid mattress, that the virtuoso has the bow, he chooses the music, and if the violin won't play, he'll turn it across his knees and snap it in two.

Time telescoped. My father faded from the house. New women youthfully engaged his hopes of future fatherhood – he'd spawned enough wrinkles on my mother's face to satisfy him there.

A stifling quilt covers my later adolescence, a time spent half asleep, half drugged up by the National Health, patrons and protectors of our children's welfare. As I surfaced from that bog, escaped to university, lived, survived, my resilience took the shape of a stout brown wallet in which I kept the early image of my father, a Medusa's head too blinding as yet to behold, but still possessing power, hence not to be discarded lightly. I saw him in the flesh quite rarely, on those obscene collective lies fostered by our society and christened Family Occasions. Those times I never looked him in the face; at first for fear of petrification, and later from revulsion as my understanding grew. Now I had come back dolled to the eyes with the territory signals of other males, stamps of ownership and ostentatious gift tags, as if tomcats in a garden had squittered on a strategic bush. He left me alone then, frightened by the smell of other males, frightened of the knowledge I had gained from them of him. In this new grey, subdued mould he continued, a mere shadow on the walls of our family, but presumably lord of his own castle somewhere else. The sepia photograph dates from this time too, when I saw he would no longer attack me openly and began cautiously to peep around the back and sides to see if he was really as two-dimensional as he'd seemed.

What I began to see was a poor, pitiable hypocrite, lying to himself and the world, clinging desperately to doctrines that he himself had originally disbelieved, but taken on as protective cloaks which were now grafted to his skin. If they could be peeled away, there would still remain an endless onion of unpeelable lies, not worth weeping over. On the contrary, how I laughed recently at a showing of *The Godfather*, mentally transferring Marlon Brando's awesome patriarchal bawling to the mouth of a baby shaking its rattle in a pram. There they sit, ensconced, clutching their rattles: kings with sceptres, judges with hammers, justice with a sword. . . . The patriarchs by definition cannot stand alone; they are doomed to lean on their Freudian crutch which every moment threatens to wilt and bend beneath them; so their power is never satisfaction; banking up on heaps of bones of yet more victims, victims willing. . . . Slaves must die to erect their pyramids: women must die to erect their sex.

Domination is in the patriarchal blood; it passes from man to man as blood bond and blood victory. Domination in sexual terms demands a victim and a willing victim, therefore an ignorant victim, one who is younger, smaller, weaker, softer, in effect, helpless, choiceless, power-less . . . yet still smaller, younger, weaker, softer, smaller, younger, smaller, younger . . . the abuse of children, specifically girl children, is the means and the end of the patriarchy and male supremacy as we know it, live it and breathe it every moment of our lives.

'Sexual reproduction,' as my father wrote to the head of my junior school, 'is the physical basis of the family. It is the normal way for children to acquire parents, and parents children. I cannot for the life of me see why anybody else should feel it incumbent on them to explain to either of the parties how they come to be related.' Like the majority of women, I got my sex education at home, taking sweets and bitter misery not from strangers but from a man I was trained to love, honour and obey. When I escaped the bars and stripes of home I expected the world outside to be a safe place – I had been terrorised by a weird, monstrous freak, but other men were kind, protecting, avuncular maybe?

Through university I met men, through men I met constant exploita-tion and abuse. Through university I met women, through women I met feminism, and knowledge, understanding, above all, communication. I began to share my experiences of oppression and learn from those of others: but all the time the danger I had undergone as a child seemed irrelevant beside the danger I was under as a woman. Meanwhile I returned to London and began to wake. Britain's first self-help group for incest survivors was surfacing as cautiously we named ourselves. We were dumbfounded by the systematic nature and extent of the abuse of girl children, and decided to organise against it. Incest, 'The Red I', as one American woman has called it, was now a brand that burnt the other way. A group of us set up a campaign in August 1981 to publicise the feminist issue of incest, expose the myths, those of old and those still being perpetrated by new 'experts'; to found refuges for girls; and to form more groups for adult women throughout the country. The campaign grew and with it our knowledge and understanding of father–daughter relationships in general, whether seen as abusive or not. All women, as sisters, nieces, granddaughters and daughters, we are all tarred with the same brush.

I made one last attempt a year ago, when I had finally amassed the distance and the courage to tell my father about the work I do for the Incest Survivors' Campaign, to understand his motivation. I asked him what he thought was the true role of a parent in the home or a leader in government, whether violence was justified in the upbringing of children and the affairs of nations, and what he now felt about my own treatment at his hands.

'Of course you didn't have a violent childhood,' he replied. 'I was a loving father. Sometimes I was forced to chastise you, but children must accept that parents are not to be challenged, instead of questioning their authority as your mother did, poisoning your minds against me and teaching you disloyalty. In any case everyone is treated as they really wish, and if you felt victimised, then that is what *you* must have willed.'

As an incest survivor I had heard that message many times before, from the lips of headmaster after social worker after judge after family therapist. It did not surprise me, but his next words did. I told him about a sixteen-year-old friend of mine who sat for eight hours in her own urine, brutally interrogated by two policemen while her stepfather shared tea, sandwiches and dirty jokes with the officers next door.

First my father asked if she was black; then he fell silent and stirred his tea thoughtfully. 'She made a serious allegation,' he concluded.

I looked at the sepia mugshot before me. He may be a serious criminal, but then he is just an ordinary man – not worth wasting any more effort on really.

But I did hand him a last Mars bar before I left. After all, he was going to need it on the desert island I'd planned for him.

Ever since she could remember he had been everything in life to her. She had had no thought since she grew up for anybody but her father. There was no room for any other thought, so completely did he fill her heart. They had done everything together, shared everything together, dodged the winters together, settled in charming places, seen the same beautiful things, read the same books, talked, laughed, had friends, – heaps of friends; wherever they were her father seemed at once to have friends, adding them to the mass he had already. She had not been away from him a day for years; she had had no wish to go away. Where and with whom could she be so happy as with him? All the years were years of sunshine. There had been no winters; nothing but summer, summer, and sweet scents and soft skies, and patient understanding with her slowness – for he had the nimblest mind – and love. He was the most amusing companion to her, the most generous friend, the most illuminating guide, the most adoring father; and now he was dead, and she felt nothing.

Elisabeth Von Arnim, *Vera*

It was awful to Harriett that her father should be ill, lying there at their mercy. She couldn't get over her sense of his parenthood, his authority. When he was obstinate, and insisted on exerting himself, she gave in. She was a bad nurse, because she couldn't set herself against his will. And when she had him under her hands to strip and wash him, she felt that she was doing something outrageous and impious; she set about it with a flaming face and fumbling hands. 'Your mother does it better,' he said gently. But she could not get her mother's feeling of him as a helpless, dependent thing.

May Sinclair, *Life and Death of Harriett Frean*

ELAINE FEINSTEIN

A Legendary Hero

I was born in Bootle in 1930; educated in Leicester at the Wyggeston Grammar School, and read English at Newnham College, Cambridge, between 1949 and 1952. For two years afterwards I solemnly ate dinners at Gray's Inn (passing Bar Finals part one without much difficulty) in the hope that I was learning a trade that would help me to cope with the masculine world. The realities of the situation (which would require considerable private funding even for a young man) were gradually brought in upon me and thereafter I taught in schools, gave WEA lectures, supervised undergraduates, joined the editorial staff of Cambridge University Press, and for two years or so commuted to the University of Essex where I was an assistant lecturer in Comparative Literature. I have been married to Dr Arnold Feinstein since 1956, and have three sons.

All my early writing had to be done in the cracks of these responsibilities. I minded less than I might have done, because I thought of myself as a poet and that situation is traditional for poets. I had always written poetry from childhood and began to publish as a poet and translator of poetry long before I wrote novels. Indeed, my first novel, *The Circle*, recognisably uses the voice of my poetry. Since then, I have written a further six novels (most recently *The Survivors*) and a volume of short stories, *The Silent Areas*, both from Hutchinson; my selected poems, *Some Unease and Angels*, also from Hutchinson, appeared in 1982. A second edition of my translations of the *Selected Poems of Marina Tsvetayeva* is now back in print from Oxford University Press. Most recently, I have written plays for radio and television and I am currently working on a twelve-part series based on the life behind *The Country Diary of an Edwardian Lady*.

I am still glad to be one of those who at least began life with a general trust of men; you often get back from life more or less what you expect from it. I doubt if it is an advantage to expect the worst.

I had a happy childhood, a lively adolescence, and (perhaps as a result of my father's demeanour) no fear of sex. But I had too much expectation of love. Probably no one else could give me the kind of loyalty which can, if you're lucky, be on offer from a parent, and no doubt it's an intolerable burden upon a mate.

Perhaps I was too much cherished as a child. My mother could carry none of the children she conceived after me – she had Rhesus negative blood – and my survival must have seemed miraculous to both of them. But my father would have been indulgent in any case; he was extravagant by nature, and all his family had a soft, Mediterranean gentleness with children.

Looking back now, I wonder that my mother connived at such uncritical idolatry. She was a gentle, bookish woman, astonished by my father's flamboyance and swagger; and quite shrewd enough to see how unwisely he ran his affairs. Alas, her strengths were invisible to me. I modelled myself on my father. And this much at least was worthy of admiration: nothing downed his spirits for long. Not all his influence was so encouraging. He left school at twelve, and had little patience with books or teachers.

His parents were Russian Jews in the wood trade who settled in Liverpool at the turn of the century. All his family were giant figures in my childhood; the women often working at the bench alongside their brothers. The family business was never likely to be one that made its way from a barrow to the stock exchange; it was probably only viable on sheer energy. And my father had clever fingers. He could make any machinery work. But he wasn't a natural salesman; he had a simple, direct style of talking and it was not in him to wheedle for business.

My grandfather had studied at a Yeshiva* in Odessa, and was genuinely learned, even erudite. He made no worldly use of these skills, however. It was expressly forbidden in the Talmud to teach for money; and he had no desire to become a salaried official of some local community. Instead, he enjoyed his reputation as a *Tsaddick*,† and worked with his hands. Always with a sense of God's especial protection. My father, who knew himself a favourite son, felt the same benevolence extending to himself, though very little of my grandfather's learning reached down to him. It was a faith that carried him sturdily through all financial calamities.

Really, he only believed in luck and hard work; and my mother's

---

*Yeshiva: A university that trained students in the Bible, Jewish thought and law.
†A holy man to whom it was customary to turn for advice.

infinitely more urbane family saw him as a hopeless dreamer. What do they know, all the clever buggers? He would dismiss scepticism. He liked the rituals, the white cloths and candles, the certainty that everything was kept in its separate and ordained place.

It was my mother who determined that my schooling should be as good as Leicester could provide. And I was grateful for that, though I was hostile to the Wyggeston School, once I understood my father was uneasy about it. I was restless and constrained by the school and never learnt how to accept its discipline. I was always in trouble for not having the right shoes, or forgetting my books, or pencils. The headmistress knew how to make me cry. But my father's shrug, whenever I told him about it, made me comfortable again. It was not an altogether harmless lesson.

When I was nine or ten, I was often taken after school to his factory on Clinton Street in Leicester. In the late thirties, it was a broken-down, three-floored monster in a slum street, facing a group of cottages (two up, two down), whose children played marbles or whipping top out on the pavement. I felt strangely removed from them. They were ill-dressed, and often snotty, for all their cheerfulness; and somehow I couldn't imagine being one of them. My father laughed when I puzzled at their lives, and said that nothing was easier than to find yourself without enough to buy a cup of tea.

There was nothing grand about the factory in Clinton Street. My father always had to take his jacket off, when he went into his office, to protect it from the dust and shavings which covered the floor. The whine of circular saws penetrated his room continuously; everywhere smelled of creosote and boiling glue. My father took his afternoon tea brewed up, like the men, on a primus stove; and he used the same chipped enamel mugs. But he was the boss, and his time was his own. He valued that. Not having to take orders.

Every afternoon he collected me from the school bench where I sat confidently waiting and looking down the hill for the snub V-nosed Armstrong Siddeley as it came up behind the cycles and smaller cars. The car seemed to have some of the qualities of the man; it was all leather and wood. Heavy and reliable and reassuringly durable.

The only time he ever failed to turn up I was so stunned with shock it took me over an hour to believe it. Even the most rigorous teachers had begun to leave the school by then; but in any case, I would have been reluctant to approach them. I had begun to cry, and my face was smeared with tears.

I had a few coppers, not quite enough to pay for the two trams which would take me across town to Groby Road where we lived then. But the conductors saw my blotchy face and let me ride free. I remember when I reached home, seeing with incredulity that his car was already outside the house. I could hardly believe it. Was it possible for him simply to have forgotten me? There was an ambulance outside the house; and as I watched a stretcher was brought from our house into the street. My father waved to me to stay where I was, without explanations. I crossed the road just the same, but he hardly seemed aware of me. He said: 'Your mother. I'll have to go with her to the hospital. One of your cousins will come round to look after you.'

And he didn't even say he was sorry I'd been left at the school.

When one of my favourite cousins came round and found me in tears, he thought I was weeping over my mother's haemorrhage; he could never have guessed it was really for the discovery that my father didn't put me first all the time. It shames me now, that I felt so little fear for my mother. Perhaps I guessed her inner strength; perhaps I needed to feel her invulnerable.

It must have been somewhere around then that I began to dream, obsessionally, that my father was being attacked by a man with a bread knife. As I watched helplessly the strength went out of my father's huge arm; I always woke, screaming, before his assailant brought down the knife on his head. I suppose it was a dream that acknowledged my fear that he was more vulnerable in the world than I wished. There are other readings. It probably sealed my own dependence on every weak man I have loved since.

As long as there was any money about, my father loved grand hotels: the swank and the magnificence of them, the flunkeys whose arrogance he had to face down; the whole excess and splendour of the tables and the trolleys. 'Just like the films, isn't it?' he often observed wonderingly, which was near as he came to analysing the pleasure he felt. Too easy, to say that this was any compensation for his slum childhood. For one thing, none of his family ever thought of themselves as underprivileged. It was much more a question of coming into his birthright, the good fortune for which he had been intended.

His ostentation was always entirely innocent. When he became President of the local Leicester synagogue no one had ever enjoyed wearing a top hat more. And he disarmed my natural greed by being too ready to supply my whims. If I hesitated between two toys, he suggested both; later, he did the same for dresses. My mother's lips might tighten at the

extravagance, but he overrode both of us. And I didn't love him for his gifts, but for the *style* of the giving. It wasn't what my mother called 'cupboard love', as she scornfully characterised those who loved where their interest lay.

For all his extravagance, my father never went bankrupt, though an unexpected disaster in the mid-fifties meant he had to sell up and start over again. As far as I can piece it together, his factory in Clinton Street was still profitable when the lease came up for renewal; but the landlord, perhaps seeing as much, demanded £5000 under the usual dilapidations clause. My father was outraged by the absurdity of the claim. He saw it as *chutzpah*, and refused to consider paying.

Fatally, he read the inconvenience as a sign, an opportunity, a signal to buy land in the newly developing factory area near Oadby and to have a fine modern factory instead of the rat-infested slum he'd accepted most of his working life.

163

It wasn't, of course, any time for expansion. Setting aside the general economic situation (from which I remember clearly I felt quite immune) people had already begun to prefer plastic clothes pegs to those made of wood. And then, any other considerations apart, the months my father spent first poring over new plans, and then excitedly watching them turn into concrete and glass, he wasn't trading at all.

The real blow came when the architect's bill was finally presented, and wildly exceeded his most pessimistic estimate.

I can still hear him receiving the news by the phone, and then going back to sit and look into the coal fire.

'I don't know if I'm solvent,' he said. I can remember asking him: 'Does that mean we haven't any money at all?' And my mother trying to protect him from me. But he growled: 'What do you think all this is?'

And his gesture took in the house and the furniture. I tried to reassure him that none of it mattered to me.

But I saw it mattered to him. Remembered he had put the floors down with his own hands; inlaid corner cupboards with fine cabinet-making joints. Everywhere was solid oak; the work of his hands.

He minded; but he didn't look finished to me. He had a natural resilience, which I only saw falter once, years later, when my mother developed cancer.

Now they are both dead, I understand the nature of his dependence on her quiet intelligence. Then, I still heard strength and protection in his voice, even as he told the news over the phone.

He was sombre, collecting me from the station, repeating over and over again the necessity of keeping up a brave face. I remember her thin shoulders and frail wrists, her bravery, the sweetness of her smile and the readiness in her to face whatever came.

Alone in the house, once my mother had been taken to the hospital my father's smiling strength disintegrated. He muttered again and again in disbelief: why should it come to her? She was so gentle and kind. Why to her? And, to my horror, he cried.

I had never seen him cry; I had never seen any man cry. Men don't cry easily in England. I saw; and I was afraid.

By the day of the operation he was unrecognisable in his grief. Brothers and cousins gathered; and called a doctor, who injected some strong sedative which was supposed to hold until after my mother came up from the theatre. It did not stop him moaning in his sleep.

And who was I weeping for, as I waited? Was it for my brave, sweet-faced mother facing death, or for him unable to bear the thought of her loss? Or for myself, with my legendary hero broken down altogether?

Or perhaps the sense that, after all, I lacked the wish to replace my mother.

In fact, she lived a further thirty years, and by the time I was married, with three children, what I came to fear most, I suppose, was turning *into* her; to be servant and silent support, and have all my children's love turned elsewhere.

When my mother died, my father came to live with our family and the threat of becoming my mother became palpable in a new form. It was what he expected. The resentment he felt at not being the emotional centre of the household made him unexpectedly bitter.

My children found him difficult. He dominated the place uncomfortably; settled himself in the kitchen, which was the biggest room, and the nerve centre of the house; and from there gibed at them.

'What, do you really think you're going to make a living on that *pipka*?' he would jeer at one son (now indeed a musician). So we quarrelled furiously at least once a day. I see now how alike we were, and are; then I couldn't believe in his spite. And yet, in many ways he was still his kind old self. If he went out, he always came back with presents. Even if he drove off in a huff in his car to Bournemouth, he would repent on the way, usually at the very moment my own fury had turned to anxiety, and would telephone so as not to worry me.

He tried to help me, to get my sons to do housework at my side, sadly recalling my mother's spotless house, and generating hostility he couldn't understand.

When he had a chest cold he found my behaviour callous and ugly; and his voice took on the querulous tones of a child who expects better treatment. 'Eggs,' he would say, 'I'll turn into a chicken if I have any more eggs.' He expected sitting with; bellows of healthy fury followed me round the house as I tried to give my own family a bit of cheerfulness. In his eyes, I must have seemed pitiless.

His main efforts to enter the household had a certain doomed pathos. For instance, he decided to learn to cook. Particularly Yiddisher dishes, like bread pudding, which reminded him not only of his married home, but also his own childhood. He wasn't a man for recipe books but it turned out reasonably well. The taste of cinnamon and sugar plunged me back into my childhood; and I'm hurt now to think of him, face lined with the thyroid deficiency that dried his skin, and a tea towel tucked round his waist, turning up a white tired face to me and looking for approval.

But I couldn't ever give him the sense of praise and gratitude he expected. I was drawing guide lines for my own survival. 'What *do* you do for me? Cook my meals? I could get as much from a boarding house.'

He wanted someone gentle and tireless as my mother. I knew that, and it prevented me responding warmly to his gestures of love. After our bitterest quarrels, he would open his arms. 'Doesn't matter. You still love me, don't you?' Some needle of ice in my heart prevented me agreeing. He died at seventy-four and very suddenly.

He hated Cambridge as a town from the time he first came to live with us. He could find no way to make friends in it. An enterprising man, he took up a surprising and altogether new set of hobbies. Painting, for instance. He bought an easel, and good paints, and set out to paint the willow trees hanging over the river near our house on Jesus Green. To his irritation, he couldn't make them look upright.

So I took him along to the Fitzwilliam Museum. He had been in art galleries before, abroad, without much interest; now he went round narrowly, looking at Corot and Constable, and marvelling at the miracle of reflections in water. 'It's more *difficult* than I thought,' he grumbled. And characteristically set out to find where he could be taught the skill. One day, when I was in London, I rang up to say I wouldn't be home till seven. And he sounded disappointed.

'Not before *then*? I've got something to show you.'

'Well, I guess I'll get the next train,' I agreed.

But he had had his heart attack before I arrived home. He had finished a picture that pleased him, and was just framing it as a present when he suddenly complained of a grinding pain in his teeth. Then he crawled up to the radiator. My son Martin saw his blue lips, and his shivering and went upstairs to call a doctor.

'Where's my daughter when I need her? Gallivanting about as usual,' he moaned.

When I came in, my own heart went cold looking at him. The ambulance had to be hurried; and when he arrived at Addenbrooke's, and they had attached him to a heart bleeper, it took a long time to find his notes.

'Can't you make them get a move on?' he asked me, 'I'm cold!'

He seemed uncharacteristically unemotional. He'd been ill once before, with a raging temperature in that last year, and then when he saw me he'd called me pet names – 'Elainela', 'Elainski', all the old Yiddish/Russian diminuitives. Now – and it was rare, and oddly hurtful – he called me 'Elaine'. Quite coolly.

'Is it all ending?' he asked.

I wish I had told him the truth I feared. Instead, I spoke more brusquely than intended.

'Nonsense. You're as tough as old boots.'

Of course, I wasn't sure. And a few moments later, spelling out his

166

name for a nurse ('Isidore Cooklin,' he insisted, 'and get the spelling right!'), I even wondered if I wasn't mistaken.

So I never said a true goodbye. Not as I would have wanted. That night he suffered a massive second attack, and that was that.

For a year, I grieved over every unkind word I had spoken. The tears rose whenever I thought of his goodness.

It has been my experience that daughters who felt less love for their fathers, and some who particularly disliked them, are more independent than I am; detach themselves more easily from damaging relationships; and have less need to see the men at their side as strong protectors. I have been left instinctively monogamous, in an age where such a condition is rare and may become comic.

I have had few dealings with psychotherapy, but even without that exploration of my psyche I can see that, in imitating my father, my virtues were notably those that fitted a male stereotype better than the female stereotype current in my early married years. Things have changed since the fifties. I was resourceful, enterprising, busy and potentially entrepreneurial. But I could not cope with getting dishes washed before they were used, let alone deal with shitty nappies in an age before automatic washing machines. I would have made somebody a good husband. But all my best friends were men in those days.

If nowadays so many of my closest friends are women it may indeed be a sign of that enforced growing up which followed on my father's death.

Father, forgive me, lying under the earth, unforgotten still. Forgive me my cowardice. The way my life has bent since you died. Forgive me living without your fierce courage. I have been cowed, I have been downed, I have let small shocks better me; as you never did.

And if I still feel under your protection it is not from some imagined heaven (you lie next to my mother in the cemetery in Groby Road, Leicester) but as a voice in my own heart pointing up my anxieties in contemptuous Yiddish phrases. The *why worry?* of my childhood which would serve me so well now.

And my prayer?

It is to make me bolder.

Dad

Your old hat hurts me, and those black
   fat raisins you liked to press into
my palm from your soft heavy hand:
   I see you staggering back up the path
with sacks of potatoes from some local farm,
   fresh eggs, flowers. Every day I grieve

for your great heart broken and you gone.
   You loved to watch the trees. This year
you did not see their Spring.
   The sky was freezing over the fen
as on that somewhere secretly appointed day
   you beached: cold, white-faced, shivering.

What happened, old bull, my loyal
   hoarse-voiced warrior? The hammer
blow that stopped you in your track
   and brought you to a hospital monitor
could not destroy your courage
   to the end you were
uncowed and unconcerned with pleasing anyone.

I think of you now as once again safely
   at my mother's side, the earth as
chosen as a bed, and feel most sorrow for
   all that was gentle in
my childhood buried there
   already forfeit, now forever lost.

Elaine Feinstein

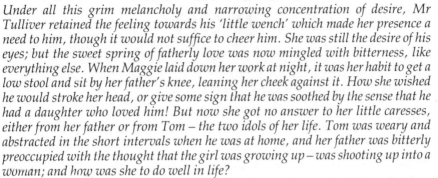

Under all this grim melancholy and narrowing concentration of desire, Mr Tulliver retained the feeling towards his 'little wench' which made her presence a need to him, though it would not suffice to cheer him. She was still the desire of his eyes; but the sweet spring of fatherly love was now mingled with bitterness, like everything else. When Maggie laid down her work at night, it was her habit to get a low stool and sit by her father's knee, leaning her cheek against it. How she wished he would stroke her head, or give some sign that he was soothed by the sense that he had a daughter who loved him! But now she got no answer to her little caresses, either from her father or from Tom – the two idols of her life. Tom was weary and abstracted in the short intervals when he was at home, and her father was bitterly preoccupied with the thought that the girl was growing up – was shooting up into a woman; and how was she to do well in life?

George Eliot, *The Mill on the Floss*

The infantile fixation in the fathers then was, it is clear, a strong force, and all the stronger because it was a concealed force. But the fathers were met, as the nineteenth century drew on, by a force which had become so strong in its turn that it is much to be hoped that the psychologists will find some name for it. The old names as we have seen are futile and false. 'Feminism', we have had to destroy. 'The emancipation of women' is equally inexpressive and corrupt. To say that the daughters were inspired prematurely by the principles of anti-Fascism is merely to repeat the fashionable and hideous jargon of the moment. To call them champions of intellectual liberty and culture is to cloud the air with the dust of lecture halls and the damp dowdiness of public meetings. Moreover, none of these tags and labels express the real emotions that inspired the daughters' opposition to the infantile fixation of the fathers, because, as biography shows, that force had behind it many different emotions, and many that were contradictory. Tears were behind it, of course – tears, bitter tears: the tears of those whose desire for knowledge was frustrated.

Virginia Woolf, *Three Guineas*

ADRIENNE RICH

Split at the Root

Through working on the essay included here – and through the readings, conversations, reflections, dreams, memories and angers that have gone into it – I can now write, at the age of fifty-four, without ambivalence or strangeness, *I am a Jewish lesbian feminist, and for me this means an expanding politics*. What these words mean to me is a path of entrance, a map of connections. I am tired of parallel lines that never meet.

I live in northwestern New England with the writer Michelle Cliff, and together we edit the lesbian/feminist journal, *Sinister Wisdom*. I have published twelve books of poems and two of prose. *Of Woman Born: Motherhood As Experience and Institution*, and *On Lies, Secrets and Silence*; both are published in England by Virago.

For about fifteen minutes I have been sitting chin in hand in front of the typewriter, staring out at the snow. Trying to be honest with myself, trying to figure out why writing this seems to me so dangerous an act, filled with fear and shame, and why it seems so necessary. It comes to me that I have to claim my father, for I have my Jewishness from him and not from my gentile mother; and I have to break *his* silence, *his* taboos; in order to claim him I have in a sense to expose him.

And then I have to face the sources and the flickering presence of my own ambivalence as a Jew; the daily, mundane anti-Semitisms of my entire life.

These are stories I have never tried to tell before. And yet I've been on the track of this longer than I think.

In a long poem written in 1960, when I was thirty-one years old, I described myself as 'Split at the root, neither Gentile nor Jew, Yankee nor

Rebel.'* I was still trying to have it both ways: to be neither/nor, trying to live (with my Jewish husband and three children more Jewish in ancestry than I) in the predominantly gentile Yankee academic world of Cambridge, Massachusetts.

But this begins, for me, in Baltimore, where I was born in a hospital in the Black ghetto, whose lobby contained an immense, white marble statue of Christ.

My father was then a young teacher and researcher in the Department of Pathology at the Johns Hopkins Medical School, one of the very few Jews to attend or teach at that institution. He was from Birmingham, Alabama; his father, Samuel, was an immigrant from Austria-Hungary and his mother, Hattie Rice, a Sephardic Jew from Vicksburg, Mississippi. My grandfather had had a shoe store in Birmingham, which did well enough to allow him to retire comfortably, and to leave my grandmother, on his death, a small income. The only souvenirs of my grandfather, Samuel Rich, were his ivory flute, which lay on our living-room mantel and was not to be played with; his thin gold pocket-watch, which my father wore; and his Hebrew prayerbook, which I discovered among my father's books in the course of reading my way through his library. In this prayer book there was a newspaper clipping about my grandparents' wedding, which took place in a synagogue.

My father, Arnold, was sent in adolescence to a military school in the Tennessee mountains, a place for training white Southern Christian gentlemen. I suspect that there were few if any other Jewish boys at Colonel Bingham's. Or at 'Mr Jefferson's university', in Charlottesville, where he studied as an undergraduate. With whatever conscious forethought, Samuel and Hattie sent their son into the dominant Southern WASP culture, to become an 'exception', to enter the professional class. Never, in describing these experiences, did he ever speak of having suffered – from loneliness, cultural alienation, or outsiderhood. I never heard him use the word 'anti-Semitism'.

It was only in college, when I read a poem by Karl Shapiro beginning: 'To hate the Negro and avoid the Jew/is the curriculum' that it flashed on me that there was an untold side to my father's story of his student years. He looked recognisably Jewish, was short and slender in build with dark wiry hair and deep-set eyes, high forehead and curved nose.

My mother is a gentile. In Jewish law I cannot count myself a Jew. If it is

* 'Readings of History' in Adrienne Rich, *Snapshots of a Daughter in Law*, W. W. Norton, New York, 1967, pp. 36–40.

true that 'We think back through our mothers if we are women' (Virginia Woolf) – and I myself have affirmed this – then even according to lesbian theory, I cannot (or need not?) count myself a Jew.

The white Southern Protestant woman, the gentile, has always been there for me to peel back into. That's a whole piece of history in itself, for my gentile grandmother and my mother were also frustrated artists and intellectuals, a lost writer and a lost composer between them. Readers and annotators of books, note-takers, my mother a good pianist still, in their eighties. But there was also the obsession with ancestry, with 'background', the Southern talk of family, not as people you would necessarily know and depend on, but as heritage, the guarantee of 'good breeding'. There was the inveterate romantic heterosexual fantasy, the mother telling the daughter how to attract men (my mother often used the word 'fascinate'); the assumption that relations between the sexes could only be romantic, that it was in the woman's interest to cultivate 'mystery', conceal her actual feelings. Survival tactics, of a kind, I think today, knowing what I know about the white woman's sexual role in the Southern racist scenario. Heterosexuality as protection, but also drawing white women deeper into collusion with white men.

It would be easy to push away and deny the gentile in me: that white Southern woman, that social Christian. At different times in my life, I suppose, I have wanted to push away one or the other burden of inheritance, to say merely, *I am a woman; I am a lesbian*. If I call myself a Jewish lesbian do I thereby try to shed some of my Southern gentile guilt, my white woman's culpability? If I call myself only through my mother, is it because I pass more easily through a world where being a lesbian often seems like outsiderhood enough?

According to Nazi logic, my two Jewish grandparents would have made me a *Mischling, first-degree*: non-exempt from the Final Solution.

The social world in which I grew up was Christian virtually without needing to say so; Christian imagery, music, language, symbols, assumptions everywhere. It was also a genteel, white middle-class world in which 'common' was a term of deep opprobrium. 'Common' white people might speak of 'niggers'; *we* were taught never to use that word; *we* said 'Negroes' (even as we accepted segregation, the eating taboo, the assumption that Black people were simply of a separate species). Our language was more polite, distinguishing us from the 'rednecks', or the lynch mob mentality. So charged with negative meaning was even the word 'Negro' that as children we were taught never to use it in front of Black people. We were taught that any mention of skin colour in the

presence of coloured people was treacherous forbidden ground. In a parallel way, the word 'Jew' was not used by polite gentiles. I sometimes heard my best friend's father, a Presbyterian minister, allude to 'the Hebrew people', or 'people of the Jewish faith'. The world of acceptable folk was white, gentile (Christian, really) and had 'ideals' (which coloured people, white 'common' people, were not supposed to have). 'Ideals' and 'manners' included not hurting someone's feelings by calling her or him a Negro or a Jew – naming the hated identity. This is the mental framework of the 1930s and 1940s in which I was raised.

(Writing this I feel, dimly, like the betrayer: of my father, who did not speak the word; of my mother, who must have trained me in the messages; of my caste and class; of my whiteness itself.)

Two memories: I am in a play reading at school, of *The Merchant of Venice*. Whatever Jewish law says, I am quite sure I was *seen* as Jewish (with a reassuringly gentile mother) in that double vision that bigotry allows. I am the only Jewish girl in the class and I am playing Portia. As always, I read my part aloud for my father the night before, and he tells me to convey, with my voice, more scorn and contempt with the word 'Jew': 'Therefore, Jew . . .' I have to say the word out, and say it loudly. I was encouraged to pretend to be a non-Jewish child acting a non-Jewish character who has to speak the word 'Jew' emphatically. Such a child would not have had trouble with the part. But *I* must have had trouble with the part, if only because the word itself was really taboo. I can see that there was a kind of terrible, bitter bravado about my father's way of handling this. And who would not dissociate from Shylock in order to identify with Portia? As a Jewish child who was also a female I loved Portia – and, like every other Shakespearean heroine, she proved a treacherous role model.

A year or so later I am in another play, *The School for Scandal*, in which a notorious spendthrift is described as having 'many excellent friends . . . among the Jews'. In neither case was anything explained, either to me or to the class at large about this scorn for Jews and the disgust surrounding Jews and money. Money, when Jews wanted it, had it, or lent it to others, seemed to take on a peculiar nastiness, and Jews and money had some peculiar and unspeakable relation.

At this same school – in which we had Christian hymns and prayers, and read aloud through the Bible morning after morning – I gained the impression that Jews were in the Bible and mentioned in English literature, had been persecuted centuries ago by the wicked Inquisition, but that they seemed not to exist in everyday life. These were the 1940s and we were told a great deal about the Battle of Britain, the noble French Resistance fighters, the brave, starving Dutch – but I did not learn of the resistance of the Warsaw Ghetto until I left home.

I was sent to the Episcopal church, baptised and confirmed, and attended it for about five years, though without belief. That religion seemed to have little to do with belief or commitment; it was liturgy that mattered, not moral passion. Neither of my parents ever entered that church, and my father would not enter *any* church for any reason – wedding or funeral. Nor did I enter a synagogue until I left Baltimore. When I came home from church, for a while, my father insisted on reading aloud to me from Thomas Paine's *The Age of Reason* – a diatribe against institutional religion. Thus, he explained, I would have a balanced view of these things, a choice. He – they – did not give me the choice to be a Jew. My mother explained to me when I was filling out forms for college that if any question was asked about 'religion' I should put down 'Episcopalian' rather than 'none' – to seem to have no religion was, she implied, dangerous.

But it was white social Christianity, rather than any particular Christian sect, that the world was founded on. The very word 'Christian' was used as a synonym for virtuous, just, peace-loving, generous, etc. etc.* The norm was Christian: 'religion: none' was indeed not acceptable. Anti-Semitism was so intrinsic as not to have a name. I don't recall exactly being taught that the Jews killed Jesus; 'Christ-killer' seems too strong a term for the bland Episcopal vocabulary; but certainly we got the impression that the Jews had been caught out in a terrible mistake, failing to recognise the true Messiah, and were thereby less advanced in moral and spiritual sensibility. The Jews had actually allowed *moneylenders in the Temple* (again, the unexplained obsession with Jews and money). They were of the past, archaic, primitive as older (and darker) cultures are supposed to be primitive: Christianity was lightness, fairness, peace on earth, and combined the feminine appeal of 'the meek shall inherit the earth' with the masculine stride of 'Onward, Christian Soldiers'.

Some time in 1946, while still in high school, I read in the newspaper that a theatre in Baltimore was showing films of the Allied liberation of the Nazi concentration camps. Alone, I went downtown after school one after-noon and watched the stark, blurry but unmistakable newsreels. When I try to go back and touch the pulse of that girl of sixteen, growing up in many ways so precocious and so ignorant, I am overwhelmed by a memory of despair, a sense of inevitability, more enveloping than any I had ever known. Anne Frank's diary and many other personal narratives of the Holocaust were still unknown or unwritten. But it came to me that every one of those piles of corpses, mountains of shoes and clothing, had contained, simply, individuals, who had believed, as I now believed of myself, that they were meant to live out a life of some kind of meaning, that the world possessed some kind of sense and order; yet *this* had happened to them. And I, who believed my life was intended to be so interesting and meaningful, was connected to those dead by something – not just mortality but a taboo name, a hated identity. Or was I – did I really have to be? Writing this now, I feel belated rage, that I was so impover-ished by the family and social worlds I lived in, that I had to try to figure out by myself what this did indeed mean for me. That I have never been taught about resistance, only about passing. That I had no language for anti-Semitism itself.

*In a similar way the phrase 'that's white of you' implied that you were behaving with the superior decency and morality expected of white, but not of Black people.

When I went home and told my parents where I had been, they were not pleased. I felt accused of being morbidly curious, not healthy, sniffing around death for the thrill of it. And since, at sixteen, I was often not sure of the sources of my feelings or of my motives for doing what I did, I probably accused myself as well. One thing was clear: there was nobody in my world with whom I could discuss those films. Probably at the same time I was reading accounts of the camps in magazines and newspapers; what I remember was the films, and having questions that I could not even phrase: such as, are those men and women 'them' or 'us'?

To be able to ask even the child's astonished question *Why do they hate us so?* means knowing how to say 'we'. The guilt of not knowing, the guilt of perhaps having betrayed my parents, or even those victims, those survivors, through mere curiosity – these also froze in me for years the impulse to find out more about the Holocaust.

1947: I left Baltimore to go to college in Cambridge, Massachusetts, left (I thought) the backward, enervating South for the intellectual, vital North. New England also had for me some vibration of higher moral rectitude, of moral passion even, with its seventeenth-century Puritan inner security, its Abolitionist righteousness, Colonel Shaw and his Black Civil War regiment depicted in granite on Boston Common, its nineteenth-century literary 'flowering'. At the same time, I found myself, at Radcliffe, among Jewish women. I described my background – for the first time to strangers – and they took me on, some with amusement at my illiteracy, some arguing that I could never marry into a strict Jewish family, some convinced I didn't 'look Jewish', others that I did. For these young Jewish women, students in the late 1940s, it was acceptable, perhaps even necessary, to strive to look as gentile as possible, but they stuck proudly to being Jewish; expected to marry a Jew, have children, keep the holidays, carry on the culture.

I felt I was testing a forbidden current, that there was danger in these revelations, I bought a reproduction of a Chagall portrait of a rabbi in striped prayer shawl and hung it on the wall of my room. I was admittedly young and trying to educate myself, but I was also doing something that *is* dangerous: I was flirting with identity.

One day that year I was in a small shop where I had bought a dress with a too-long skirt. The shop employed a seamstress who did alterations, and she came in to pin up the skirt on me. I am sure that she was a recent immigrant, a survivor. I remember a short, dark woman wearing heavy glasses, with an accent so foreign I could not understand her words.

Something about her presence was very powerful and disturbing to me. After marking and pinning up the skirt she sat back on her knees, looked up at me, and asked in a hurried whisper: 'You Jewish?' Eighteen years of training in assimilation sprang into the reflex by which I shook my head, rejecting her, and muttered, 'No.'

What was I actually saying 'no' to? She was poor, older, struggling with a foreign tongue, anxious; she had escaped the death that had been intended for her, but I had no imagination of her possible courage and foresight, her resistance; I did not see in her a heroine who had perhaps saved many lives including her own. I saw the frightened immigrant, the seamstress hemming the skirts of college girls, the wandering Jew. But I was an American college girl, having her skirt hemmed. And I was frightened myself, I think, because she had recognised me ('It takes one to know one,' my friend Edie at Radcliffe had said) even if I refused to recognise myself or her; even if her recognition was sharpened by loneliness, or the need to feel safe with me.

But why should she have felt safe with me? I myself was living in a false sense of safety.

There are betrayals in my life that I have known at the very moment were betrayals: this was one of them. There are other betrayals committed so repeatedly, so mundanely, that they leave no memory trace behind: only a growing residue of misery, of dull, accreted self-hatred. Often these take the form not of words but of silence. Silence before the joke at which everyone is laughing: the anti-woman joke, the racist joke, the anti-Semitic joke. Silence and then amnesia. Blocking it out when the oppressor's language starts coming from the lips of one we admire, whose courage and eloquence have touched us: *She didn't really mean that: he didn't really say that.* But the accretions build up out of sight, like scale inside a kettle.

1948: I come home from my freshman year at college flaming with new insights, new information. I am the daughter who has gone out into the world, to the pinnacle of intellectual prestige, Harvard, fulfilling my father's hopes for me, but also exposed to dangerous influences. I have already been reproved for attending a rally for Henry Wallace and the Progressive Party. I challenge my father: 'Why haven't you told me that I am Jewish? Why do you never talk about being a Jew?' He answers measuredly, 'You know that I have never denied that I am a Jew. But it's not important to me. I am a scientist, a Deist. I have no use for organised religion. I choose to live in a world of many kinds of people. There are Jews I admire and others whom I despise. I am a person, not simply a Jew.' The words are as I remember them, not perhaps exactly as spoken.

177

But that was the message. And it contained enough truth – as all denial drugs itself on partial truth – so that it remained for the time being unanswerable, even though it left me high and dry, split at the root, gasping for clarity, for air.

At that time Arnold Rich was living in suspension, waiting to be appointed to the professorship of pathology at Johns Hopkins. The appointment was delayed for years, no Jew ever having held a professorial chair in that medical school. And he wanted it badly. It must have been a very bitter time for him, since he had believed so greatly in the redeeming power of excellence, of being the most brilliant, inspired man for the job. With enough excellence, you could presumably make it stop mattering that you were Jewish; you could become the *only* Jew in the gentile world, a Jew so 'civilised,' so far from 'common,' so attractively combining Southern gentility with European cultural values that no one would ever confuse you with the raw, 'pushy' Jews of New York, the 'loud, hysterical' refugees from Eastern Europe, the 'overdressed' Jews of the urban South.

We – my sister, mother and I – were constantly urged to speak quietly in public, to dress without ostentation, to repress all vividness or spontaneity, to assimilate with a world which might see us as too flamboyant. I suppose that my mother, pure gentile though she was, could be seen as acting 'common' or 'Jewish' if she laughed too loudly or spoke aggressively. My father's mother, who lived with us half the year, was a model of circumspect behaviour, dressed in dark blue or lavender, retiring in company, ladylike to an extreme, wearing no jewellery except a good gold chain, a narrow brooch, a string of pearls. A few times, within the family, I saw her anger flare, felt the passion she was repressing. But when Arnold took us out to a restaurant, or on a trip, the Rich women were always turned down to some WASP level my father believed, surely, would protect us all – maybe also make us unrecognisable to the 'real Jews' who wanted to seize us, drag us back to the *shtetl*, the ghetto, in its many manifestations.

For, yes: that *was* a message – that some Jews would be after you, once they 'knew', to rejoin them, to re-enter a world that was messy, noisy, unpredictable, maybe poor – 'even though,' as my mother once wrote me, criticising my largely Jewish choice of friends in college, 'some of them will be the most brilliant, fascinating people you'll ever meet.' I wonder if that isn't one message of assimilation – of America – that the unlucky or the unachieving want to pull you backward, that to identify with them is to court downward mobility, lose the precious chance of passing, of token existence. There was always, within this sense of Jewish identity, a strong class discrimination. Jews might be 'fascinating' as individuals but came with huge unruly families who 'poured chicken soup over everyone's head' (in the phrase of a white Southern male poet). Anti-Semitism could thus be justified by the bad behaviour of certain Jews; and if you did not effectively deny family and community, there would always be a cousin claiming kinship with you, who was the 'wrong kind' of Jew.

I have always believed his attitude toward other Jews depended on who they were. . . . It was my impression that Jews of this background looked down on Eastern European Jews, including Polish Jews and Russian Jews, who generally were not as well educated. This from a letter written to me recently by a gentile who had worked in my father's department, whom I had asked about anti-Semitism there and in particular regarding my father. This informant also wrote me that it was hard to perceive anti-Semitism in Baltimore because the racism made so much more intense an impression. *I would almost have to think that Blacks went to a different heaven than the whites; because the bodies were kept in a separate morgue, and some white persons did not even want blood transfusions from Black donors.* My father's mind was racist and misogynist, yet as a medical student he noted in his journal that Southern male chivalry stopped at the point of any white man in a streetcar giving his seat to an old, weary, Black woman standing in the aisle. Was this a Jewish insight – an outsider's insight, even though the outsider was striving to be on the inside?

Because what isn't named is often more permeating than what is. I believe that my father's Jewishness profoundly shaped my own identity, and our family existence. They were shaped both by external anti-Semitism and my father's self-hatred, and by his Jewish pride. What Arnold did, I think, was call his Jewish pride something else: achievement, aspiration, genius, idealism. Whatever was unacceptable got left back under the rubric of Jewishness, or the 'wrong kind' of Jews: uneducated, aggressive, loud. The message I got was that we were really superior: nobody else's father had collected so many books, had travelled so far, knew so many languages. Baltimore was a musical city, but for the most part, in the families of my school friends, culture was for women. My father was an amateur musician, read poetry, adored encyclopaedic knowledge. He prowled and pounced over my school papers, insisting I use 'grown-up' sources; he criticised my poems for faulty technique and gave me books on rhyme and metre and form. His investment in my intellect and talent was egotistical, tyrannical, opinionated and terribly wearing. He taught me nevertheless to believe in hard work, to mistrust easy inspiration, to write and rewrite; to feel that I *was* a person of the book, even though a woman; to take ideas seriously. He made me feel, at a very young age, the power of language, and that I could share in it.

The Riches were proud, but we also had to be very careful. Our behaviour had to be more impeccable than other people's. Strangers were not to be trusted, nor even friends; family issues must never go beyond the family; the world was full of potential slanderers, betrayers, *people who could not understand*. Even within the family, I realise that I never in my whole life knew what he was really feeling. Yet he spoke – monologued – with driving intensity. You could grow up in such a house mesmerised by the local electricity, the crucial meanings assumed by the merest things. This used to seem to me a sign that we were all living on some high emotional plane. It was a difficult force-field for a favoured daughter to disengage from.

Easy to call that intensity Jewish; and I have no doubt that passion is one of the qualities required for survival over generations of persecution. But what happens when passion is rent from its original base, when the white gentile world is softly saying: 'Be more like us and you can be almost one of us'? What happens when survival seems to mean closing off one emotional artery after another? His forebears in Europe had been forbidden to travel, or expelled from one country after another, had special taxes levied on them if they left the city walls, had been forced to wear special clothes and badges, restricted to the poorest neighbourhoods. He had wanted to be a 'free spirit', to travel widely, among 'all kinds of people'. Yet in his prime of life he lived in an increasingly withdrawn world, in his house up on a hill in a neighbourhood where Jews were not supposed to be able to buy property, depending almost exclusively on interactions with his wife and daughters to provide emotional connectedness. In his home, he created a private defence system so elaborate that even as he was dying my mother felt unable to talk freely with his colleagues, or others who might have helped her.

I imagine that the loneliness of the 'only', the token, often doesn't feel like loneliness but like a kind of dead echo chamber. Certain things that ought to, don't resonate. Somewhere Beverly Smith writes of women of colour 'inspiring the behaviour' in each other. When there's nobody to 'inspire the behaviour,' act out of the culture, there is an atrophy, a dwindling, which is partly invisible.

I was married in 1953, in the Hillel House at Harvard, under a portrait of Albert Einstein. My parents refused to come. I was marrying a Jew of the 'wrong kind' from an Orthodox Eastern European background. Brooklyn born, he had gone to Harvard, changed his name, was both indissolubly

180

connected to his childhood world, and terribly ambivalent about it. My father saw this marriage as my having fallen prey to the Jewish family, Eastern European division.

Like many women I knew in the fifties, living under a then-unquestioned heterosexual imperative, I married in part because I knew no better way to disconnect from my first family. I married a 'real Jew' who was himself almost equally divided between a troubled yet ingrained Jewish identity, and the pull toward Yankee approval, assimilation. But at least he was not adrift as a single token in a gentile world. We lived in a world where there was much intermarriage, where a certain 'Jewish flavour' was accepted within the dominant gentile culture. People talked glibly of 'Jewish self-hatred' but anti-Semitism was rarely identified. It was as if you could have it both ways, identity and assimilation, without having to think about it very much.

I was moved and gratefully amazed by the affection and kindliness my husband's parents showed me, the half-*shiksa*. I longed to embrace that family, that new and mysterious Jewish world. It was never a question of conversation – my husband had long since ceased being observant – but of a burning desire to do well, please these new parents, heal the split consciousness in which I had been raised, and, of course, to belong. In the big sunny apartment on Eastern Parkway, the table would be spread on Saturday afternoons with a white or embroidered cloth and plates of coffee cake, sponge cake, *mohn* cake, cookies, for a family gathering where everyone ate and drank – coffee, milk, cake – and later the talk eddied among the women still around the table or in the kitchen, while the men ended up in the living room watching the ball game. I had never known this kind of family, in which mock insults were cheerfully exchanged, secrets whispered in corners among two or three, children and grand-children boasted about, and the new daughter-in-law openly inspected. I was profoundly attracted by all this, including the punctilious observance of *kashruth*, the symbolism lurking behind daily kitchen tasks. I saw it all as quintessentially and authentically Jewish, and thus I objectified both the people and the culture. My unexamined anti-Semitism allowed me to do this. But also, I had not yet recognised that as a woman I stood in a particular and equally unexamined relationship to the Jewish family and to Jewish culture.

There were several years during which I did not see, and barely communicated with my parents. At the same time, my father's personality haunted my life. Such had been the force of his will in our household that for a long time I felt I would have to pay in some terrible way for having disobeyed him. When finally we were reconciled, and my husband and I and our children began to have some minimal formal contact with my parents, the obsessional power of Arnold's voice or handwriting had given way to a dull sense of useless anger and pain. I wanted him to cherish and approve of me not as he had when I was a child, but as the woman I was, who had her own mind and had made her own choices. This, I finally realised, was not to be; Arnold demanded absolute loyalty, absolute submission to his will. In my separation from him, in my realisation at what a price that once intoxicating approval had been bought, I was learning in concrete ways a great deal about patriarchy, in particular how the 'special' woman, the favoured daughter, is controlled and rewarded.

Arnold Rich died in 1968 after a long deteriorating illness; his mind had gone and he had been losing his sight for years. It was a year of intensifying political awareness for me, the Martin Luther King and Robert Kennedy assassinations, the Columbia University strike. But it was not that these events and the meetings and demonstrations that surrounded them pre-empted the time of mourning for my father; I had been mourning a long time for an early, primary and intense relationship, by no means always benign, but in which I had been ceaselessly made to feel that what I did with my life, the choices I made, the attitudes I held, were of the utmost consequence.

Sometimes in my thirties, on visits to Brooklyn, I sat on Eastern Parkway, a baby-stroller at my feet: one of many rows of young Jewish women on benches with children in that neighbourhood. I used to see the Lubavitcher Hassidim – then beginning to move into the Crown Heights neighbourhood – walking out on *shabbas*, the women in their *sheitels* a little behind the men. My father-in-law pointed them out as rather exotic – too old-country, perhaps, too unassimilated even for his devout sense of Jewish identity. It took many years for me to understand – partly because I understood so little about class in America – how in my own family, and in the very different family of my in-laws, there were degrees and hierarchies of assimilation which looked askance upon each other – and also geographic lines of difference, as between Southern Jews and New York Jews, whose manners and customs varied along class as well as regional lines.

I had three sons before I was thirty, and during those years I often felt that to be a Jewish woman, a Jewish mother, was to be perceived in the Jewish family as an entirely physical being, a producer and nourisher of children. The experience of motherhood was eventually to radicalise me; but before that I was encountering the institution of motherhood most directly in a Jewish cultural version; and I felt rebellious, moody, defensive, unable to sort out what was Jewish from what was simply motherhood, or female destiny.

My children were taken irregularly to Seders, to Bar Mitzvahs, and to special services in their grandfather's temple. Their father lit Hanukkah candles while I stood by, having relearned each year the English meaning of the Hebrew blessing. We all celebrated a secular, liberal Christmas. I read aloud from books about Esther and the Maccabees and Moses, and also from books about Norse goblins and Chinese grandmothers and Celtic dragon slayers. Their father told stories of his boyhood in Brooklyn, his grandmother in the Bronx who had to be visited on the subway every week, of misdeeds in Hebrew school, of being a bright Jewish kid at Boys' High. In the permissive liberalism of academic Cambridge, you could raise your children to be vaguely or distinctly Jewish as you would, but Christian myth and calendar organised the year. My sons grew up knowing far more about the existence and concrete meaning of Jewish culture than I had. But I don't recall sitting down with them and telling them that millions of people like themselves, many of them children, had been rounded up and murdered in Europe in their parents' lifetime. Nor was I able to tell them that they came in part out of the rich, thousand-year-old, Ashkenazic culture of Eastern Europe, which the Holocaust destroyed; or that they came from a people whose secular tradition had included a hatred of oppression and a willingness to fight for justice – an anti-racist, a socialist and even sometimes a feminist vision. I could not tell them these things because they were still too blurred in outline in my own mind.

The emergence of the Civil Rights movement in the sixties I remember as lifting me out of a sense of personal frustration and hopelessness. Reading James Baldwin's early essays, in the fifties, had stirred me with a sense that apparently 'given' situations like racism could be analysed and described and that this could lead to action, to change. Racism had been so utter and implicit a fact of my childhood and adolescence, had felt so central among the silences, negations, cruelties, fears, superstitions of my early life, that somewhere among my feelings must have been the hope that if Black people could become free, of the immense political and social burdens they were forced to bear, I too could become free, of all the ghosts and shadows of my childhood, named and unnamed. When 'the Movement' began it felt extremely personal to me. And it was often Jews who spoke up for the justice of the cause, Jewish civil rights lawyers who were travelling South; it was two young Jews who were found murdered with a young Black man in Mississippi. Schwerner, Goodman, Chaney.

Moving to New York in the mid-sixties meant almost immediately being plunged into the debate over community control of public schools, in which Black and Jewish teachers and parents were often an opposite sides of extremely militant barricades. It was easy as a white liberal to deplore and condemn the racism of middle-class Jewish parents or angry Jewish schoolteachers, many of them older women; to displace our own racism onto them; or to feel it as too painful to think about. The struggle for Black civil rights had such clarity about it for me: I knew that segregation was wrong, that unequal opportunity was wrong, I knew that segregation in particular was more than a set of social and legal rules, it meant that even 'decent' white people lived in a network of lies and arrogance and moral collusion. In the world of Jewish assimilationist and liberal politics which I knew best, however, things were far less clear to me, and anti-Semitism went almost unmentioned. It was even possible to view anti-Semitism as a reactionary agenda, a concern of *Commentary* magazine or, later, the Jewish Defense League. Most of the political work I was doing in the late 1960s was on racial issues, in particular as a teacher in the City University during the struggle for Open Admissions. The white colleagues I thought of as allies were, I think, mostly Jewish. Yet it was easy to see other New York Jews, who had climbed out of poverty and exploitation through the public school system and the free city colleges, as now trying to block Black and Puerto Rican students trying to do likewise. I didn't understand then that I was living between two strains of Jewish social identity: the Jew as radical visionary and activist who understands oppression first-hand; and the Jew as part of America's devouring plan in which the persecuted, called to assimilation, learn that the price is to engage in persecution.

By the time I left my marriage, after seventeen years and three children, I had become identified with the women's liberation movement. It was an astonishing time to be a woman of my age. In the 1950s seeking a way to grasp the pain I seemed to be feeling most of the time, to set it in some larger context, I had read all kinds of things, but it was James Baldwin and Simone de Beauvoir who had described the world – though differently – in terms that made the most sense to me. By the end of the sixties there were two political movements, one already meeting severe repression, one just emerging – which addressed those descriptions of the world.
    And there was, of course, a third movement, or a movement-within-a-

movement – the early lesbian manifestos, the new visibility and activism of lesbians everywhere. I had known very early on that the women's movement was not going to be a simple walk across an open field; that it would pull on every fibre of my existence; that it would mean going back and searching the shadows of my consciousness. Reading *The Second Sex* in 1950s isolation as an academic housewife had felt less dangerous than reading 'The Myth of Vaginal Orgasm' or 'Woman-Identified Woman' in a world where I was in constant debate and discussion with women over every aspect of our lives that we could as yet name. De Beauvoir had placed 'The Lesbian' on the margins, and there was little in her book to suggest the power of woman-bonding. But the passion of debating ideas with women was an erotic passion for me, and the risking of self with women that was necessary in order to win some truth out of the lies of the past was also erotic. The suppressed lesbian I had been carrying in me since adolescence began to stretch her limbs and her first full-fledged act was to fall in love with a Jewish woman.

Some time during the early months of that relationship, I dreamed that I was arguing feminist politics with my lover. *Of course*, I said to her in this dream, *if you're going to bring up the Holocaust against me, there's nothing I can do*. If, as I believe, I was both myself and her in this dream, it spoke of the split in my consciousness. I had been, more or less, a Jewish heterosexual woman; but what did it mean to be a Jewish lesbian? What did it mean to feel myself, as I did, both anti-Semite and Jew? And, as a feminist, how was I charting for myself the oppressions within oppression?

The earliest feminist papers on Jewish identity that I read were critiques of the patriarchal and misogynist elements in Judaism, or of the caricaturing of a Jewish women in literature by Jewish men. I was soon after in correspondence with a former student who had emigrated to Israel, was a passionate feminist, and wrote me at length of the legal and social constraints on women there, the stirrings of contemporary Israeli feminism, and the contradictions she felt in her daily life. With the new politics, activism, literature of a tumultuous feminist movement around me, a movement which claimed universality though it had not yet acknowledged its own racial, class and ethnic perspectives, or its fears of the differences among women – I pushed aside for one last time thinking further about myself as a Jewish woman. I saw Judaism, simply, as yet another strand of patriarchy; if asked to choose I might have said (as my father had said in other language): *I am a woman, not a Jew*. (But, I always added mentally, if Jews had to wear yellow stars again, I too would wear one. As if I would have the choice to wear it or not.)

Sometimes I feel I have seen too long from too many disconnected

185

angles: white, Jewish, anti-Semite, racist, anti-racist, once-married, lesbian, middleclass, feminist, exmatriate Southerner *split at the root*; that I will never bring them whole. I would have liked, in this essay, to bring together the meanings of anti-Semitism and racism as I have experienced them and as I believe they intersect in the world beyond my life. But I'm not able to do this yet. I feel the tension as I think, make notes: *if you really look at the one reality, the other will waver and disperse.* Trying in one week to read Angela Davis and Lucy Dawidowicz.* Trying to hold throughout a feminist, a lesbian, perspective – what does this mean? Nothing has trained me for this. And sometimes I feel inadequate to make any statement as a Jew; I feel the history of denial within me like an injury, a scar – for assimilation has affected *my* perceptions, those early lapses in meaning, those blanks, are with me still. My ignorance can be dangerous to me, and to others.

Yet we can't wait for the undamaged to make our connections for us; we can't wait to speak until we are wholly clear and righteous. There is no purity, and, in our lifetimes, no end to this process.

This essay, then, has no conclusions: it is another beginning, for me. Not just a way of saying, in 1982 right-wing America, *I too will wear the yellow star*. It's a moving into accountability, enlarging the range of accountability. I know that in the rest of my life, the next half-century or so, every aspect of my identity will have to be engaged. The middle-class white girl taught to trade obedience for privilege. The Jewish lesbian raised to be a heterosexual gentile. The woman who first heard oppression named and analysed in the Black civil rights struggle. The woman with three sons, the feminist who hates male violence. The woman limping with a cane, the woman who has stopped bleeding, are also accountable. The poet who knows that beautiful language can lie, that the oppressor's language sometimes sounds beautiful. The woman trying, as part of her resistance, to clean up her act.

*Angela Y. Davis, *Women, Race and Class*, Women's Press,1982; Lucy S. Dawidowicz, *The War Against the Jews 1933–1945* (1975), Bantam Books, 1979.

At last he has performed his function as a father. He has given life, and nourishment to sustain life. Money is not enough to sustain life. The mysterious movements of credit, the magical transformations of goods into money, the symbolic relations of fatherhood collapse. Strains, cracks, fissures appear when fatherhood becomes the transfer of currency. That is not what I want. Children scream violently, struggling, hissing with rage, daughters become avenging demons. What is required is nourishment. Love. We will fight forever, we will never give up. We will spew up your aid, your allowances, your falseness, we will struggle for what we need. We cannot be denied. Our desires are as old and powerful as the earth. They are also your desires. If you deny them you will die. If we cannot be nourished by your love your corpse will nourish us. Do not be afraid. Your agony is enormous, but it is not so great as ours. You should be afraid of one thing only, and that is if we should believe in our own weakness. If we should fall, and weep, and give up, cringing and being kind. That is what you should fear. Fear the good daughter, deprived, the sleeping snake, the subservient poor, the bland and lying face that you demand from us. Then you see nothing. You give nothing. Your desires and mine remain hidden. We will all be hidden by the hidden, silent, secret desire, never expressed. You have created such a huge world, such a stack of card houses, such false structures of governments, and bombs and money and boarding schools and ministries and hotels and banks and factories and development projects and armies to hide you, to protect you from your own desires. But do not be afraid. We will pursue you. We are your daughter, your soul. We will sneak up on you in the night and in the afternoon. We are your salvation. We will have you. We will find you out in spite of all your struggles and your power. Your power is nothing. It will scream, melt, explode in the heat of our desire, and of your own.

Dinah Brooke, Games of Love and Death

EILEEN FAIRWEATHER

The Man in the Orange Box

I was born in June 1954 in north London. My father was a police sergeant, my mother a school meals assistant. I went to a girls' Catholic grammar school where, somewhat confusingly, I was encouraged to aim for the academic heights and to be the mother of many children. But the nuns, in their own stern, loving, contradictory way, did give me a strong sense of 'girls can do anything'. At any rate, I survived various sojourns in bedsits, supported by shop and cleaning work, to get through A levels and to Sussex University. There I studied English, ecstatically discovered the then fledgling women's liberation movement, and thought, and still do, that it was wonderful to be paid for three years to read and to think. After graduating I worked in fringe theatre as a performer and playwright, and wrote a novel which I hated as soon as I finished it. From 1979–80 I worked full-time for the feminist magazine, *Spare Rib*, and since then have managed to support myself, albeit precariously, as a freelance writer. I am coauthor with Melanie McFadyean and Roisin McDonough of *Women in Belfast*, based on interviews with women in Northern Ireland, and my features have appeared in a wide variety of publications, ranging from *Cosmopolitan* to the *Leveller*, *New Statesman* to *She* and *Honey*, the *Sunday People* to the *Guardian*. Currently I divide my time between England and Finland, am writing a novel to be published by Michael Joseph, and, with the man who's 'much too good for me', raising our baby daughter.

At Daddy's Knee

My real father was the film star Robert Mitchum. So at least I consoled myself from the age of eight or so. After all, Mitchum was everything a man was supposed to be: reliable, charming, gallant and protective.

Attractively authoritative, but respectful of women and – above all – loving. The perfect daddy. How very different from my own.

My father's looks utterly belied the sourness of his nature. He had a handsome, open face and a smile which, when he thought to use it, was eminently charming. Physically he always seemed relaxed, and far, far younger than his years. As a relative once commented, comparing my mother's worn appearance with his, 'Well, boy, you've obviously looked after Number One,' – a sarcasm which Dad proudly accepted as a compliment. Presumably he really did feel as he looked – a man who had not a care in the world, if only because he was so ready to have others shoulder them.

Blaming other people was Dad's speciality, and from knee-high I was picked out as the child most to blame for Mum not exactly being fond of him. But for my loyalty to her, Mum apparently would be A Real Woman instead of 'colder than a witch's tit'. Did I, my father solemnly asked, understand how terrible it was for a virile man like him 'to live in a monastery'? I didn't, but for years felt guilty for seemingly having forced him to. The fact that the late night fights followed by the creaking of bed-springs gave the lie to his supposed celibacy was no consolation at all. I then just felt guilty that Mum had to endure this for the sake of diverting his wrath from us children.

At Daddy's knee, I was exposed to the full range of male prejudices, stripped bare of any chivalrous gloss. I learnt that all women drivers were Bloody Women Drivers, and most females either loose-knickered scrubbers or, as he would graphically revile my mother, 'colder than an eskimo's dick'. When I and my two sisters hit pubescent plumpness he called us Shapeless Fat Lumps, and when insecurity set in, Typical Female Neurotics. He thought educating girls an expensive waste of time and something that his Shiftless Trio were, anyway, bound to fail at. Courtship might have seemed our only other escape route as females but that too, he dourly prophesised, could only lead to one thing, saddling him with dozens of bastard grandchildren.

Although Dad was a policeman, he didn't score very high on protection. When any of us were ill, he would scream that *he* shouldn't have to put up with our whining, then off he would stomp for the pub or the betting shop, after forcing our mother to beg for prescription money. It was a pattern from which he didn't waver even when one of my sisters nearly died.

A master of divide and rule, my father encouraged myself and my sisters to despise our mother, and each other. He preferred his daughters in descending order of age, thus setting up a history of jealousy between us from which we have never quite recovered. Our loyalty to each other is fierce but jagged, scarred by the years we spent competing for the day's ration of approval, dodging blows and insults, and hoping, guiltily, that today it would be the *other* one who was labelled mad, bad, or dumb.

The less approval Dad gave us, the more we yearned for it. Even when my elder sister went through her 'Mod' phase, all gum-chewing Sod-You mascara-ed tough talk, she still burst into tears the one time Dad reached for her head to pat it rather than to yank out some more of her hair. Even after I became a self-styled Hard Line Feminist, and ceased to talk to my 'pig' policeman father, I burst into tears the time I met him on a demonstration and instead of reviling me he muttered, 'Well – at least you don't look so bloody scruffy as the rest of this rent-a-mob.' For hours afterwards I was as happy and excited as a five-year-old.

My father's few words of affection on that demo were enough to jolt me instantly from bitter hatred to desperate hope. For years I jostled between such extremes. I *wanted* to believe him when he said, in his more mellow moments, that he dearly loved me, my sisters and mother, and that why we all turned out so rotten and ungrateful was to him a total mystery. I wanted to forgive him, to believe that he hurt us out of carelessness rather than malice, for that way at least I could retain the illusion of being loved by him. After my mother finally left him, that illusion increased.

The homecoming

Suddenly he needed me. He was totally alone: his wife fled, his daughters grown, friendless and facing retirement. My phone would ring at all hours, Dad seeking advice and comfort. In the months before my mother left him we had hardly been on speaking terms, yet now he acted as though we had always been loving and close. I was wary, but touched. Perhaps my dad loved me after all, and something could be rescued.

For a year or more Dad solicited my company and served me no insults. He even ceased to blame me for the divorce. Then Dad found a girlfriend and decided to move in with her. I was, he said, to pick up whatever I wanted before he left our old family home.

There was absolutely nothing of intrinsic value to take: our family's furniture and ornaments were mostly cheap, worn and ugly. But for sentimental reasons I did want some of the clutter from my childhood and teens, as well as the possessions I had stored at home during my early moves from flat to flat. I guessed that I would also want to rescue the odd memento for my mother: in her haste to leave Dad, she had taken nothing with her save her clothes.

190

A couple of days before I was due to make this last visit home, Dad sent me two documents through the post: my birth certificate, and certificate of First Holy Communion. There was no covering letter. I should have twigged then, but didn't – not until I got to the house, and found that it was almost totally bare. With one of his infuriatingly innocent, genial smiles, Dad informed me that after clearing out what he wanted, he had taken everything of mine and my mother's to the council rubbish tip. Why was I upset, he asked in apparently hurt bewilderment? After all, he had been thoughtful enough to save for me what he thought I might need from my earlier life. Oh yes – those certificates. One proving that I had been born, and the other that once at least I had been a good Catholic girl.

I didn't cry then, in front of him, or even rage. I was too numb, too shocked. As I wondered through the empty house, past the shelves where Mum had displayed the misshapen pots we made for her at school, and the photos of us as babies, I heard Dad whistle cheerfully over the last of his packing. And I remembered something my mother used to say: that causing other people pain was the only thing that ever really made him happy. Well, happy or powerful – perhaps to him they were the same.

How powerless he must have felt, to have so resented even his own children. Myself in particular, because I was the one who made it to grammar school, had the education he felt he had been cheated of by poverty. From my room, every single sign of the Stuck-Up, Namby-Pamby Learning he affected to despise had been cleared away: the shelves were stripped of their books, the cupboard of my school and university essays, and only some dents in the lino served as a reminder of where my prize possession had stood: The Desk.

Mum had given it to me when I was sixteen. It was a high, old-fashioned teacher's bureau, and to our minds very romantic with its ink well and wooden flaps and secret cubby holes. She had bought it as a surprise for me at a school sale, while I was away one summer working in a holiday camp. When I came home, it was to find Mum crying as desperately she applied the last licks of paint to the legs, while Dad yelled, 'That girl's not worth that amount of bloody work, she's too shiftless ever to sit at any bloody desk!' The desk was Mum's gift to me for having just passed nine O levels. It was also her way of indulging or simply approving my fantasies about being a serious scholar, and maybe even one day A Serious Writer. Well, now Dad had finally got his revenge on my presumptious dreams by throwing away that hated desk, and absolutely everything in it.

That 'everything' included the certificates for my O and A levels, and my university degree; the first innocent love letters and valentines I ever

received, the diaries I kept daily from the age of ten or so, and my few photos of schoolfriends, pets and family; the buff envelope which contained my first wages, and the collar of my dog, Micky, whom Dad got rid of after he dirtied the carpet. In the desk I had also stored my first attempts as a writer, the teenage stories and plays and poems. Purple prose efforts, no doubt, but still important to me. They were my 'juvenilia', my youth, things I might have liked one day to look over, to cry or laugh about, regain a sense of where I had come from, whom once I had been.

And now that all the tangible milestones in my life up to the age of twenty or so had been fed to municipal shredding machines, I felt grazed and helpless and lost, as though my past and very identity had been stolen from me. I remember wondering numbly whether my father had read through my life before rejecting it. Presumably he had, in order to find all he thought worth salvaging: those two certificates.

And my doll's house, the beloved doll's house that I had long planned to give to my own future children, that was gone too. It had been another of Mum's presents, a large hand-made wooden house, none of your

192

plastic rubbish, that she had lovingly repainted and fitted out with scraps of curtain and carpet, and which Dad of course had also hated. For it was the main friend of my childhood, and even early teens; I could spend hour after hour in front of it on my knees, dividing up the house and its tiny dolls into homes, villages, schools and hospitals, writing newspapers for them on Mum's curling papers, love letters, suicide notes and diagnoses of terminal illnesses. Theirs was a soap opera world of rape and hardship and family discord, but I, their creator, always had the power to mend and to heal and provide happy endings.

Most parents would probably have been glad of a child who could quietly amuse herself for hours, but Dad constantly threatened to chop up my house and throw it out. Presumably what he resented was my ability to withdraw, and what he perhaps sensed was my positive *need* to fantasise. 'They're only bleeding dolls!' he would rage, just as he screamed, 'It's only a bleeding film!' when I sobbed indiscriminately over the fate of both the cowboys and the Indians in the TV Westerns. He despised my excusions into fantasy as time-wasting, childish, and excessively female. When he came upstairs to tell me off for playing with my house, he would sternly remind me of the old biblical wisdom, quoting, 'When I was a child, I spake as a child, I understood as a child, I thought as a child: but when I became a man I put away childish things.' Eventually, I hit back. 'If your own world isn't sufficient,' I said as levelly as I could, 'then you have to create your own.' I was ten years old, and as he said, A Precocious Little Bugger. If throughout my teens Dad resented and constantly tried to end my education, I presume it was because it gave me the power to answer him back.

I cried for two days after he had thrown my things away. I even rang him and begged him to explain. But he seemed totally unable to accept the enormity of what he had done. To him, throwing away my life had been no more than slightly ruthless spring cleaning.

From a rusty tin lying forgotten at the back of the pantry, I rescued a handful of tiny, plastic curlers. They were my mother's, and are the only memento I have from my childhood home.

Eventually I forgave him. After all, he was going to be remarried – he deserved the chance to turn over a new leaf.

Second chance

In the absence of any other offers I made the good luck speech at his wedding, and cried happily, just as I had when the registrar intoned, 'I now pronounce you . . . man and wife.' Whatever my cynicism about marriage, or my father, today he looked so young and handsome and hopeful – so what the hell. Even if he had been a bad old bastard, he was going to have his second chance.

And so, perhaps, was I. That day, Dad threw various small scraps of approval my way, and I was duly thrilled. Even though he dryly introduced me to everyone as, 'the daughter I don't often talk about', he still felt ready to boast about my having a degree, published this and that, and (oh, ultimate proof of success) appeared on TV. He praised me for wearing a dress ('Didn't know you'd got legs') and for no longer being Quite So Fat. And I was as grateful for this attention as if I were again the small child who had frenetically yelled, 'Look, Dad, look, Dad!' after I first learned to stay upright on a bike, and swim with my feet off the bottom of the pool. For once, Dad didn't make me feel I was a failure, in my work life or as a woman. The crowning glory came when, after meeting the love of my life, Dad gave his approval – even if afterwards he did thoughtfully add, 'Of course he's much too good for you.'

Within a very short space of time, and after my father had thrown out his wife's grandson whom she was bringing up, the new Happy Family collapsed. It was only when my father blamed me for the failure of his second marriage, when despite my enormous capacity for guilt even I knew this wasn't just, that something clicked into place. If I knew I wasn't to blame second time round, maybe I hadn't been the first? As a child, I had desperately shovelled aside my father's accusations that it was my fault if my mother hated him, but on an irrational level the accusation had stuck. Now, for perhaps the first time, I had a true sense of my innocence. And it was this which enabled me finally to break off from my father, to accept that I would never get his approval, and didn't in fact *need* it. It was not I who had ruined his marriages and his life: I did not need his forgiveness.

This freed me from the futile struggle to win my father's love. But of course it did not free me completely from the longing for it. It is highly unlikely that my father will ever read this book, but when I think of him doing so, I imagine him reacting not with rage but with regret and enlightenment – that Dad, Daddy, would cry, 'Oh my God, my little girl, what have I done,' and beg my forgiveness, which of course I would give, then sweep me into his arms.

There is the spectre of the dutiful daughter. I wonder sometimes what I will do if, as seems likely, my father ends up on his own: old, lonely, and perhaps sick and poor. Will I make him food, roll his cigarettes, keep him company? I doubt if my father will ever lose his power to wound me, and yet . . .

There was a softer, romantic side to my father's nature, expressed by the hours he spent fondly tending his roses and vegetables, and enjoying the splendours of the Latin mass. Perhaps my father was simply 'a real man' at his overconditioned worst; scared that it was unmasculine to show or reciprocate feeling. For his were all solitary pleasures, or shared with nature and God – those who couldn't, in human terms, communicate back.

His relationship with my mother was fraught, his religion held him back from having affairs; perhaps we, his daughters, therefore, exacerbated his frustration. Certainly puberty was the point at which he cut off from us, and when my elder sister married he blurted out to me, on the way to her wedding, that he had long felt jealous of our boyfriends.

I have often wondered, too, how much my father's work affected his outlook. An ordinary cop does see some of the ugliest, most brutal and brutalising sides of life, and my father did more than his share of scraping up dead bodies, including, once, the mangled remains of a family friend. And he could show compassion: once he received a commendation, at the request of a woman whom he had comforted for hours, having had to break the news that her entire family had been killed abroad. It was an award he never told us, his family, about: we learnt of it from local paper.

And how much, I wonder, was my father soured by early poverty? I remember the farm labourer's cottage where he grew up in the thirties as dank, dark and tiny; and the bitterness in his voice as he described how until he was three or four he had to sleep hunched up in an orange box. Even his sole Christmas treat – jam on his bread instead of the usual dripping – came from a British Legion charity parcel, for which, said Dad dryly, you paid with the humiliation of having your name pasted on the village notice board, 'as one of the grateful effing poor'.

And yet at the end of the day I'm not sure that even the orange box and the dead bodies are excuses enough. My father relied on his uniform to overcome his sense of being 'just a poor ignorant peasant'. He boosted himself by putting down others, like Ginger Beers (queers), Toms (pros), and Our Coloured Brethren (Blacks). Dad's attitude was: 'I've had splinters in the face, so why shouldn't you.' Whichever way I look at it, he was as mean of spirit as he was of pocket. And so, in the end, I simply got out of range.

Our culture is top-heavy with images and indeed impossible ideals about what constitutes good *mothering*, our concept of good fathering is almost nonexistent. Our society does not, even now, expect much from fathers. A good father is one who does *not* drink all the housekeeping, and does *not* scar the children.

I have little doubt that, for a girl, having a father who gives you a sense of dignity and of strength is a huge bonus. In myself, I have long been aware of a conflict between my hunger for independence and for male approval. It is a conflict which, I am sure, helps explain the 'inexplicable' mood swings of so many women, making even the most energetic and confident prey to sudden self-doubt and self-destructive behaviour. The root of the conflict is deceptively simple: you long to be free *and* to be loved. When the first man in your life teaches you that the two are irreconcilable, the price of freedom can seem impossibly high.

The boy thinks of his father's superiority with a feeling of rivalry; but the girl has to accept it with impotent admiration. I have already pointed out that what Freud calls the Electra complex is not, as he supposes, a sexual desire; it is a full abdication of the subject, consenting to become object in submission and adoration. If her father shows affection for his daughter, she feels that her existence is magnificently justified; she is endowed with all the merits that others have to acquire with difficulty; she is fulfilled and deified. All her life she may longingly seek that lost state of plenitude and peace. If the father's love is withheld, she may ever after feel herself guilty and condemned; or she may look elsewhere for appreciation of herself and become indifferent to her father or even hostile. Moreover, it is not alone the father who holds the keys to the world; men in general share normally in the prestige of manhood; there is no occasion for regarding them as 'father substitutes'. It is directly, as men, that grandfathers, older brothers, uncles, playmates, fathers, family friends, teachers, priests, doctors, fascinate the little girl. The emotional concern shown by the adult women towards Man would of itself suffice to perch him on a pedestal.

Simone de Beauvoir, *The Second Sex*

In the period in which the main interest was directed to discovering infantile sexual traumas, almost all my women patients told me that they had been seduced by their father. I was driven to recognise in the end that these reports were untrue and so came to understand that hysterical symptoms are derived from phantasies and not from real occurrences. It was only later that I was able to recognise in this phantasy of being seduced by the father the expression of the typical Oedipus complex in women.

Sigmund Freud on 'Femininity', *New Introductory Lectures*

MELANIE McFADYEAN

Looking for Daddy

I am a freelance journalist. I live in London. I am in my early thirties.

This story was written in an attempt to exorcise my frequent return to a day in 1959 when it seemed as if everything began to fall apart.

My parents did what they had to do and there is no intentional indictment of them. Both are happily re-married.

The story has a strange significance to me now. When my sister read it she passed me the Snopake and laughing asked me to paint out some details about her. A few months later she died. Bleak and meagre as the story is, it tells of an experience we shared that shaped our lives. We fought all the time, but she protected me after it happened and I'll always love her for it.

Lastly, I realise now that 'real' men do feel the cold even though they're not very good at showing it.

'Come into the front room, we've something to tell you, children.' That's how they began the episode. They were very big, I remember, Mamma and Dadda.

On his trip to America Dadda seemed to have grown – he was even taller, even handsomer. Naturally one day he'd marry me, when I was twenty-five. There'd be at least two children. It always seemed odd that they only had two, me and my older sister.

During his trip to America, Mamma seemed to have become ice-edged. Something had seized up in her. She was even more beautiful and thin and distant.

While he was in America, I had felt unsafe every night without him to protect us. I knew that one night, a man broke in and prowled about my sister's bedroom as she slept. Nobody told me, I just knew.

My sister became strange while he was away. She took to drawing faces on her fingers and talking to them. I played in the street more and more, dreading his absence about the house after school and at weekends.

My sister stayed at home and organised events to which the street kids were invited but never came. She wouldn't let my gang into the house. She slammed the front door in my friend Penny's face and moved me to fits of violent rage and then displayed the scratches I'd made on her hands, saying nobody would marry her and it was all my fault. But I knew it wasn't and I felt all right because Dadda and I would marry one day, of that I could be certain. She told me that Dadda and Mamma had found me in a bag of string in the gutter, but I shouldn't tell them I knew. She ruined her own story by coming out with another one – surely, she said, I could remember being born? Surely I could remember being inside Mamma? Everyone could remember that, I'd better not let on I couldn't, nobody would like me any more. But then, she added, I was mad anyway and everyone had been told to treat me kindly as though I were normal, and I shouldn't say she'd told me or else.

It was a Saturday – I always thought of Saturdays as being red, because they were exciting. They were the days when Dadda would take you downtown to the old-fashioned bookshop where the fat lady let you play with the switchboard with all those tubes out of which voices came like miracles. Dadda treated you and let you sit on the back of the Ford Continental convertible which he drove with the roof down all year round. But only when Mamma wasn't looking.

That Saturday started out even redder than most because it was the day that Dadda came home from his trip to America. But he never took off the suit, and at weekends he always wore old shorts and a leather jacket and was in the garden digging and pruning and swearing. In summer he'd ride me about in the wheelbarrow and feed me raspberries, and in autumn I played with the bonfires he built.

He didn't even go into the garden that Saturday. He and Mamma stood in front of the piano under which I used to hide and talk to a mythical creature. They were enormous by the time we stood before them for the announcement. She wore a fitted suit and her hair was very tidy. They didn't look like they'd kissed. She was almost lifeless, Dadda unreal.

He said he had presents for us from America. He turned to the piano and passed us each a brown paper parcel. Usually you tore open such a parcel. But I remember opening it slowly as if delaying what would happen after the parcel. Because you loved Dadda, even when he gave you a raspberry from the garden you were happy, but I didn't like the gaudy red nylon cardigan with a big collar and white plastic buttons. I

199

pretended it was lovely and put it on. I was a noisy child, but something made me very quiet that day. My sister put her cardigan on too, and we showed them. Dadda said we looked lovely, Mamma didn't say a word. She stood there very proud and icy and tragic.

After the announcement, my sister fled to the garden and we didn't see her for hours. Nobody could make her leave the tree in the wild part far from the house. I sat under the table, the one with the iron curly bits beneath it, and listened to what he had said over and over again. 'Your mother and I are getting divorced.' They always got divorced on the TV and in the films from America, so it should have been quite normal, and I'd heard them fighting many times at night. Once I saw Mamma crying as I hid on the stairs and was shocked to discover that grown-ups cry. I found Dadda as I crept past her, head in hands, his shirt torn to strips and red marks down his back. This must be something to do with them getting divorced.

Mamma sat at her desk and made phone calls. I didn't listen. She used to sit with her legs up on the desk and talk to people in German – I liked her being foreign even though I couldn't understand what she said. She was very thin and wore smart clothes and all her softness went. Before, she used sometimes to sit at the piano and sing 'Over the Hills and Far Away' and 'Johnny's Not Back From the Fair'. I felt that mood of wind and hills and people who never come back. The house was like the songs but empty and hollow. Dadda must have left immediately after the announcement because when I went to their bedroom his things had gone, he must have packed before he told us. In a hurry to leave us. Only her things were in their room – the hairbrushes and makeup and bottles of perfume, nylons over the chair and photographs of her family.

He had a cupboard at the end of the room. I searched each shelf, they were all papered over and there was a smell of sandalwood. He'd left a pair of socks. I picked them up and held them against my cheek and thought of him, not that it was like thinking. The street was dead which was unusual because at weekends kids played out there. It was one of those colourless, shadowless days, neither warm nor cold. Sometimes I think I remember seeing him disappear round the corner, past the letter box.

Dadda never came back. The weeks passed into deepening winter, his garden shrinking under the frost. Life went on but it wasn't real. Mamma tried to smile. My grandmother, her mother, had always lived upstairs. She used to give us slices of deep frozen butter and drinks of tinned orange juice. My sister used to send me up to our gran's room with stomach aches and I had to get her to tell me stories while my sister

sneaked behind the sofa to watch the adult programmes on the TV. But she went, she was paralysed and Mamma couldn't look after her. I stayed out until bedtime, roller skating in the street lamp light.

One evening I came in at bed time and Mamma and my sister were sitting on a big armchair crying. They said our grandmother had died. I think I cried a bit, but mostly the shock just silenced everything.

Sometimes on Saturdays he took me out. My sister wouldn't come with us. He took me to self-service restaurants and gave me so much to eat that I felt sick. Once he took me on the motorway and tried his new red Ford Convertible to see if it would go 100 miles an hour, but I wasn't to tell my mother. Sometimes he took me to the zoo and made the elephants curtsy, and imitated the orang-utan. He showed me the Egyptian mummies in the British Museum and we went to the pictures now and again.

I always wondered what he meant when he talked about 'real' men. He said they didn't wear overcoats or pullovers. They didn't drink tea or feel the cold. For a long time I believed him. I supposed they were like him. They'd love me and take me out, treat me and thrill me when they chose to and then go to their other lives which were nothing to do with me.

'There are plenty of things a girl can find to do at home.'
'Until someone takes pity on me and marries me?'
He raised his eyebrows in mild appeal. His foot tapped impatiently, and he took up the papers.
'Look here, father,' she said, with a change in her voice, 'suppose I won't stand it?'
He regarded her as though this was a new idea.
'Suppose, for example, I go to this dance?'
'You won't.'
'Well' – her breath failed her for a moment. 'How would you prevent it?' she asked.
'But I have forbidden it!' he said, raising his voice.
'Yes, I know. But suppose I go?'
'Now, Veronica! No, no. This won't do. Understand me! I forbid it. I do not want to hear from you even the threat of disobedience.' He spoke loudly. 'The thing is forbidden!'
'I am ready to give up anything that you show to be wrong.'
'You will give up anything I wish you to give up.'

H. G. Wells, Ann Veronica

What was I doing with David, in my own bed, in my father's house, in the middle of the afternoon? In the middle of the afternoon in the middle of summer when my father would of course not be teaching and liable at any moment to walk through the door? I have never been able to understand why, given the precision with which up to that time I handled my life, I made such an amateur blunder. Perhaps it is that the intrusion of sexuality marks the end of precision. Or perhaps it was something more complicated, for I have never given myself the luxury or insisted upon the humility of thinking my motivations simple. Was I trying to punish my father for something; for his lack of attention to my obvious adulthood, for his lack of jealousy at the intrusion of so clear a rival? He didn't even tease me about David. Perhaps I was outraged at his lack of outrage at what could so obviously have separated us. Would it be so easy for him to let me go? Perhaps the prospect so deeply appalled me that I had to construct the scene that would forbid me marriage during my father's lifetime, that would make impossible the one match he might have approved.

Mary Gordon, Final Payments

SHEILA ROWBOTHAM

Our Lance

I was born in 1943, in Yorkshire, and studied history at St Hilda's College, Oxford. I've taught in secondary schools, further education and the Workers' Educational Association, and have been involved in the women's liberation movement since it began in the late 1960s. Apart from working on socialist and feminist journals over the years, I've written several books, on the history of socialism and feminism, including *Women, Resistance and Revolution, Hidden from History* and *A New World for Women*. With Jean McCrindle I edited a book of interviews with women, *Dutiful Daughters*; and with Hilary Wainwright and Lynne Segal I wrote *Beyond the Fragments*. A collection of my essays, *Dreams and Dilemmas*, was published by Virago. For the last two years I've been a visiting professor in the Women's Studies Department of the University of Amsterdam, and I'm now working in the Economic Policy Unit of the Greater London Council. I live in Hackney, in East London, and have one son, Will.

My father was in his fifties when I was born. We were separated in age by half a century and the gulf only seemed to grow wider. Our placings in the world and our relationship to where we found ourselves were contrary and apart.

Born in 1888, he was the seventh in a family of fourteen. The joke went that grandmother Rowbotham was running out of names for the boys by the time he came along. From sober Charles and Tommy she began to branch out into Lancelot, Clifford and Randal. Combined with Rowbotham, these lofty names became somewhat absurd and Lancelot was reduced to 'our Lance'.

Grandfather Rowbotham had a small farm in a village called Aston near Sheffield. He had worked in the mines, checking the wooden props and beams to make sure they were safe. The money he earned had been used to build up the farm. It was assumed all the children would work on the farm as it was unthrifty to employ labour. Children worked for their keep.

My father remembered grandfather as a harsh man who beat his children each day *in case* they had done something wrong which he had not found out about. Grandfather Rowbotham certainly assumed he had total rights over his children's lives. As he had so many to keep an eye on he could not really maintain complete control over his unruly brood. According to Auntie Glad, the daughters were locked in their rooms at night to prevent them going with their boyfriends, but they somehow found the means to escape.

My father went against his father. He sought a world beyond the farm and beyond the village. He won a scholarship to grammar school. Then he worked on the farm in the day and studied at evening classes in Sheffield to become an engineer. 'I walked both ways in all weathers.' As an apprentice he began converting clocks so that they would run off electricity. Still in his early twenties, he got a good job as an electrical engineer in a colliery nearby. It was unusual to get a post like this so young. He was enterprising and rebellious, designing a safety lamp that became used in the nearby mines, reading the socialist paper *Clarion* and exposing the council in the local newspaper. He had done well. But I always felt he retained a sense of hurt that his father put obstacles in the way of his studies and never acknowledged his accomplishments.

Despite these early successes, the rest of his life was to be full of ups and downs, partly because he was a rebellious individualist, partly because of what my mother described as his 'bulldog' sexual approach. He pursued too many women by the standards of the village, according to Auntie Glad. Rather to everyone's surprise, he was quite successful in his amorous philandering. As no one remembers him as either handsome or the life and soul of the party, his attraction was assumed by his sisters to be based on craftiness, flattery and persistence. He possessed more generally tremendous will-power and a dogged determination to live and think as he pleased, which remained with him until the end of his days.

He met my mother, Jean Turner, when he was in his mid-thirties and was already married. She was in her late teens and visiting a farm near Aston for her holidays from Sheffield.

Her family were (she thought) a cut above the Rowbothams. Her father owned a factory which made guns and ammunition. But the Rowbothams' version of themselves tended to prevail through sheer will and weight of numbers. They were as good as anybody and a great deal better than most.

When my mother returned to Sheffield, Lance continued his courtship.

She portrayed him to me as a country bumpkin who drove off her other suitors with his rude manners and farm clothes and won her, by elimination, through perseverance. Once she stormed off and left him. He pursued her. She got on a tram. But he ran alongside it until the mirth of the other passengers forced her to get off.

My father maintained the other suitors were shallow city slickers in spats. As a young girl, pondering these tales of the distant courtship in Sheffield just after the First World War, I was always a little disappointed in the other suitors' lack of grit, gump and heroism. It seemed to me that they could at least have challenged my father to a duel for my mother's hand, or something. I was somewhat hazy about what spats were; they were not to be seen on the streets of Leeds in the 1950s. Perhaps the spats had made combat impossible. Or perhaps my mother had misjudged the chivalrous suitors. Perhaps they were shallow city slickers after all and my mother well rid of them.

She gave the impression that it was a matter of chance that she was telling me the story more than thirty years on. 'He swept me off my feet, your father did.' Once you were swept, apparently fate took its course.

After they both died I was to learn that despite living together all those years they never married. My father's legal wife was a Catholic and regarded by the Rowbothams as socially inferior. Lance had married her in his teens amidst the disapproval of his family. Only his favourite sister Glad stood by him. By the time he met my mother his wife had already left him for someone else, but because she was a Catholic refused him a divorce.

When my mother died in the early 1960s I found letters from Lance during this period which she had kept all those years. They revealed a man I did not recognise as my father. The atmosphere they evoked was reminiscent of the characters which had fascinated me in H. G. Wells's novels. The feel of a new century, a new rising man, coming up in the world through technical expertise and evening classes, impatient of upper-class privilege, determined to make his own way, blunt and passionate.

Lance and Jean left England for India in the early 1920s. He had been offered a job there and my mother said she was keen to get out of Sheffield and pushed him to go. Such a step was clearly pretty scandalous in those days. But in defying her family and going to India with Lance, she was from this point on totally dependent upon him materially, without legal security. It cast a new light on her insistence on the importance of me being educated so I could earn my own living, and on the fierceness of her love of freedom.

Lance worked as a mining engineer near Calcutta for twelve years under the British Raj, with the nationalist movement rumbling threateningly on the outskirts of their world of colonial privilege.

Stories of India in this period filled my childhood. My father would pontificate on the unappreciated virtues of Empire – all rashly given to the Indians by the Labour Party in their ignorance. Other stories came from my mother. They were long explorations of character and coincidence, embellished with observations and reflections. 'Tell me about the time . . .' I would say, longing for her to breathe life into all the household objects, imperial booty of elephants, embroidered paintings, Buddhas and carved screens which had found their way to Harehills (in Leeds) by some quirk of history.

The picture she communicated was very much *her* India, not his. Her relief when the monsoon rains came made her run naked, delighting in the water on her body. But he pursued her. At first she thought he was playing, and laughed, but he was enraged at the thought that an Indian might see her naked. She became friendly with a retired army officer who played her Beethoven and introduced her to Indian culture. My mother giggled years after about the woman who came back from leave with contraceptive pessaries which melted, was still romantic about young men she danced with at the club, nostalgic for the *ayah* who had looked after my brother Peter who was born in India.

My father's India differed from my mother's. He did not talk of the details of his life and work there, perhaps partly because I was his daughter not his son. But also because he never talked much about personal relationships. His India was transmitted either through opinion or had to be inferred. It must have felt a long way from South Yorkshire to Calcutta. It was easier for Jean at the club, young, pretty, vivacious, a good dancer, her social inexperience could be excused. It hardly mattered what she thought as long as she obeyed the outer forms of colonial convention. Her friendship with a family which was part Indian, part British meant he was warned that he must stop her seeing them or lose his job. She acquiesced, but never really accepted the values of the Raj. He did. The accoutrements of Empire served as a buffer against the shock of his world at home and the world he found himself in. The Indians, he maintained, did not care for their own, nor appreciate how much the British had done for them. Years later, with my newly acquired Marxist analysis, I pointed out in vain that imperialism had destroyed domestic industry, forced up rents, caused famine, aggravated religious conflict. Indians lacked moral integrity, repeated Lance. They had no idea of the virtues of hard work. He liked the Sikhs and the Chinese, however.

Highly honoured, they came somewhere just below Yorkshire people in his scale of merit and worth.

Thirty years after he had left, Lance continued to see India through the eyes of a South Yorkshire man. He never shifted from a dogmatic and uncompromising stance. My mother had no more idea of the political complexities of imperialism and nationalism but she could see that there were other versions of India, not just the British one. It is possible to imagine that behind Lance's British identity there was considerable social discomfort among his 'betters' at the club, where he played bridge seriously and ponderously and joined the freemasons half-heartedly. He was too stubborn to be socially mobile, too proud not to smart before an upper-class accent. Years later he kept his Kipling poems proudly amidst Agatha Christie thrillers and adventure novels.

They stayed twelve years in India. They had to leave because Lance got the sack. This story he *did* tell me and I always felt very proud of him. His boss was away on leave in Britain. The next in command tried to lower the wages of the miners. Lance had to sign for the reduction to take effect. He refused because he said the wages were below starvation level already and no human being could be expected to live on them. Amidst the Tory paternalism there was a fierce sense of fair play which contradicted the small businessman's approach to the world of measured self-interest. Because he had worked in the mines he appreciated the risks, discomfort, health hazards.

They returned to Britain during the depression. Eventually he got work as an electrician in a colliery: this was a comedown after India. He was in his forties and no longer used to manual work. Eventually grandfather Turner relented and lent Lance the money to buy a car. He got a Morris and a sales job and went into partnership. Around the late 1930s they settled in lodgings with a family in Leeds. My mother loved this period and the stories of this era were all cheery. But Lance's partner ran off with the money.

My father never told me of his business failures and difficulties. He presented himself to me very much as the sagacious wordly-wise businessman. Treat the other chap fairly but if he does not play square knock him down. Neither a borrower nor a lender be. Never have an overdraft as the bank makes money out of you.

In the 1940s they moved to a house in Harehills, Leeds. Lance got a job as a salesman for a firm in Keighley which made pit motors. He prospered with the expansion of the coal industry. He assured me it was by dint of his ability to judge character, read writing upside down, hear several conversations at once and other entrepreneurial skills. My mother implied it was all hot air, luck and grandfather Turner's loan.

By this time Lance was in his fifties and Jean in her early forties. But still their life together was full of upheavals. She became ill with breast cancer and had to have a breast removed. The operation left her weak and frail. I was born just after this, a 'mistake', in 1943. Peter was seventeen.

Jean talked of sex with my father as an onerous chore. As long as I can remember they slept apart. She tried to buy quinine to abort me but it had been withdrawn from the shops. She fell down stairs with me but did not miscarry. She told me she had had a lot of miscarriages and I wondered as I grew older if some of them had been abortions.

My father never talked to me about his feelings about sexuality. But all the time I knew him he must have been sexually unhappy. I found it impossible to imagine this as a teenager. The idea that my father had sexual desires was unthinkable and merely ludicrous. My mother also communicated to me her sexual revulsion and the bitterness which she had accumulated in the course of his numerous sexual infidelities. With old age he became very respectable, moralised sternly and watched the clock if I went out at night. 'The dirty old buggers are always the worst with their daughters. They know what you can get up to,' said Jean who had no sympathy with hypocrisy.

Arguments were persistent between them. I would lie in bed hearing him upbraid her and the softer rhythm of her petulant defiance. He almost – but never quite – wore her spirit down. She would curse her misfortune that he worked at home and was always under her feet.

She chain-smoked and absentmindedly put her lighted cigarettes on window sills while she did the housework. They burned brown scars into the wood. 'Jeannie, do you want to burn the house down?' he'd roar, filling the whole house with male rage which still makes me wince and tremble at the anger of it. I suppose Jean Turner *did* want to burn the house down. But she had nowhere else to live and thus resorted to unmitigating guerilla warfare.

As I grew older, I became the cause of arguments. My beloved dog Simon urinated on bushes specially bought from a market garden for our new posh house in Roundhay. I began to drink coffee without putting cups on saucers. 'Nice people won't have you in their house,' he said. Simon and I were protected by an elaborate domestic underground which consisted of my mother and a series of home helps. My brother was an occasional member but he worked with my father and it was implicitly recognised that, as a man, he was not to understand some things. The underground collected information, planned strategy, had a laugh and indefatigably worked out the best way to achieve objectives. My father,

officially all-powerful in his home, had to resort to creeping up on the kitchen in his carpet slippers to gain access to information.

For years, passionate resentment against my father made it impossible for me to imagine how this affected him. To me he was simply a tyrant to be resisted. The pattern was set by a childhood game my mother and I used to play. We were two waitresses, Rosie and Posie, who would get up to all kind of tricks until the boss came home. 'When the cat's away the mice will play,' she would say. He controlled the material world but she found freedom of the spirit in fantasy and imagination. My brother was old enough to see their conflict as tragic on both sides. I saw only how her life was constrained and thwarted and I blamed him for his domineering and masterful ways.

Our moments of closeness were rare. Even as a small child my father suffocated me with instructions. We battled over the formal politeness he thought children should show to adults, over my clothes, my table manners, my books. By the time I reached my early teens I had moved from guerilla resistance to frontal attack and the area of struggle expanded to take in religion, Suez, the Queen, race, class, the Empire, my friends, the time I spent on the phone, the time I came in at night. Eventually all these found a name – 'socialism'.

Well, my father was not one for debate for the sake of it. The saying 'I'm not arguing I'm telling tha'' was more like it. He simply *was* in the world. His views were how things were.

When he died in 1967 we were still unreconciled and locked in a mutual incomprehension – though outsiders pointed out similarities between us. 'She takes after you, Lance,' they'd remark. After his death I felt only a numbness and behind that a relief at being rid of the anger. No wild grief like the anguish of my mother's death. The sadness remained deeply buried. Only an uneasy stirring at his memory over the years.

Then in 1976 a woman read my astrology chart. In the course of the reading she looked at me and said with force, 'You were a terrible daughter.' She said I should try and sort out my feelings about him. I might have still closed up on what she said and dismissed it. But I knew she was a feminist and the remark came from her commitment to women's freedom. Real freedom could not be based on evasion. I could recognise in my heart the truth of what she said. For while it was true that he had been a dominating man, he had also loved me and was very proud of me. I had unfinished matters to explore with the spirit of my father. Death is not the end of such affairs.

I spent time on the moments of warmth and affection which had existed between us. They were rare but I dredged them up. In the kitchen one night when I was in my teens my mother interrupted him mischievously in the midst of a spate of moralising: 'What about the woman with the fish tail dress?' Out came the story. Travelling to India once, he had been playing bridge with a woman who my mother said was very haughty, dressed in a tight evening dress with frills in a kind of fish tail. One night when they were meant to be playing bridge my father had contrived to take her up on deck. When they both eventually appeared again in the dance hall she was rather flustered. The fish-tail frills were all standing on end and try as she would she could not flatten them – much to the mirth and amusement of my mother and the other passengers. Years later, the moraliser, caught in the act again, grinned boyishly and disarmingly and subsided.

When I got into a women's college at Oxford my father was very chuffed. 'She'll get funny ideas, Lance, and won't want to get married,' warned his friend Mr Kessler who kept an electrical shop and believed in educating sons not daughters. But my father let me go. He had dreams that I would dress in tweed suits, hobnob with the gentry, become a teacher, enter the Foreign Office. He gave a large sum of money to the

210

college building fund. Believing that colliery managers and dons were basically the same breed of humanity, he took the view that just as presents to the managers secured orders this was how you got your daughter a good reference for a job. I caught him by chance sneaking out of the college in a new hat he had bought in London. He had come to Oxford secretly because he knew I would be cross at him giving money. There were many parents with more money. And how to explain that the upper-middle-class intelligentsia played the capitalist system with slightly different rules? However, taken by surprise, we both enjoyed meeting in this way and he took me and some friends out for a meal. It was one of the happiest times I remember with him.

When I was nineteen I went on an anti-nuclear march and a section of the march broke off to invade a regional seat of government the whereabouts of which had been leaked. We tramped through the woods near Reading and hit the headlines. We were denounced in *Tribune* and Peggy Duff said we were anarchists. My father boasted to his National Coal Board friends that his daughter had done this. They were horrified, but he thought it showed grit and moral fibre, especially when he heard the military police, whom he disliked, were there.

Always my staunch protector, when I went off with my boyfriend to build a library in Poland, organised by Progressive Tours, Lance took his passport out. He was ready to come and rescue me in case I was captured behind the Iron Curtain. In vain I explained that the Polish communists wanted students and young people to go on work camps. At the time it was infuriating, but in retrospect I can appreciate his concern for me and his readiness to stand by me in strange worlds, whether they were women dons, the police or the Polish authorities.

I struggled through these memories to understand how a man like my father must have had love choked at the source until its only expression became either possessing and controlling or protective.

I tried to find out more about him when he was young, before I was born, by talking to Auntie Glad, one of the few people he ever allowed close to him as an equal. My aunt described him as socially awkward, not joining in family games and dances in the evenings. He went his own way with his studying and his courting as if he were somehow apart from the rest of them. After making his own break with the farm, he felt responsible for getting his younger brothers started as engineers.

I began to find certain recognitions across the gulf. The course of our lives were so different, yet there was a shared substance which he had imparted somehow to me. I knew his pride and stubborn determination in myself.

I played the tape I had made of the conversation with my aunt to the women's group I was in and talked about my father's influence on my life when we were discussing our families.

As I heard friends who were in men's groups talking about the experience of masculinity it became easier to find openings through which I could enter my father's vision of the world. By realising that to become a man was a social relationship, I could begin to connect his responses and his silences to those I could observe among men who were closer to me. This provided the tissue for speculation beyond my subjective reaction to him. I could begin to stretch my imagination towards him. There remain significant points where this just blanks out – for instance, as soon as I venture near to trying to work out how he has marked my sexual feelings towards men. For a long time I thought I simply fancied men who were not like him. As time passes it is evident that this is far too simple. It is more that I fancy men who appear at first glance to be unlike him. At second glance, of course, there is more going on than immediately meets the eye. It is here I find my ability to observe and distinguish starts to fuzz over.

Early in 1977, I had a son, Will. I was a parent and I had a different relation to another father – Will's father. This accelerated the urgency, for not only was my own relationship to my father involved but the possibility of someone being a father differently from my father and my father's father. Or, put more generally, how do we develop relationships in which love can be expressed which does not seek to own and control? No more *padre padrone*.

When Will was about one, some women who lived nearby formed a consciousness-raising group to explore collectively as feminists our relationships to our fathers. About half of us had children. Our class backgrounds (donated by our fathers) ranged from working class to intellectual middle class. Our fathers were Londoners, Scots, Yorkshire, a Polish Jew, a Viennese Jew. Brought together by the accident of feminism, it would have been a bizarre social occasion if they had met one another in the flesh.

Considerable diversity in the patterns of relating soon emerged, even in our tiny group. Some of the women had fathers who were very obviously dominating men, who, like mine, had believed their word should be law. Others had mild-mannered fathers who went into retreat in the family. One woman had an exciting romantic father whom she adored, and who even taught her to poach. One had no father because he had died when she was a baby. She developed an idea of fatherhood by scrutinising other people's fathers. Another had only met her father

212

when she was eighteen because he had vanished when she was little.

One meeting turned into two, three. They continued. There was a depth to the discussions, an openness to complexity and a trust of one another. They became for me part of a quiet process of renewal, both of self and of my political understanding of feminism. They clarified for me an uneasiness about an assumption which is often accepted without much examination by feminists and men who support feminism. Characteristics which are commonly associated in our culture with 'masculinity' are often just dismissed as bad. Opposition to sexism is thus equated with switching these qualities. Instead I think we should be looking at the potential which is thwarted when characteristics are confined by the existing relationship between the sexes and seeking to open out new possibilities. Instead of just repressing all manifestations of, for instance, 'aggression', we can recognise that elements can be good or bad depending on circumstance. In a changing context they can be reshuffled and redistributed between the sexes in the process of reworking their social meanings.

Because we were not dealing with abstractions of a vaguely defined 'patriarchy' but talking about actual men, a complex picture began to emerge of 'manhood' and 'fatherhood' and our contradictory needs and images of both. Because these were men with whom we were connected passionately and intimately, however painfully, it was impossible to settle for an oversimplified stereotype in which they could be objectified as 'the enemy' or even 'the other'. Whatever the diversity of the social relationship as daughters to fathers, we were still flesh of their flesh. We carried noses, eyes, ears and memories.

By looking at the way in which our fathers had become men, we were exploring how versions of masculinity were taken on by real living men in the specific historical confines of their lives. They appeared not as helplessly moulded by an omnipresent unchanging sex-gender structure but as individuals acting upon and shaped by the values and relationships within which they found themselves. Even within one small consciousness-raising group of feminists, and even within the confines of our restricted understandings of our fathers, these blew open stereotypes of masculinity.

They thus emerged as individuals, not just as 'men'; struggling and resistant, vulnerable, trapped, enraged, isolated, cut off. We wept at the gulf in communication which became acute in our adolescence. Suddenly it had seemed to dawn on them that they had reared girls and that we were not going to turn into boys. Our fathers sat stiffly in armchairs, clutching newspapers to protect themselves from female invasion. What was it they feared? What were they protecting? Why? Were they pre-ordained, these patterns of incommunication? Or were they, like other relationships between people, subject to social transformation? This is a big question not only for feminists but for all people who seek to make a world without hierarchy and inequality in which men and women will be able to experience extensions in our present understandings of freedom and love.

We did not find the answer in one small group. Men retained their perplexing mystery for us as women in many ways. But something moved as a result of these collective discussions. For me personally the process effected certain significant shifts in my feelings about my father, which in turn altered my perception of the wider meaning of fatherhood.

In one meeting we talked about our ideal fathers. Mine were thoughtful, sensitive, humane socialists with whom you could discuss ideas and relationships and with whom there was space for your inner being to move outwards. They were sea beings, red Neptunes who could be devoured by Saturn and be born again and were not afraid of the dark flow of the ocean.

But as I described these Neptunes I became aware that I would have been a very different person with such a father. One woman pointed out that even in thinking of an ideal I was expressing a kind of pride in his difference from my ideal. For whatever the scars of conflict, I had been partly formed by the kind of person my father was. An aspect of self-realisation was thus bound up with recognising him as both apart and linked to my own sense of identity.

His life still echoes within me. The echoes are half-finished words, phrases which I cannot quite pick up with my everyday ears. I have to turn my ears inward to resonances to be reminded of what I know through him. Then it is as if I can almost remember fragments of a social order he both reverenced from his village boyhood and rebelled against. I carry scraps of an archaic countryman's world before the 1914–18 war, a smarting Wellsian class consciousness of the upwardly mobile 'little man', a peculiar mixture of the radical who read *Clarion* and the conservative who defended Empire, the staunch Yorkshire patriot who thought nothing of buying on the black market in the Second World War. I know the awkward engineer in the British Raj, the paternalist racialist white boss, the Tory who voted Labour in 1945 for a better deal for the unemployed, the affable salesman passing round cigarettes and over-tipping waiters to show he had money, the skilled tradesman white with responsibility at news of a pit disaster. These were just parts of a man and the man my father.

214

But in the moment of touching his past and the past of the fathers which were also within him, it all dissolves in me.

> Full fathom five thy father lies,
> Of his bones are coral made,
> Those are pearls that were his eyes.
> Nothing of him that doth fade
> But doth suffer a sea-change
> Into something rich and strange.

I am not him, nor his father or father's father. Not only because I am a woman or because I was his child late in life, but because changes outside our immediate family have worked upon our lives. So the gulf and the lack of shared assumptions are not simply a matter of our being different sexes or separated by half a century. I am a townswoman, educated at Oxford, part of the educated middle class, a Marxist, a feminist. This journey in one generation would have been inconceivable in an earlier historical period in our family history. The placings have gone all askew.

Reading Virginia Woolf's *A Room of One's Own* I was struck by her assumption that feminists with the self-consciousness to seek an autonomous relation to culture and to the past would be the daughters of educated fathers. This was probably too narrow a judgement even in her own day. But in the context of the modern women's movement it is true only for a minority within even the middle class. It indicates the enormous social change which the expansion of higher education has had upon the lives of women in my generation. For many of us there has been a break between the lives of our parents which has brought us into a new relationship to the external public world of education, ideas, work.

But the problems Virginia Woolf describes in our relationship as women to male-dominated culture are still very much there. Certain entrances to even considering the extent of the problem are deeply embedded in those unfinished feelings towards my father. The tussle to open the wounds where our love for one another congealed is a means of casting light on more general timidities, fears of authority, the reliance on ideas which are received as authority. I had to be able to feel him as a person hewing at his world and shaped by its confines. I could not make do with an emblem of political contest, 'the enemy', or a symbol, 'the patriarchy'. These would both mean that I would continue to see him only as the authority I had opposed. I could not simply oppose the cast of my own fears, because that failed to shift them at source. It would have left me for ever resisting aspects of male-defined culture while allowing men the power to intimidate me.

Lance Rowbotham – a man on the grand scale – had always been in the world, had travelled its length and breadth and could not be gainsaid. His knowledge came not from books, mere flibbertigibbet bits of paper, but from some source through which life itself was repeated, familiar as the earth and the sky but unknown since time began. This was what I wanted to encounter.

However, he became at once more complex and more vulnerable as I tried to glimpse him as he was to himself, rather than how he over-whelmed me. It was a terrible struggle to reach even this threshold. I cannot do more than glimpse aspects through chinks in the gate, never sure if the light is deceptive, a little fearful that as I gaze my eyes will harden like stones.

There is no absolute answer as to how you maintain a connection with aspects of male-dominated culture which are needed by women and men, and how you oppose aspects of this power which thwarts and destroys us in different ways. Anger and struggle against oppression and subordination are necessary, but not adequate alone, for we must de-velop resources to bring the new social order into being, not merely resist the old. This must involve not only the slogans of rebellion but more profoundly a changed relationship to the past, a lived cultural trans-formation. Creativity implies flowing into the process of metamorphosis, into something 'rich and strange'. It means the ability to emerge anew out of the moment of immersion. For those of us who seek a new relationship in the world as women it means a constant process of negating what one dwells within while going beyond the denial to understand how such an opposition came about. It is not just a redefinition of femininity. It means turning the understanding inside out so that what it is to be a man is no longer just 'there' in the world. It requires that the cultural experience of being a man is made partly by the reason and imagination of women, just as men have appropriated the social meaning of what it is to be a woman.

The existence of a movement for the liberation of women makes it possible to conceive such a transformation. It means that women's quest towards a self-conscious place in human culture becomes a collective possibility. But it does not ensure its safe arrival. If the resolution, in which every person in the world would be free to live and create in love is far away, we can still catch glimpses along the path.

In searching for a different way of knowing my father's life I am groping towards an understanding which brings freedom, seeking the love and creativity behind anger and resentment.

It is sad that he died when I was only able to deny him love. Bitter the death of a father I never really met.

The case of Sophia Jex-Blake is so typical an instance of the great Victorian fight between the victims of the patriarchal system and the patriarchs, of the daughters against the fathers, that it deserves a moment's examination. Sophia's father was an admirable specimen of the Victorian educated man, kindly, cultivated and well-to-do. He was a proctor of Doctors' Commons. He could afford to keep six servants, horses and carriages, and could provide his daughter not only with food and lodging but with 'handsome furniture' and 'a cosy fire' in her bedroom. For salary, 'for dress and private money', he gave her £40 a year. For some reason she found this sum insufficient. In 1859, in view of the fact that she had only nine shillings and ninepence left to last her till next quarter, she wished to earn money herself. And she was offered a tutorship with the pay of five shillings an hour. She told her father of the offer. He replied, 'Dearest, I have only this moment heard that you contemplate being paid *for the tutorship. It would be quite beneath you, darling, and I cannot consent to it,' She argued: 'Why should I not take it? You as a man did your work and received your payment, and no one thought it any degradation, but a fair exchange . . . Tom is doing on a large scale what I am doing on a small one.' He replied: 'The cases you cite, darling, are not to the point . . . T. W. . . . feels bound as a* man *. . . to support his wife and family, and his position is a high one, which can only be filled by a first-class man of character, and yielding him nearer two than one thousand a year. . . . How entirely different is my darling's case! You want for nothing, and know that (humanly speaking) you will want for nothing. If you married tomorrow – to my liking – and I don't believe you would ever marry otherwise – I should give you a good fortune.' Upon which her comment, in a private diary, was: 'Like a fool I have consented to give up the fees for this term only – though I am miserably poor. It was foolish. It only defers the struggle.'*

Virginia Woolf, *Three Guineas*

And my life is a perfectly dutiful life, with the sweetness of self-devotion to another, whom I have loved, and love still, though his spirit is slowly dying. The bleak suicidal despair has vanished, given way to a steady religious melancholy, the deep sadness of the sunset of life changing with darkest shadows to the night of death. After that death, which will break my only tie to life, there will be thought and action – based on maturity of feeling. *It will be a sad life; God grant that it may be a useful one.*

The Diary of Beatrice Webb, Volume I

GRACE PALEY

❦

A Conversation
with My Father

This man my father was a smart man, a funny story teller for company, but of course he was invisible behind the *New York Times* at breakfast and maybe Gibbon at midday dinner. He was a hardworking doctor in a poor neighbourhood, a Russian Jewish immigrant who had been released from political prison in Siberia. In 1905 he jammed himself and my mother into the dense slums of the great city New York to live free of pogroms and the Tsar's police. My mother had come out of exile to join him. She was serious, intelligent and kind, but her life was spoiled by early sickness and death.

A useful fact in my life: My father liked me a lot, but was, for many years disappointed in me. This disappointment was shared by the entire loving family so it didn't seem quite so bad. They could diffuse it by talking sadly among themselves, and of course in the first years of living away from home, I didn't think of them too often anyway. I lived in that exciting and not too dangerous World War II country of US army camps with my soldier husband. A little later they looked at my children, agreed that the babies were beautiful and brilliant, so I forgave them for thinking I might be a dud, and they passed hope over my head to the next generation.

For the eventual making of literature, that early life was probably healthy – lots of women in the kitchen talking, two strong languages, English and Russian in my ear at home, and the language of my grandmother and the grownups in the street – Yiddish – to remind me of the person I really was, the middle-class child of working people, the comfortable daughter of hounded wanderers, resting for a generation between languages. Right now, of course, still in New York, but 60 years old, it seems inevitable that I would have become a writer, natural that I would not be happy without children and a good kitchen table, natural that I would spend a lot of lifetime trying to improve the world in legal and illegal ways and, full of my mother's and father's stories of youth and rebellion, natural that I would regard political struggle as something serious and worthwhile, but also joyful because of the possible happy ending.

My father is eighty-six years old and in bed. His heart, that bloody motor, is equally old and will not do certain jobs any more. It still floods his head with brainy light. But it won't let his legs carry the weight of his body around the house. Despite my metaphors, this muscle failure is not due to his old heart, he says, but to a potassium shortage. Sitting on one pillow, leaning on three, he offers last-minute advice and makes a request.

'I would like you to write a simple story just once more,' he says, 'the kind de Maupassant wrote, or Chekhov, the kind you used to write. Just recognisable people and then write down what happened to them next.'

I say, 'Yes, why not? That's possible.' I want to please him, though I don't remember writing that way. I *would* like to try to tell such a story, if he means the kind that begins: 'There was a woman . . .' followed by plot, the absolute line between two points which I've always despised. Not for literary reasons, but because it takes all hope away. Everyone, real or invented, deserves the open destiny of life.

Finally I thought of a story that had been happening for a couple of years right across the street. I wrote it down, then read it aloud. 'Pa,' I said, 'how about this? Do you mean something like this?'

Once in my time there was a woman and she had a son. They lived nicely, in a small apartment in Manhattan. This boy at about fifteen became a junkie, which is not unusual in our neighbourhood. In order to maintain her close friendship with him, she became a junkie too. She said it was part of the youth culture, with which she felt very much at home. After a while, for a number of reasons, the boy gave it all up and left the city and his mother in disgust. Hopeless and alone, she grieved. We all visit her.

'OK, Pa, that's it,' I said, 'an unadorned and miserable tale.'

'But that's not what I mean,' my father said. 'You misunderstood me on purpose. You know there's a lot more to it. You know that. You left everything out. Turgenev wouldn't do that. Chekhov wouldn't do that. There are in fact Russian writers you never heard of, you don't have an inkling of, as good as anyone, who can write a plain ordinary story, who would not leave out what you have left out. I object not to facts but to people sitting in trees talking senselessly, voices from who knows where . . .'

'Forget that one, Pa, what have I left out now? In this one?'

'Her looks, for instance.'

'Oh. Quite handsome, I think. Yes.'

'Her hair?'

'Dark, with heavy braids, as though she were a girl or a foreigner.'

219

Grace Paley on her father's knee.

'What were her parents like, her stock? That she became such a person. It's interesting, you know.'

'From out of town. Professional people. The first to be divorced in their county. How's that? Enough?' I asked.

'With you, it's all a joke,' he said. 'What about the boy's father? Why didn't you mention him? Who was he? Or was the boy born out of wedlock?'

'Yes,' I said. 'He was born out of wedlock.'

'For Godsakes, doesn't anyone in your stories get married? Doesn't anyone have the time to run down to City Hall before they jump into bed?'

'No,' I said. 'In real life, yes. But in my stories, no.'

'Why do you answer me like that?'

'Oh, Pa, this is a simple story about a smart woman who came to NYC full of interest love trust excitement very up to date, and about her son, what a hard time she had in this world. Married or not, it's of small consequence.'

'It is of great consequence,' he said.

'OK,' I said.

'OK. OK yourself,' he said, 'but listen. I believe you that she's good-looking, but I don't think she was so smart.'

'That's true,' I said. 'Actually that's the trouble with stories. People start out fantastic. You think they're extraordinary, but it turns out as the work goes along, they're just average with a good education. Sometimes the other way around, the person's a kind of dumb innocent, but he outwits you and you can't even think of an ending good enough.'

'What do you do then?' he asked. He had been a doctor for a couple of decades and then an artist for a couple of decades and he's still interested in details, craft, technique.

'Well, you just have to let the story lie around till some agreement can be reached between you and the stubborn hero.'

'Aren't you talking silly, now?' he asked. 'Start again,' he said. 'It so happens I'm not going out this evening. Tell the story again. See what you can do this time.'

'OK,' I said. 'But it's not a five-minute job.' Second attempt:

Once, across the street from us, there was a fine handsome woman, our neighbour. She had a son whom she loved because she'd known him since birth (in helpless chubby infancy, and in the wrestling, hugging ages, seven to ten, as well as earlier and later). This boy, when he fell into the fist of adolescence, became a junkie. He was not a hopeless one. He was in fact hopeful, an ideologue and successful converter. With his busy brilliance, he wrote persuasive articles for his high-school newspaper. Seeking a wider audience, using important connections, he drummed into Lower Manhattan newsstand distribution a periodical called *Oh! Golden Horse!*

In order to keep him from feeling guilty (because guilt is the stony heart of nine-tenths of all clinically diagnosed cancers in America today, she said), and because she had always believed in giving bad habits room at home where one could keep an eye on them, she too became a junkie. Her kitchen was famous for a while – a centre for intellectual addicts who knew what they were doing. A few felt artistic like Coleridge and others were scientific and revolutionary like Leary. Although she was often high herself, certain good mothering reflexes remained, and she saw to it that there was lots of orange juice around and honey and milk and vitamin pills. However, she never cooked anything but chilli, and that no more than once a week. She explained, when we talked to her, seriously, with neighbourly concern, that it was her part in the youth culture and she would rather be with the young, it was an honour, than with her own generation.

One week, while nodding through an Antonioni film, this boy was severely jabbed by the elbow of a stern and proselytising girl, sitting beside him. She offered immediate apricots and nuts for his sugar level, spoke to him sharply, and took him home.

She had heard of him and his work and she herself published, edited, and wrote a competitive journal called *Man Does Live By Bread Alone*. In the organic heat of her continuous presence he could not help but become interested once more in his muscles, his arteries, and nerve connections. In fact he began to love them, treasure them, praise them with funny little songs in *Man Does Live* . . .

> *the fingers of my flesh transcend*
> *my transcendental soul*
> *the tightness in my shoulders end*
> *my teeth have made me whole*

To the mouth of his head (that glory of will and determination) he brought hard apples, nuts, wheat germ, and soy-bean oil. He said to his old friends, From now on, I guess I'll keep my wits about me. I'm going on the natch. He said he was about to begin a spiritual deep-breathing journey. How about you too, Mom? he asked kindly.

His conversion was so radiant, splendid, that neighbourhood kids his age began to say that he had never been a real addict at all, only a journalist along for the smell of the story. The mother tried several times to give up what had become without her son and his friends a lonely habit. This effort only brought it to supportable levels. The boy and his girl took their electronic mimeograph and moved to the bushy edge of another borough. They were very strict. They said they would not see her again until she had been off drugs for sixty days.

At home alone in the evening, weeping, the mother read and reread the seven issues of *Oh! Golden Horse!* They seemed to her as truthful as ever. We often crossed the street to visit and console. But if we mentioned any of our children who were at college or in the hospital or dropouts at home, she would cry out, My baby! My baby! and burst into terrible, face-scarring, time-consuming tears. The End.

First my father was silent, then he said, 'Number One: You have a nice sense of humour. Number Two: I see you can't tell a plain story. So don't waste time.' Then he said sadly, 'Number Three: I suppose that means she was alone, she was left like that, his mother. Alone. Probably sick?'

I said, 'Yes.'

'Poor woman. Poor girl, to be born in a time of fools, to live among fools. The end. The end. You were right to put that down. The end.'

I didn't want to argue, but I had to say, 'Well, it is not necessarily the end, Pa.'

'Yes,' he said, 'what a tragedy. The end of a person.'

'No, Pa,' I begged him. 'It doesn't have to be. She's only about forty. She could be a hundred different things in this world as time goes on. A teacher or a social worker. An ex-junkie! Sometimes it's better than having a master's in education.'

'Jokes,' he said. 'As a writer that's your main trouble. You don't want to recognise it. Tragedy! Plain tragedy! Historical tragedy! No hope. The end.'

'Oh, Pa,' I said. 'She could change.'

'In your own life, too, you have to look it in the face.' He took a couple of nitroglycerin. 'Turn to five,' he said, pointing to the dial on the oxygen tank. He inserted the tubes into his nostrils and breathed deep. He closed his eyes and said, 'No.'

I had promised the family to always let him have the last word when arguing, but in this case I had a different responsibility. That woman lives across the street. She's my knowledge and my invention. I'm sorry for her. I'm not going to leave her there in that house crying. (Actually neither would Life, which unlike me has no pity.)

Therefore: She did change. Of course her son never came home again. But right now, she's the receptionist in a storefront community clinic in the East Village. Most of the customers are young people, some old friends. The head doctor has said to her, 'If we only had three people in this clinic with your experiences . . .'

'The doctor said that?' My father took the oxygen tubes out of his nostrils and said, 'Jokes. Jokes again.'

'No, Pa, it could really happen that way, it's a funny world nowadays.'

'No,' he said. 'Truth first. She will slide back. A person must have character. She does not.'

'No, Pa,' I said. 'That's it. She's got a job. Forget it. She's in that storefront working.'

'How long will it be?' he asked. 'Tragedy! You too. When will you look it in the face?'

One day lying on my stomach in the afternoon trying to sleep
I suffered penis envy (much
             to my surprise
and with no belief in Freud for years
             in fact extreme
antipathy) What could I do but turn around
and close my eyes and dream of summer
             in those days I
             was a boy
whistled at the gate
             for Tom

Then I woke up
Then I slept
and dreamed another dream
In my drowned father's empty pocket
there were nine dollars and the salty sea
he said   I know you   my darling girl
you're the one that's me

Grace Paley